For:

Ossie Jenkins Jr.
Larry Eugene Ford
John Albert Jr.
Arthur Ashe Jr.
Dr. Robert Walter Johnson
Paul Robeson
Ralph Wiley
Curt Flood
Julius Thompson
Hubert "Dickey" Ballentine

# CONTENTS

# ACKNOWLEDGMENTS

I am greatly indebted to many people who contributed to the conception and writing of this book. I would like to thank my friend Ishmael Latiff, who during my *St. Louis American* columnist days suggested I write a book of essays about sports. I would also like to thank my beloved brothers Bakari Kitwana, who convinced me to narrow my subject, and Don Matthews, who took me by the hand and helped to guide me. Don kept saying, "Just write the thing." Of course, I could never forget my man Eric Clarke, who offered me a weekly newspaper column with the *St. Louis American*. I am also indebted to colleagues and friends like Scot Brown, Hashim X, Tara Green, Dana Williams, Lawrence Jackson, Lisa Alexander, and Olympia Vernon for their support. A huge shout-out to academic Baller, my soul brother from another, Davarian Baldwin for keeping me focused and constantly challenging me with great ideas.

I would also like to thank my long-standing support group of Anita Lewis, Gilman Whiting, Tracy Sharpley-Whiting, the late Julius Thompson, and Haki Madhubuti to whom I owe so much. Of course, how could I forget my friends Joe Pugh and Joe Mac, Nigel, Victor, June, James, Yvonne, Walter, Levell, Arvis, Julie, Lou, Josh, Imara, Normund, and Kerry for their support, conversation, and consistent inquiries about the progress of my project.

I would also like to thank the Carter G. Woodson Public Library in Chicago for the use of its research materials, the Schomburg Library in New York, the Black Coaches Association, the Negro League Museum, the Lilly Library, and the Football Hall of Fame Archives. However, I would be remiss if I forgot students that took my course "Writing Race and Sport in American Culture" at Willamette University. They courageously shared their personal knowledge, feelings, experiences, and were unafraid of didactic race/sport discussions. I would also like to thank my parents, Sharon Lewis and Wali Hassan, along with my aunts Gina and Ayango, and my uncles Stan, Muriel, and George, who supported my endeavors over the years.

However, I am most grateful to Angele, my biggest fan, who has graciously and patiently endured the pace of this project. And finally, I want to thank my daughters, Safina and Ayodele, for granting me space to work when they would rather have me play with them.

PRE
GAME

# INTRODUCTION

## RACE AND SPORT IN AMERICA

In 2008, on the April cover of *Vogue* magazine, basketball superstar LeBron James stands holding thin, blond, fair maiden Gisele Bündchen in his muscular tattooed arms. His mouth is open, much like the fabled gorilla King Kong, and he is clad in black. This young beast of a man, standing six feet and eight inches tall and looking primal, holds what many consider the epitome of beauty in his large hand and muscular arm. Is this image race at play? Yes. In fact race is in play in sport more than most want to admit. Subtle and overt racial messages, images (like the one above) and half-truths are interrogated in this book. People often ask me how I can justify mentioning race in the same breath as sports when two of the most respected and iconic individuals in American culture (Michael Jordan and Muhammad Ali) are African American. "Is not the greatest professional golfer Black or at least part Black, Asian, and Caucasian? Are not two of the best women's tennis players Black? Is not the home-run king Black (previous and current)? Is this not proof positive that racism does not rear its ugly head in spaces where sporting events take place? See, non-Whites are excelling—what more do you want?" I am sometimes scolded. Of course, these same people also argue that long before Dr. King was marching on Washington and describing his "dreams," Jackie Robinson marched onto all-White baseball fields living the reality of desegregation that King only dreamed about.

It has been argued that the Black male intelligentsia is generally unprepared to think critically about the role of sports in black life.[1] *Ballers of the New School* reflects a Black intellectual prepared to consider, critique, and dissect the nature and structure of American culture and race relations. In a "Baller" spirit, I challenge ideas that shape sports culture, casting myself as a Black intellectual unafraid of deconstructing notions of supremacy and the role of sports in validating such notions. This is a book that unabashedly scrutinizes a sports culture that cultivates and reinforces much of the mythology, paranoia, silence, alienation, and pathology that defines the racial scene in America.

A young James Baldwin, living in France, once wrote in a letter to Bill Russa Cole explaining that: "One writes out of one thing only—one's own experience. Everything depends on how relentlessly one forces from this experience the last drop, sweet, bitter, it can possibly give. This is the real concern of the artist, to recreate out of the disorder of life, and his own life, that order which is art." Here I have done just that, mining personal experiences, facts, and a lifetime of perceptions regarding sport and what it means in American culture.

As a writer, I deem it my duty to utilize sport as a vehicle for discussing and correcting the subtle nuances of the complex images and realities of race. It is essential if we desire a clearer understanding of the impact of sport in America. Because I use sport to broach this, it is unfortunate that some will read this book and attempt to box me into the category of being a race-embracing rebel. Some might mistake my discussion of race in sport as stirring hierarchies and as playing the proverbial "race card" (yet I am not the dealer). But the bitter truth is that in American sports culture—like American society—the treatment and depiction of athletes of color is plagued by race, which influences White self-perception, while attacking Black self-reliance, self-culture, and individual expression.

My goal here is to create the milieu of what Cornell West terms "race-transcending prophets" who are each "courageous and prolific, a political intellectual."[2] And sport is my medium because it provides our most blatant markers for exploring stalled racial progress. Modern athletes (whom I refer to as Ballers of the New School, or BNS)—through their frustrations, hopes, and cultural influences—show us how far we have to go as a society. Just as race was a hurdle for Jack Johnson and Jackie

Robinson, it was an issue for me as a little boy scoring touchdowns against my White peers. We were on the same field together, but still segregated because of race. I engage race and American culture through sport and a hip-hop-influenced generation that plays in the modern era via its own set of rules. This book uses sport to examine Black and White masculinity, White supremacy, sexism, racism, and American culture.

In many ways this book retorts the fallacy inherent in sports, as well as other facets of contemporary society, instructing us that we have transcended race as a major problem. It is also a response to the incorrect notion that racial acrimony is a minor issue, especially in sport. While undeniably there has been some progress, the paucity of women and non-White representation in leadership positions in college and professional sports is but a microcosm of the work that remains to be done to eradicate racism and discrimination in the modern world.

Modern athletes, Ballers of the New School, are members of the post–civil rights and hip-hop generation that refuse to be reconstructed, disrespected, or patronized (not too different from their civil rights and Black Power foremothers and forefathers). They will not be exempted from social, political, economic, and educational opportunities in American society, but ironically they often lack the collective political acumen and activism of previous generations of athletes. This generation is not burdened with the fear of improper conduct that may dishonor their community (this is unfortunate) and the struggle for opportunity. The BNS, in all their beauty and imperfections, are the focus of this book because they represent independent, collective members of a specific generation that has not reaped the changes that the movement for civil rights promised. Yet the marketing of modern athletes gives a false sense of American culture as one that embraces pluralism, equity, and progress. While it is profitable to market their demeanor and values, these same marketable attributes pose a direct threat to "Whiteness" as normal. They also prove that our racial progress, while real, is quite shallow and minimal without conformity or acquiescence to the dominant narrative and ideology as superior or "the right way." BNS are the ideal site to build a discussion around race and contemporary American culture.

The guiding mantra of the essays assembled here is "keepin' it real," thus *Ballers of the New School* uses sport as a tool for a progressive race theory. Such theory agrees with liberals that the goal of full and meaningful participation in America has been frustrated, but that it must move beyond immigrant analogies and cultural pathology to explain the failure of Blacks and other non-Whites to integrate. Therefore, I link minority oppression to an analysis of the conditions and culture of sport to address structural root causes that reproduce oppression over space and time. Using sport, I contest and attempt to redefine racial meaning in an interpretative way that roots itself in a liberating vision of society, politics, economics, and culture. The final analysis is that sports culture is a real site of practiced racism, as well as a mechanism for projecting colonial domination over people of color. A racial contract is what modern athletes of color struggle against. Some articulate this struggle better than others, but race is at the core of the conflicts, myths, and inequities in American sports culture and society.

Sure, you may say, everyone knows that sports culture is a real site of practiced racism. But the problem is that the narrative is often the exact opposite. Few want to discuss why people of color may dominate many of the high-profile sports in American culture (boxing, football, baseball, and basketball), but are absent in positions of real power. Rarely engaged is a discourse in sport that addresses what philosopher Charles Mills terms a "racial contract" that is structured around White privilege in all aspects of our society. Unfortunately, the visibility of Black athletes in high-profile sports detracts attention from the inequities that continue to plague our society. Thus, I broach what few want to touch without gloves: that racism thrives in American sports culture.

*Ballers of the New School* falls within a body of literature that examines racism in American sport culture from David Wiggins's *Glory Bound: Black Athletes in White America* (1997), Kenneth L. Shropshire's

*In Black and White: Race and Sports in America* (1996), and Harry Edwards's *The Revolt of the Black Athlete* (1969), to Gerald Early's *Culture of Bruising* (1994), and of course Arthur R. Ashe Jr.'s *A Hard Road to Glory* (1988), to name a few important books. There are also problematic texts on race and sport that tend to blame the victim, such as John Hoberman's *Darwin's Athlete* (1997) and Jon Entine's *Taboo: Why Black Athletes Dominate Sports and Why We're Afraid to Talk about It* (2000).

Since the Civil Rights Act of 1964, Blacks and other minorities saw many of the barriers to the American dream tumble as they suddenly gained access to integrated schools, neighborhoods, and career opportunities. Yet new subtle barriers have systematically "resegregated" the nation, increasing the rate of non-White incarceration, retarding affirmative action gains, and dousing the civil rights movement's fire of change. In 2008, forty years after the historic Kerner Commission unveiled grave racial disparities in America, the Eisenhower Foundation recently surmised that America failed to meet the goals laid out by the commission, and that racism remains a primary problem. The Eisenhower Foundation gave America a D in meeting goals such as increasing school integration, combating chronic unemployment, closing the poverty gap, and eliminating segregated housing.

Amid these facts, modern America breathes easier believing that the one arena of society considered a theater of progress and reconciliation—free from the burden of racial tensions, segregation, and discrimination—is sports. This is a flawed comfort. In fact, so much has been invested in the mythic integration saga that commentators, critics, sportswriters, fans, and athletes cry foul when racial issues sneak onto the playing fields of conversation. During the 1990s much of the talk about racism involved the nature of racism's existence and the evidence that proved its existence. We no longer have to prove it exists, but we do have to prove it remains a significant issue.

Hence, because of some of the obvious progress and the high profile of modern athletes, many need to see proof that race is an issue at all in society—especially in the world of sport. While it is true that some very significant progress has occurred in the past fifty years in sport, it is for precisely this reason that I find sport culture a perfect model to absorb an examination of the infrastructure that tolerates and reflects racism in America in the twenty-first century. Sport is a good model because it denies the existence of race while cultivating it. For example, in May 2007 Justin Wolfers, a business and public policy professor at the University of Pennsylvania's Wharton School, and Joseph Price, a Cornell graduate student in economics, detailed how in the NBA White referees call fouls at a higher rate against Black players than they do against White players. Although this study reviewed box scores from 1991 to 2004 to determine that Black players received 4.5 percent more fouls called against them by White officials, the NBA called the study by these academics "flawed."

In fact, Billy Hunter, the executive director of the players union, minimized the results of the study as more a reflection of society than the NBA. The NBA then responded with its own study that, of course, found "no bias." Whichever report one chooses to believe, we can all agree that the politics and practices expressed and reinforced in American sport culture, where people go for an escape, remind us of how much remains to be done in society. And as Billy Hunter pointed out, society does still suffer from racial discrimination; it is an issue that requires greater investigation.

Thus *Ballers of the New School* challenges, without apology, the notion that the modern institution and culture of sports are models of harmony and equal opportunity exempt from racism. A close scrutiny of the symbols, subjectivities, power dynamics, and sentiments of the complex system of American sports culture will reveal the racial signs of empire and racial supremacy. Indeed, sport in American culture is often a site for racial performance; where persons of color are made or unmade in public. Athletes who dare challenge the power of the dominant culture pay a heavy price. It is a myth to presume that sport has significantly decreased racism, created racial harmony, or alleviated racial prejudice.

It often appears that the contemporary American media's agenda is to shroud overt and subtle truths about racism in sport to confirm a unitary American identity. And such efforts are often successful because of the difficulty in the present landscape to effectively confront a clearly visible racism. The clear and distinct set of social, economic, and political ideas and practices of the past that explicitly expressed and reinforced the prevailing ideological framework of racial supremacy is a bit trickier in the twenty-first century. It is tough to visualize the Cartesian clarity of the racial contract when LeBron James is the leading highlight on ESPN, Tiger Woods is encouraging you to use American Express, and Michael Jordan is selling you boxers along with his own line of athletic apparel featuring an insignia of him in his classic jump pose. Moreover, American media works overtime, terrified that the non-White "other," whose cultural style dominates high-profile sports, might superimpose the dominant culture, or that the populace might see that society is, to paraphrase Edward Said, unmonolithic, complex, but not reductively unified.

The true challenge is to discuss race amid the high media visibility of a few Black male athletes selling hot dogs, candy bars, batteries, underwear, hamburgers, and sneakers, among other things, which lulls Americans into believing inequality and racism are dead. Quiet as it is kept, the true challenge is to confront color-blind perceptions of contemporary sports culture in America, to expose the farce or mockery of the real racial smudges within sport culture that often go unnoticed or are minimized. One racial contract stipulation for non-White success is a willingness to transcend, obscure, or erase Blackness. Therefore, I use sport to rekindle progressive resistance to racism, and reclaim the battle of language that dictates and spins a narrative of sport and racial progress that benefits American conservatives, who conceal the abated and still malicious expressions of racism.

Quite frankly, this book is an affront to the false impression that the American sports world is a theater of progress and reconciliation, untroubled by racial tensions. I fearlessly challenge the myth of sport as a site of public symbolic progress, a space that champions equality, justice, and progress. In many ways, *Ballers of the New School* compliments courageous works like William Rhoden's *Forty Million Dollar Slaves* (2006), and the pioneering efforts of sports sociologist Harry Edwards. It is also a response to critics like John Hoberman, who believe that "black male intelligentsia is generally unprepared to think critically about the role of sport in black life" (xv). As a member of that group, I am prepared and eager to broach this topic, particularly how race has always mattered in sport and conjured, even reinforced, America's racial contract of oppression and non-White inferiority. Yet, despite illuminating the significance of race, I do not trivialize the opportunity, change, and progress that have occurred via sports.

This book challenges America's race/sport progress narratives. For example, the rapper Ice Cube remarked in Charles Barkley's book *Who's Afraid of a Large Black Man?* that three things transcending race are music, entertainment, and athletics. These are the types of fallacies that I challenge. While Cube is correct that spectacular plays (by athletes) make fans forget color, I contend this amnesia is momentary, and usually does not extend to their workplace, neighborhood, or a stranger in the seat next to them and, certainly not the one on the street. When you stop to look at the structure of the institutions, the harsh racial truth stares you in the face. On the surface, race might be transcended, but the truth is that sport culture often reifies many racist stereotypes, helping to maintain a racial social order that privileges Whites in all aspects of our society, or what scholar Charles Mills calls the racial contract of White privilege.

Because of the exaggerated presence of a few Black athletes in the global media, there is a false sense of racial calm; that racism is a thing of the past. Meanwhile, the reality of Black presence in America suggests otherwise. Young Blacks and other minorities in American society are drowning in unemployment, inferior education, increasing probabilities of time in prison, and ever-rising incidents of police brutality. Somehow in the midst of these depressing facts, America promotes the fallacy that sports transcend race, that, in fact, the greatest racial strides made in America have been and continue to be through sports.

As a responsible Black male intellectual, I feel it is my duty to use sports to interrogate Whiteness and move toward cultural transformation. My hope is that people will read this book and ponder the deeper role of race in sport culture. I want readers to challenge the status quo of franchises, college and professional leagues that exclude at the top, and to consider who writes the sports news, who shapes subsequent discourses and images, and what those images convey regarding race in America.

While sports culture may reinforce the racial contract, oddly sport is a site where individuals have triumphed over stupid notions of racial inferiority. I believe many modern athletes of color understand and resent the reality that if not for the games they play so well, they could easily have found themselves in America's jails. My narrative is the antithesis of the "work hard, stay focused, and you will get a fair chance" narrative so often used in reference to successful athletes.

*A Brief Time-Out*

The discriminatory nature of the racial contract reinforces White privilege through sports. It is this very same racial contract that claims there is nothing wrong with professional sports, Hollywood, schools, and universities appropriating Native American names and spiritual and cultural symbols.

Let us examine for a second sports' role in perpetuating racism when professional team images and names are Chief Wahoo (Cleveland), the Redskins (Washington), the Chiefs (Kansas City), and the Braves (Atlanta). As the National Coalition on Racism in Sports and Media points out, "The American public has been conditioned by sports industry, educational institutions, and media to trivialize representations of Indigenous culture as common and harmless entertainment. Reducing the victims of genocide to a mascot, perpetuating ignorance behind racist stereotypes, and using a Chief, the highest political position you can attain in Native American society," is not harmless. Having American Indians as mascots is akin to naming a team the Honkies, the Coolies, the Sambos, or the Black Bucks. How progressive is American sport culture when collegiate and professional teams present these images on fields of play, given the history of Native American genocide and colonization in this country?

The misrepresentation and abuse of American Indian images and the role that sports play in stoking and perpetuating these tensions are unacceptable. In sports culture, as in society, past and present racial asymmetries are explained away, or the inequalities are simply elided to narratives of progress and change. At the same time, sport culture's notions of empire, race, and power are steeped in images of White leaders to reinforce America's racial reality. It is a reality that pervasively privileges Whiteness, while devaluing and demeaning non-White bodies, culture, and intelligence. Coaches like Phil Jackson and Bill Parcells loom larger than life given the scarcity of White star players in contemporary high-profile sports. A simple glance at the racial reality in terms of the hierarchy of player, owner, general manager, team president, and coach in the highest-profile sports (football, baseball, and basketball) prove my contention. This speaks volumes regarding the realities of power and race in sports culture.

Whereas some cultural critics argue that the issue of race is normalized while class warfare is the major issue, I do not completely agree. There is much proof that sports strive to instill beliefs in both White and non-White people of White standards, principles, and values as superior. Intelligent individuals must acknowledge the prevalence of race in the twenty-first century. Unfortunately, it is as much an issue now as it was during slavery, Reconstruction, and Civil Rights America. A major contention throughout this book is that sports possess a modicum of color-blindness and meritocracy—at least on fields of play (those who can play usually get to play, players tend to look past race on playing fields, and at least for two to four hours they are united in a common cause), but the rules change when it is time to hire for coaching and executive-level positions. Still, the common thought is that race does not matter. While sports encourage racial interaction and improve racial harmony, opportunity and achievement are often consciously and sometimes unconsciously hindered by race.

*Game Plan*

We have to assess the racial cultural meaning embedded in the reality that Black Americans, here well before twentieth-century Eastern Europeans, remain tied to sports as the most viable avenue of social mobility. What are the racial implications when sport hope springs eternal in the Black community over education? What does this say about the state of racial progress in America? Why has so much been invested in the mythic sports integration saga that few acknowledge or even ponder what Bill Russell, Jack Johnson, Tommy Smith, John Carlos, Curt Flood, Althea Gibson, Arthur Ashe, Doug Williams, or Jackie Robinson's careers really did and did not achieve? We also have to break glass ceilings that remain in the executive arenas of American sports culture. Finally, more modern athletes have to cultivate a true Baller spirit and become better activists and intellectuals.

Part of the game plan is to ask whether it is safe or sane to claim that race conceived of exclusively in terms of Black and White *was* a problem but is now nullified (particularly in athletics) because of attitudinal, institutional, and social changes. Does the election of America's first Black president (Barack Obama) or Black coaches leading teams to championships make us post–race? Of course, the answer is no. Race is still a problem. Hence the plan is to change the game so that racism can be discussed in sports without fear. This book is meant to be proof that one can enjoy sport without being blind to the racial, cultural, and social issues that strain and strangle it. Further, it is proof that sport can be enjoyed without turning a deaf ear to a discourse on Whiteness, racial privilege, and real cultural transformation in sports culture.

One of my goals is to suggest that while social progress is undeniable, much of what has been promised has yet to be delivered. Thus, we continue to apply pressure for change because the racial tensions plaguing contemporary America, silently play out in sports culture as well. Although the first strain of post–civil rights athletes used "two-ness" to their advantage to gain modicums of acceptance, I examine how the hip-hop generation's Ballers of the New School (BNS) refuse to grapple with the "two-ness" that DuBois spoke of, thus inviting heightened criticism and peeling back the racial layers that envelope contemporary American society. Armed with Charles Mills's "Racial Contract" theory, which attempts to understand the inner logic of racial domination and how it structures the politics and policies of the world—namely, maintaining and reproducing a racial order that "secures the privileges and advantages of the full white citizens" while "maintaining the subordination of nonwhites" (*The Racial Contract* 14)—I hope to clothesline myths that modern sport is absolved of committing fouls, penalties, or errors of racism.

From media to collegiate and professional sports, racial inequity exists and it engenders blind patriotic nationalism that encourages class and racial privilege, while judging non-Whites as immoral, less intelligent, and inhumane or not human at all. Precisely because it is considered taboo to pose any racial questions in sports, each chapter in this book examines myriad facets of racism in American sports culture from education to film.

*The Playbook*
The first chapter, "A Letter," is an intimate plea to my young cousin (now a Ph.D. candidate in Engineering) to choose the path of intellectualism, or to at least explore options other than sport. It is also my plea to young men and women in America to allow nothing to limit them-especially racism.

In chapter two, "Ballers in Contemporary America," I introduce contemporary athletes, whom I call "Ballers of the New School" (BNS). I define the term "Baller" and describe how they function in discussions of race and American culture. Further, I attack the myth that sports transcend race by framing discussions of racism and sports in what philosopher Charles Mills calls the "Racial Contract," which according to Mills is akin to a racial state and racial judicial system that clearly demarcates the status of Whites and non-Whites by both law and custom to maintain and reproduce a racial order that secures privileges and advantages of full White citizens and maintains the subordination of non-Whites.[3]

Chapter three, "Original Ballers and New School Ballers," makes clear that there is a tradition of African American resistance that finds voice in the aesthetics and function of Black vernacular tradition and culture. I briefly profile some key pioneer Ballers like Jack Johnson, Jim Brown, Satchel Paige, and Curt Flood, and compare them to contemporary Ballers like Venus and Serena Williams and Allen Iverson. I reemphasize what it means to be a Baller of the New School, while paying homage to the pioneer Ballers and critiquing the shortcomings of modern Ballers.

Chapter four—"Where the Brothers and Sisters At?"—examines how the lack of female and non-white authority figures such as coaches, owners, general managers, vice presidents, athletics directors, quarterbacks, and so on confirm the reality of the racial contract and discrimination in sports. It explores the lack of level racial and sexual playing fields in terms of diversity in positions of leadership. I am equally critical of the athletes for their role in perpetuating these disparities. My argument is that one must seize all power they have to force diversity into existence, which might require drastic measures like athletes boycotting predominately White institutions.

Chapter five, "Big Pimpin' in Amateur Sport" and chapter six, "All about the Benjamins!" continues my scrutiny of issues of race, inequality, and exploitation that engulf the economics and social ethics of professional and amateur athletics in America. In both of these chapters I stress the business of sport, in addition to the subtle negative perceptions of greed and avarice applied to non-White athletes. In chapter five, I specifically scrutinize the history of amateur sport, as well as its current economic and racial underpinnings, which generate huge revenue despite claims of nonprofit status. In addition, I argue that college athletes in the top two revenue-generating sports (football, basketball) should get paid beyond a scholarship. My impetus is to launch an attack on the greed of the NCAA and universities that generate enormous profits from sports without paying athletes in high revenue-producing sports for their services under the ruse of being nonprofit entities. In short, chapter six interrogates notions of greed, worth, and race in professional sports. My goal, as I recast issues like the Jackie Robinson narrative of Branch Rickey's good will, is to dispel notions of racial progress as less an act of morality and more an act of avarice.

Chapter seven, "The Making of Men in Sports Films," is a review of images of White and Black male portrayals in contemporary sports films. I look at films like *Jerry Maguire, Any Given Sunday, Rocky I, II,* and *III,* and *Blue Chips* to show how the racial contract is played out on the silver screen to conjure images of "Super Niggers," "the Super Jock," "the Bad Nigger," "the Stud," and "Great White Moral Saviors." These cinematic racial contracts uphold traditional stereotypes and construct new ones. I argue that rarely do sport films give honest or balanced portrayals of modern Black athletes, while usually situating paternalistic Whites that function on higher moral and intellectual ground.

Chapter eight, "Average Joes, Complacency, Politics, and Sport," explores how organized sport encourages and promotes an intellectually passive populace that runs counter to a culture of intellectualism necessary in the new millennium. Here I question the role of sport to send, subliminal racial messages that contribute to myths, stereotypes, and social distance that often go unchallenged.

Chapter nine, the final chapter, "Challenging All Ballers," offers some final recommendations and observations for improving race relations in America, and in sports culture. It is a fitting ending to a discourse on race, sports, and American culture. It is intended to remind the reader that breaking down stereotypes, limiting categories, and exposing the racism that limits human thought and communication will move society forward in a productive manner.

"Man," my buddies always grumble, "you ruin my enjoyment of sports with politics and race. Don't you know that sports are apolitical, nonracial regions of escape? You need to chill." But who can chill knowing that we live in a society that, like it or not, is a propaganda machine working a triple shift. Sports are an important cog that fuel and keep the machine running. Who can be calm knowing that racism, anti-intellectualism, and discrimination are so prevalent in America or that the Black community gravitates toward sports as the most viable career option? I am certainly uncomfortable knowing that African American athletes from middle class and poor communities (Third World countries in their own right) often lack the consciousness, commitment, and vision to make sports a third option at best for upward mobility. Can any of us be comfortable when critical analysis or intellectualism rank lower than box scores or the rankings of sports teams?

If we are not careful, sport might give the false perception that discrimination and oppression are invisible. Indeed, sport is capable of lulling us into believing that great racial strides have been made; that non-Whites, especially athletes (a small number concentrated into three or four sports), are among the wealthiest professions in America, instead of corporate CEOs and investment bankers. Naive youth are also fooled into believing sport is *the* viable path out of poverty and oppression; and that the disproportionate representation of non-Whites on the playing fields in the big three (football, basketball, baseball) is proof that Martin Luther King Jr.'s "Dream" has come true. As luck would have it, sports, which give us leisurely pleasure from the comforts of our couches, also telegraph racial hierarchies and political messages that do serious damage. However, with the right focus, sports can become an arena for challenging the ideas of difference, distance, and separation, and perhaps bring awareness to issues people might ignore. Or as Dave Zirin eloquently urges in *What's My Name, Fool?*, sport can be transformed "from a kind of mindless escape into a site of resistance."

I am convinced that conversations on race and sport can be a site of resistance that ushers forth real social cohesion. For example, on one level I want to consider what really might have been going through the minds of individuals sitting at home and in the Palace of Auburn Hills on November 19, 2004, when a fight broke out between players and fans because a White fan doused Ron Artest, then of the Indiana Pacers, who was lying prone on the scorers' table after a brief scuffle with Ben Wallace (then of the Detroit Pistons)? Was "Average Joe" outraged by the offensive, degrading act of throwing a drink at a human being? Was "Average Joe" outraged that Artest refused to lie there, know his place, and take it (in the spirit of Jackie Robinson or Martin Luther King, Jr.)? Or was Joe more outraged that Artest charged into the stands for retribution, which resulted in one of the most frightening eruptions of sustained violence in an American sports arena?

Confrontations like the one that occurred in the Palace in Detroit, and the answers to the questions posed above suggest that sports culture and American culture is filled with unacknowledged racial tensions waiting to ignite.[4] *Ballers of the New School* fearlessly broaches these tensions. My ruminations here explore why modern athletes of color refuse to turn the other cheek, reject patience, subservience, or passivity, and why they are labeled aggressor and violent. Equally explored is how in the modern world, issues of finance, corporate appeal, and mainstream marketability complicate race and humble BNS in a manner similar to that of Jackie Robinson when he broke the color line.

Although America looks to sport culture for escape, what we find if we open our eyes is a tense racial climate. And, this uncomfortable tension must be addressed. A quick scan of sports magazines and news shows confirms that if a person of color makes one false move, American society will usually bury them. Sports writers cannot wait to label athletes of color as vicious, criminal, or amoral. White players with similar or more extensive criminal troubles rarely deal with the same level of vehement public exposure or denunciations (compare media treatment of Kevin Greene, Christian Peter, Roger Clemens, Andy Pettitte, or John Daley, for example).

John Gerdy is correct in *Sport: The All-American Addiction* that sports' influence on our lives and culture is immense because everywhere we turn, sport-related images, attitudes, and behaviors are there. And while the racial contract compels differential treatment of White athletes, the criminalization of athletes of color influences our culture, maintaining perceptions and attitudes that keep old racial politics in play. Indeed, these dynamics impact hero images, where people work and what happens in the workplace, the schools we attend, what we see on television, even the taxes we pay. In the end, we cannot ignore the importance of sport. It is a great tool that can allow us to straddle over racial fences to discover that we have more in common than not. But to discover our commonalities, we cannot be afraid to leap fences to interrogate its impact on the racial politics of our culture.

Thus *Ballers of the New School* asks you to consider the role of race in the sweaty as well as the sweat-free zones of society. By flipping the script of the well-worn narrative of sport as America's most significant site of racial progress, we can scrutinize the true role of sport in mobilizing and shaping definitions, social relations, and public life. We can better discern why the once familiar "hero" who is now often non-White is often criminalized in the media as enemy, stranger, and antisocial thug.

Indeed, American sport culture performs and propagates rituals, symbols, and expressions of fear and difference that sustain racism, and notions of racial supremacy that block bridges to racial progress. By examining and restructuring the power of the racial subtexts thrust into sporting arenas, upon the bodies of athletes of color, and into the mind and hearts of spectators via the racial contract, we emerge with more truthful narratives, more honest dialogues, better American values, better social relations, and hopefully, real change.[5]

# FIRST HALF

# CHAPTER ONE

## A LETTER TO MY COUSIN

*He was the tallest tree in the forest*
*Stood above all the rest*
*And many people have said*
*That he was the very best*

*(Refrain)*
*The tallest tree*
*The tallest tree*
*The tallest tree in the forest*

*There was no one quite like him*
*Because he did so many things*
*He was a man of all seasons*
*And he could really sing*

*He was also a famous actor*
*And a great lawyer, too*
*Became an All-American football player*
*There were few things he couldn't do*

*But most of all he was a man*
*Who believed in justice for all*
*And in his struggle for freedom*
*He always stood proud and tall*

—Useni Eugene Perkins

*The Streets is a short stop/either you're slingin' crack rock/*
*Or you got a wicked jump shot.*

—The Notorious B.I.G.

*Children can't achieve unless we raise their expectations and turn off the television sets and eradicate the slander that says a black youth with a book is acting white.*

—Barack Obama

Dear Lutalo,

Your birthday recently passed and I did not send you a gift or call. For your previous landmark birthday when you became a teenager, I bought you a leather basketball, invited you out for the week, and schooled you in several games of basketball. I promised to give you another chance after you worked on your game some more. This year you turned sixteen—an important age for most young men and women. I did not send a sports-related gift this year because I was having trouble with your gift: this letter. Indeed, it has given me trouble, as I have been trying to figure a way to begin. Several times over the past few weeks, I have stopped and started composing it, in search of the precise words, the correct message that alarms, even frightens without nihilism. Finally, inspired by my rereading of James Baldwin's classic essay "My Dungeon Shook," which he composed for his nephew, I realized that if I let my heart and truth guide me, the proper words would follow.

As I write this message to you and young women and men of your generation, James Baldwin's accusations in his letter to his nephew that we are not expected to succeed, nor aspire for much beyond life in ghettos, continues to haunt me. I cannot bear to watch you or other youth limit yourselves to professional athletic aspirations to fulfill expectations of social mobility. I am aware that your generation represents an era of somewhat different young men and women who see mega-rich Black entertainers and athletes "shining" for an adoring public in society that looks to be "all good" or to have achieved the dream of equality and economic success. I am also not far removed from this generation that has taken a term like "nigger" and attempted to poetically turn it into a term of endearment, detonate its racial sting, and flatten its bite by changing the spelling to "niggas." While I understand the intent, history will not allow me to swallow such reasoning. It is a bitter pill, for the implications and outcomes are too regressive. The true travesty is that descendants of those once enslaved, who risked death for resisting such degrading terms, or for literacy, find education to be out of reach or not a viable option for making it in the twenty-first century.

Now that you have turned sixteen, you should feel that the entire world is at your fingertips, and it is. Instead, the only thing you see at your fingertips is a basketball. Believe me, there is so much more.

Perhaps you now are certain you can best me in a game of one-on-one basketball (however, I doubt it, although I am certain your skills have improved markedly since your summer visit with me a few years ago when we played daily for one week!). Your boundless energy reminds me of my youth. Just as my pressured breath, the urgency of each of my possessions, and my reliance on guile for victory made me painfully aware of my age. I was once like you and like most young Black males today. You work hard on your game and little else because you have Allen Iverson–like aspirations of going pro. That is "all good," as they say.

However, allow me to entreat you in a one-on-one dialogue about life, educational pursuits, and opportunities. Despite the visible barriers that surround the lives of many youth of color in America, they can win if they diversify their options. I beseech this one-on-one with you because it bothers me that two-thirds of young Black males between the ages of thirteen and eighteen are obsessed with using sports as a route to riches and fame. It also bothers me that so many Black youth are without a sense of their role or purpose in history, their origins, or a vision for the future that does not include sports. I feel that perhaps I am partially to blame. My generation has not effectively attacked the poverty, nihilism, and bouts of self-loathing that afflicts so many young women and men today.

One culprit is the propagation of entertainment or athletic success as the most viable paths to living the high life. Most young people admire wealthy entertainers or athletes, while eschewing academic ambitions. Too many Black youth dedicate themselves to sports in hopes of such success. Sadly, despite the heavy competition and the slim odds (of turning professional) this remains the goal of many young brothers like you in America. Now, I am sure that you have heard this all before from your mother and father. You have perhaps heard it so much that you can no longer hear them—their lips shaping the words that you have tuned out, my words on this page forming a blur. But believe me, hear me, see this: You have many options; YOU ARE DIFFERENT!

While it is true that many young Black brothers have professional athletic aspirations, what we don't hear about is that one-third or more of White males have similar aspirations. A close examination of sports culture will reveal that White athletes dominate 80 percent of American sports! Yet there is no fear that sports are prioritized in their communities. Why? African Americans are segregated/concentrated into two or three sports (economics play a huge role in this) while White athletes dominate swimming, golf, tennis, diving, racing, water polo, badminton, snowboarding, skateboarding, gymnastics, auto racing, and soccer. However, their aspirations are not limited to sport. This, along with racial privilege, explains why they often become the owners, coaches, athletic directors, marketers, lawyers, and agents for "brothers" like you who comprise roughly 70 percent of professional football and basketball rosters. You see, White males obsessed with a professional career in sports are privileged with more options if they fail to "make it." You, my dear cousin, are without this luxury.

Let me give you an example. I was looking at an article in the newspaper about how the son of the former Denver Broncos head coach Mike Shanahan (Kyle) was hired by the Tampa Bay Buccaneers as the offensive quality control coach. What the hell is that position? Whether conjured as a favor or legitimate, Kyle, all of twenty-five, is on his way to a professional sports coaching or management career. It reminded me again of the reality of the racial contract that philosopher Charles Mills, in his book *The Racial Contract*, contends privileges Whites in all polities. It also made me realize how my generation has failed to carve out space for our youth. But despite the inequities of the racial contract, opportunities, though they don't come easy, can be yours. I know my words sound contradictory, but success is there for you if you approach life with a proper vision.

In the meantime, the cycle of the majority of young Black youth your age striving to be a professional athlete, a hustler, or a rapper has to be curtailed with the promise of jobs in the post-industrial, technology-driven economy of today. Poverty is real, and jobs are even scarce for those with four-year college degrees. The flipside of athletic aspirations suggests that the reality of economic opportunity and advancement is bleak in poor Black communities in the twenty-first century! What troubles me most is that American sports marketing and entertainment will have you believe that every Black is an athlete, wealthy, that all entertainers are living large, and that we have effectively "overcome."

I am further bothered that Black masculinity is all too often defined by athletic or physical prowess. What we need are more lawyers, doctors, college professors, accountants, financial analysts, and other professionals, as well as hardworking non-professionals, to stand as symbols of masculinity. However, this is not a viable option with so few visible role models in communities of color. People strive for what they can see. Unfortunately, as I already stated, the visible "success" for too many youths is athletes living the American dream of money and material excess. Although the odds are stacked against making it in a sport career, this is what too many young soul brothers see as attainable. Regrettably there is lax criticism of sports as a viable option of social mobility. A critique must be made of youth and elders in the community who embrace this hope at the perils of academic pursuits. Pioneers like Harry Edwards and a few scholars have dared speak out against the limits of sports and how the Black community has failed to critique sport as a viable option of social mobility.

Blacks typically confine the scope of their sports career aspirations to just a few high-profile sports. For example, a brief scan of professional sports leagues, teams, and administrative positions in periphery sports entities confirms this assertion. Still, the disproportionate voluntary and involuntary channeling of Blacks into a few sports (three or four!) is rarely criticized among Black parents. Sadly, there is not enough audible anger that there are so few non-sport or sports-related options visible and accessible to people of color.

The tough irony is that *unlike* many White team presidents or CEOs, the lynchpin to opportunities for athletes of color is their ability to play the game. More team officials of color are former athletes, whereas far more Whites in these positions are *not* former athletes. As a result, the message being sent in non-white communities is that sports careers are the key to success, even on administrative levels. And if that were not true, if there was parity in opportunity, organizations like the NFL would never have needed the "Rooney Rule" to force teams to interview "minorities" for head coaching jobs.

Lutalo, a career playing sports for a young Black man is only available for those who are damn good. Those less than damn good better start working on their intellectual game. The unfortunate truth is that even in sports, the bar is raised higher for you. What more young men have to learn is that despite the obvious racial obstacles in America, there are nearly twenty times more Black lawyers and physicians than there are athletes playing top-level professional sports! Clearly, we are in a crisis if young brothers like you, whose parents are college-educated professionals and exposing you to intellectual pursuits, make sports a priority over education. What it tells me is that our generation must do a better job of promoting education as a viable avenue to a better life.

Listen, every African American child needs to study and cherish the lessons from *Narrative of the Life of Frederick Douglass*. This autobiography places education and our struggle into the proper perspective. You should walk away from Douglass's narrative both angry and committed to lifelong intellectual pursuits. Here is why. Douglass tells of his master's wife teaching him to spell words of three or four letters when he was but a young boy. But when the husband learned of what was going on, he instructed her that it was unlawful, as well as unsafe, to teach a slave to read. Douglass explains how Mr. Auld told his wife: "If you give a nigger an inch, he will take an ell [45 inches]. A nigger should know nothing but to obey his master—to do as he is told to do. Learning would spoil the best nigger in the world. . . . [I]f you teach that nigger how to read . . . there will be no keeping him. It would forever unfit him to be a slave. He would once become unmanageable, and of no value to his master. . . It would make him discontented and unhappy.[1]" Just as "these words sank deep" into Douglass's heart and "stirred up sentiments" that "lay slumbering," so too should they stir contemporary youth against anti-intellectualism. All Black American people, with a history of being denied literacy and education, should be weary of claims of democracy, as well as deterrents to education.

A quick glance at the low literacy level of those in American prisons in the twenty-first century confirms Douglass's master's belief that teaching someone to read makes him unfit for confinement. Lutalo, did you know that more than half of all Black men do not finish high school? It is alarming because this demographic of Black men comprises a large percentage of the growing number of Black men that are increasingly disconnected from the mainstream society. Meanwhile modern prisons have taken the place of slavery as a place to contain and profit from people of color; it is education/literacy, or the lack thereof, that is the key to unlocking prison doors.

What further compounds the situation is the general lack of respect Americans hold for genuine intellectual effort, which is worse in poor communities. It is true. Educators and intellectuals are grossly undervalued in our culture. Accepting the sports dream is what destroys so many young boys in this world, lulling those who fail in this pursuit down the path of criminal, shiftless, "uneducable," or believing they are what the White world calls a nigger. Ironically, sports are a last link to the many Black people disconnected from the majority of the institutional structures in society.

Of course, the downside for Black males, regardless of the path they choose, is that they are haunted by the "Bad Nigger" myth. It lurks around every corner. Historically, Black male subjectivity has been circumscribed by a hypermasculine ethos engendered by the historic demonization of Black men in America. Case in point, there are roughly 193,900 black males in prison between the ages of 18–24, while there are 469,000 Black males enrolled in college between the ages of 18–24. And although more young men are in college than prison (which is still a very high rate), the message often conveyed is that contemporary Black youth, with their rap music and black culture, are "badass niggers" or criminals capable of some violent or illegal act.

Another problem Black men face, which few will admit, is that White masculinist discourse continues to set the standards for masculinity. And because of this, the real struggle is over proper ideals of masculine identity, representative role models, and voice. The current conundrum is one where young Black millionaires become the new models who will allow themselves to be shaped by media image makers, but who are unwilling to continue the legacy of the suffering Black male defined solely by his victimhood. This generation of athletes unconsciously plays sports in a way that conflicts with what image makers want to convey. Modern athletes of color unconsciously and consciously dictate identity that does not eradicate the Black self (keeping it real). When we hear of conflicts between contemporary athletes and teams and leagues, the real struggle is over cultural power permeated by race. The real question is "who gon' be the bitch" in this Black/White male power struggle? The struggle is fierce. So much so that displays of Black identity often result in negative media calibrations aimed at bringing down all would-be "bad niggers" in film, sports news, and even dress-code mandates from leagues like the NBA.

Okay, cool, so I have gotten a bit sidetracked. What you really want to know is why I am burdening you with my thoughts about sport, racism, and American culture? I have known you for all of your life, held you when you were just a baby, watched you grow from baby to "little fella" to "lad" to young man and soon to be grown man. I know your potential and what you can become. When I was a young lad of nine, I recall your father accompanying my mother, recently divorced from my father, to Homer G. Phillips Hospital so I could to take a physical to play football for the Mathews-Dickey Boys' Club Bulldogs. Your dad made certain I got an opportunity to play. I have no idea what he had going on that particular day, but he halted his busy schedule to make certain I took my physical and joined a team. The rest you know about. Well, in a similar spirit I halt my schedule to see how you are doing, talk to you, remind you of your intellectual gifts that rival Allen Iverson's killer crossover dribble.

My own intrigue with sport stemmed from my father, who played football at Soldan High School then Sumner High School. Listening to tales of his exploits as a tight end inspired me to give it a try. I was especially fond of him telling me how during his senior season he played tight end for Sumner High School after being kicked out of Soldan High for fighting. According to him, he caught a slant pass against his former Soldan teammates (a top team in the state at the time) and got caught at the one-yard line because he kept looking back as he ran. His narrative excited me; he was animated, acting out the scene for my brothers and me (feigning exhaustion and looking over his shoulder as he ran in place). Obviously he had never heard Satchel Paige's mantra to "never look back, someone might be gaining on you," or he would have kept his eyes on the goal line and scored. Of course, my brothers and I were mesmerized by this story of how he was nearly the only person to score a touchdown against Soldan that season! I was seven at the time, and up to that point I cannot recall ever having a conversation with him. Football was an early connection for us. In an odd way, sports brought me closer to my father, yet allowed me room to cultivate my own identity separate from his over the years. This is one of the many powers of sport.

I would like to tell you that when I reached high school I quit playing because it did not fit my plans for the future. Or that I saw early on the damage sports could bring to a young man's life, pulling him from studies and other necessary facets of social development. But that would be a lie. The truth is that three incidents (that I thought were most unfortunate at the time) conflated to present me with alternate options. First, my growth was slower than my peers, topping me out at around five foot six and 135 pounds (not ideal for varsity football) in ninth grade. Second, I lived in the wrong school district. (I had planned to attend Sumner High, the football powerhouse in the city of St. Louis.) As a result, I was enrolled at Central High, which was six blocks from my house and infamous for having the absolute worst football team in the city, perhaps in the entire state! The third unfortunate incident for me was that before my freshman year, budget cuts forced all city schools to eliminate junior varsity sports programs. You either made varsity or you did not play. Since I refused to play halfback on a football team whose linemen were only a few inches taller than me and not much heavier, I skipped football. When I transferred to Sumner late in the fall of my junior year, the season was nearly over. By default the only thing left to focus on was school—which I did, joining the Drama Club as an after-school activity. (It changed my life.) Although I missed playing, I never quite looked back. In a funny sort of way I got lucky.

However, you are even more fortunate because you have a strong support network, plus you are very smart—school comes easy for you.

Everyone wants to make it big, become rich and get their momma a new house, buy rims, Tims, gems, phat cribs, and bling. Playing ball seems to be the easiest route to achieving these dreams and staying safe in tough neighborhoods. But don't believe the hype. One needs only look at the disproportionately high number of unemployed, undereducated, and incarcerated to see that we are running in the wrong direction.

As your older first cousin, I want to convey to you that you must not allow this culture or your immediate community to sell you false hopes and shallow stereotypes regarding sport glamour or Black intellectual ineptitude. We live in a culture that values sports and entertainment more than education; it is a battle all of America must struggle hard against.

You are fortunate to be very smart. I also know that in Black communities it is difficult to juggle being smart and proving your masculinity. Trust me, I understand the perils of being "smart." It got me picked on and into numerous fights or near fights with classmates. The stigma of being smart is a rough one to live down for males in most poor communities unless you can kick lots of ass or play your ass off. Lucky for me, I was able to do more of the latter. My sports skills made getting good grades permissible among my peers.

Indeed, it is insane that athletic prowess gives permission for more than marginal educational performance in Black communities. The film *Finding Forrester* depicts this conflict or irony extremely well. The main character, Jamal, negotiates his superior intellect with his skills on the court among his homies at all times. Because academic intelligence is a sin, Jamal literally stuffs his intellectual skills into his backpack, hiding it in his locker, reserving the exertion of his intellectual skills for the prestigious private school that also rebuffs him, making clear that efficacy is reserved for Whites only.[2] So you see the struggle is complex: the hood won't let you to be smart, and the dominant culture rejects your intellect, even when it is undeniable. So your goal is to beat them both.

And you can do it because your strong support network gives you greater advantages than most of the youth out there fighting this battle. Not only do you have family members to encourage you, but also your parents are college educated, middle class, and they emphasize education and are there to support you too. More Black families have to curtail pushing their children toward sports without encouraging the full spectrum of sports careers and primacy of intellectual pursuits. Athletics is not the panacea for Black youth.

Unfortunately American culture's marketing and propaganda forces converge to make youth of all hues believe that sports are the most exciting career option. In his autobiography *From Pieces to Weight*, the rapper 50 Cent laments that the only opportunity he felt existed for him was to sell drugs. Anyone who really listens to rap music will hear this nihilism as rappers explain what is happening to them. This is a travesty that must be addressed. Instead of pointing fingers at youth, we have to point fingers at social, political, and educational systems that channel such nihilism. Modern youth (much like yourself) are bombarded with messages proclaiming Black athletic superiority—a narrow, subliminal message that sports are *the* most accessible route to Black economic mobility. This merely confirms my belief that while sports is presented as the opium of success; it is potentially as detrimental as crack cocaine in a world where racial inequities make it the drug of choice.

Now that was very difficult for me to say, for I love sport and competition. Sports helped to shape me in many positive ways. In fact, denouncing the perils of something I derive great pleasure from, something that kept me out of trouble as a youth, places me in a conundrum. Although I will be the first to admit the positive possibilities derived from a professional sports career, I am not blind to the numerous pitfalls that accompany this quest. Indeed, for the large majority who fail (and this number is *large*), sports are a dead-end trap, particularly for the vast number of Black athletes. Further compounding athletics is that our culture sanctions the construction of masculinity in competitiveness, dominance, violence, sexism, misogyny, and homophobia in sports.[3]

If not through sports, how do American males identify their masculinity in the urban landscape? Diminished social and economic opportunities give the false impression of a singular outlet for expressions, confirmations, financial security and masculinity in the Black community. What is often missed is that just like society, diversity is a problem in sports, especially among executives, front-office personnel, trainers, coaches, and so on. The opportunities for people of color in sports careers—beyond running, jumping, catching, shooting or tackling—are somewhat elusive.

When I was your age, your mom once told me that a career in football was a long shot (as I am certain she tells you the same about your B-ball aspirations). I could bore you with statistics that defy the myth of financial prosperity for the professional athlete. I will not bother telling you how only 39–45 percent of Division I African American football and basketball players graduated from college. On the other hand, I could tell you how only roughly 20 percent of male athletes receive full scholarships. Worse, I could tell you that a career playing professional sports is nearly impossible. Or that of the two million or more high school boys playing football, basketball, and baseball, less than one percent go pro! And I also refuse to get into a discussion of how out of the 336 players drafted by the NFL each year, less than 200 of them make the final roster! No, I won't do that to you. But I will ask you to indulge me in a game of true and false:

True: Black males are aberrations on this nation's college campuses. At places like Willamette University (where I used to teach) and Notre Dame, the majority of the Black males on campus are athletes. Indeed, studies have shown a steady decline in young Black males attending college since the 1980s. When I was in college at the University of Rochester, we used to joke that the government would rather spend $30,000 annually for ten or twenty years to keep us locked up rather than invest $15,000 to $20,000 for four years to make us college-educated, productive members of society.

False: All you need is skills in the world of athletics to make it.

False: Every brother got mad hops, a killer crossover, a wicked jump shot, and is lightening quick. Athletes like LeBron James, Iverson, Kobe Bryant, Tracy McGrady, Steve McNair, Michael Vick, and Barry Bonds are the exceptions. There is also luck involved because many of the very best fail to make it. I played with a dude whom I was certain would make it pro in one of three sports. Sean Irons had lightning-quick wrists for turning on a baseball and knocking it out of the park, a cannon for an arm, and could play any position. In basketball he had game; a wicked jump shot, handle, and could jump. On the football field, he was the quarterback with a bazooka arm and speed. Sean was a "can't miss" prospect, an outstanding athlete. But he did miss. Thousands of talented brothers like Sean never saw a pro training camp in football, baseball, or basketball. On the other hand, Anthony Bonner, who played in the NBA for several years, fooled us all because he bloomed late, worked very hard, got lucky, listened, and specialized in rebounding, hustling, and playing defense. So, anything can happen, there are no sure things, but opportunities are not plentiful and luck is crucial.

False: American colleges and universities recruit athletes, mostly African Americans (in football and basketball), for their academic ability and diversity enrichment to campus life rather than their athletic prowess.[4]

False: Graduation rates are high among male college athletes of color, especially in football and basketball.

False: Most athletes of color take advantage of their scholarships to obtain quality education, and the coaches place the objective of obtaining a quality education above all else.

True: The majority of males playing college baseball, football, lacrosse, wrestling, swimming, golf, and tennis are White and graduate at higher rates than non-White athletes.

False: The competition for a career in professional sports is not very fierce because there are so many opportunities.

True: There are hundreds of sports-related opportunities that most people of color fail to explore or they are rarely considered for these jobs. If you go to the website of any professional team, you will find numerous positions to consider for employment.

Amateur athletes forget that professional athletes need someone to negotiate their contracts, repair their injuries and other ailments, coach them, run their teams, or manage their finances, handle promotion and advertisement, give legal advice. Orthopedic surgeons operate on lots of athletes, repairing potential career-ending injuries, and they make good money for a long time. Besides being a coach or sports agent, here are some additional sports career opportunities youth need to consider: college athletic director, baseball umpire, football or basketball official or referee, a job in stadiums and arenas, personal trainer, team trainer, team doctor, broadcasting, public relations and advertising, print media, sporting events promotion, college coordinator of athletic business, professional or college director of strength and conditioning, sports information director (college), general manager, vice president or president of operations, sports facilities manager. There are many more. One of these positions could be you.

Black youth don't realize that they have options. They have to remove the blinders to see all the sports-related career opportunities that exist. Just know that the sports industry accounts for nearly five million jobs and at least $100 billion in annual revenues, and most of these participants do not break a sweat or suffer physical career-ending injuries at the ages of twenty-five or thirty.

True: You (Lutalo) are a gem because of your brilliance in math and science. It is your academic/intellectual skills that will draw the future Iversons and LeBron James of the world into your office for some type of service.

As I mentioned earlier, you are familiar with most of these arguments and statistics, but what gets glossed over are hard questions regarding why the majority of achievement within the Black community is limited to sports in the first place and in just a few sports (football, baseball, and basketball). No one examines the racial factors that also contribute to the concentration of Blacks into so few sports and the lack of diversity in leadership positions and jobs within the industry. Rarely discussed is what it means to exist in an era that threatens to revoke affirmative action, or why a disproportionate number of people of color fill American prisons. It means these are dangerous times for people of color in American society. Can we turn a blind racial eye to statistics showing that young Black men in the United States are twice as likely to be unemployed, three times more likely to have been arrested, and at least six times more likely to have served time in prison than all other young men in the United States? Because nearly half of all Black youth live in families below the poverty line, it is no wonder that so many young men dream of the athletic lottery, but receive an inferior education, which can lead to prison. Yet despite these dreary truths, you must focus on two things: (1) resist naming yourself as victim, and (2) take control of your condition.

Unfortunately, what also gets swept under the carpet in most discussions of social mobility in athletics are nightmare stories like former football great Dexter Manley. Manley spent nearly a decade as a dominating defensive lineman for the Washington Redskins and won two Super Bowls during his tenure. Yet he managed to make it through high school and college at Oklahoma State as a functional illiterate. Manley, who survived the poverty and crime of Houston's Third Ward, was no match for the abuses of big-time sports. He was pushed through school as long as he could sack opposing quarterbacks. Like many athletes, he did not receive the alleged free education at Oklahoma State. He majored in football. Certainly Manley must take some responsibility for his situation, but so must his coaches, athletic director, and the football program at Oklahoma State. Nonetheless, few are concerned because what is expected of Black men in our culture is that they excel physically— intellectual or academic excellence is not expected from them. Race is a very real social and ideological construct that has severe economic and educational effects on non-Whites. But don't get it twisted; I want you to understand that racism should not define your potential, as long as you are unafraid of being successful.

The brilliant writer James Baldwin lamented to his nephew that this "innocent country set you down in a ghetto in which, in fact, it intended that you should perish." Actually, the consequences Baldwin so eloquently spoke of still ring true today—even for those who embrace academic excellence. Ignore the images of Black men as drug dealers, violent gangbangers, wealthy athletes, or dumb jocks.

Instead of being "Like Mike," be like the character Jamal in the film *Finding Forrester* who surprises his racist English teacher, who cannot free himself from the racial contract that guarantees the myth of White supremacy and Black inferiority, with a balance of superb athletic abilities and outstanding intellectual skills.

Lutalo, like Jamal, I want you to refuse to perish; resist the unyielding, spirit-crushing traditions that America perpetuates through racism. Do not believe them—resist! I challenge you not to make peace with mediocrity. Declare war on this issue! Do not limit your potential to a mediocre academic performance, a killer crossover, catlike quickness, a wicked jump shot, gross racist stereotypes, or trying to spit rhymes and flow like Biggie or Jay-Z. The myth in the hood, the dream, is one of escape using athletic skills instead of one's intellectual acumen. Be a living example of the latter. Make this your entryway to freedom—it is far more stable. Like Frederick Douglass, use your education to write your own pass to freedom.

Like Douglass and Jamal, you must force the world to acknowledge your intellect. However, beware, for the intellect is a much more treacherous, yet fulfilling route to safety; you will face many hurdles and detractors along the way—trust me, I have.

Sport confirmed its place as a viable avenue for raising the downtrodden Black community's pride when Jack Johnson knocked out Jim Jeffries in 1910, becoming the first Black heavyweight champion, then

Joe Louis followed him a few decades later, and Jackie Robinson broke the color barrier in baseball. These acts confirmed sports as the most stealthy and feasible way to prove equality, and gain financial success. However when notions of sport as the most viable avenue toward equality still endure in the twenty-first century, there is a severe problem. Indeed, there is a problem when most Black male constructions of masculinity revolve around sports. Historically, the physical or manly in the Western patriarchal construction has found the perfect body in athletics, but for oppressed segments of the population, the impact can be traumatic.[5]

But, Lutalo, do not allow this to sway how you situate your sense of self; you alone construct your identity as a man. Your superior intellect is perhaps the most important aspect of the subjectivity you claim. This generation of young Black men and women must aspire to professional lives besides sports or entertainment. You are one of many young Black men whose greatest asset is your mind, not your ability to play games to entertain others.

Again, don't get it twisted; I enjoy sports. In many ways, it is responsible for me being where I am today. However, accepting sports as *the* expression of Black masculinity, upward mobility, or racial progress, or believing racist myths of Black athletic superiority are foolish notions. All youth must refuse to embrace any of this nonsense. Reject it with scorn and with passion. Always resist having your identity, existence, or masculinity shaped by other men's feelings of inferiority or superiority.

African Americans turn to sports because racism tarnishes dreams of success so severely in other social parameters that they believe the only viable dream is athletic success. As a result, rather than investing countless hours studying, far too many young brothers invest countless hours developing speed, strength, agility, and endurance skills. What does this reveal about racial progress in America?

I think James Baldwin was also correct in his contention that much of America's racial strife results from the racial superiority trap too many Whites are historically enmeshed in and do not fully understand. This is unfortunate; it poses a problem for us, but you cannot sacrifice your own identity to appease their mis-education. Nor should you be willing to appease those Blacks who have accepted the limiting, inferior terms of White supremacy for non-Whites. In the modern world, the battle is against post-civil rights liberal racial politics that gracefully ignore race, thereby silencing Black bodies into what author Toni Morrison terms "shadowless participation in the dominant cultural body." Your challenge: force the issue to the contrary in every aspect of society.[6]

This will be difficult because some of the most extreme pressures you will endure will come from post–civil rights liberal racial politikers and those from your own community or peer group who have also accepted such tainted notions. If you can stand strong against the familiar forces that ridicule you in school for being smart, and those that force stringent models of race and masculinity upon you, you will have won a very strategic battle—you will also better understand what it means to "keep it real."

Finally, and perhaps most importantly, young men and women like you have to expunge the myth that the only way to escape from a life of crime, poverty, and despair is through sports. While I refuse to blame the victim, this is an essential challenge. It is equally, if not more essential for parents and communities to alter the course of the ship. We cannot buckle to the threat of anti-intellectualism or the economic and social racist reality that cultivates this posture within non-White communities. Education has historically been and will continue to be the passageway to freedom!

Now, I cannot promise you that in your lifetime you will not have to struggle twice as hard (every child of color learns early that she or he must be twice as good), because despite obvious progress, we still have racial mountains to climb. However, as you are pulling double duty, your climb should be easier if you remember that you hail from a robust stock of cerebral men and women who have scratched the surface for you. They have thrived with far less resources, mentorship, and intellectual ability than you possess. If your foremothers and forefathers who arrived in chains on these shores prevailed, certainly you can transcend the mental chains that would have you think greater returns lie down the path of sport than if you invest in your mind. I cannot overemphasize how you are at a far greater advantage than our grandparents or your parents. Certainly, if they could prosper against great odds, then truly exceptional things are possible for you! Yes, it will not be easy. And yes, racism, though more cleverly cloaked in institutions, will pose formidable resistance. But I also believe that like the great Paul Robeson—who was an All-American athlete, actor, singer, and a scholar—you too can be a Renaissance man, what Useni Perkins identifies as "a man of all seasons," unafraid to always stand proud and tall.

Your Cousin,
Thabiti

# CHAPTER TWO

## BALLERS IN CONTEMPORARY AMERICA

*It is a peculiar sensation, this double-consciousness, this sense of always looking at one's self through the eyes of others, of measuring one's soul by the tape of a world that looks on in amused contempt and pity. One ever feels his two-ness, an American, a Negro; two souls, two thoughts, two unreconciled strivings; two warring ideals in one dark body, whose dogged strength alone keeps it from being torn asunder.*

—W. E. B. DuBois

*Hip hop is . . . the spawn of many things. But, most profoundly, it is a product of schizophrenic, post–civil rights movement America.*
—Nelson George

> *Once we abandon decontextualized labels
> like "nihilism" or "outlaw" culture" we might
> discover a lot more Malcolm X's . . . hiding
> beneath hoods and baggy pants, Dolphin
> earrings and heavy lipstick, Raider's caps and
> biker shorts, than we might have ever
> imagined.*
> —Robin D. G. Kelley

Black identity, specifically Black male identity, represents several extremes in American sport from egocentric and barbaric to excessively humble (the latter being most appealing to mainstream culture). While most contemporary Black athletes do not exude the political or racial consciousness of Curt Flood, Andrew "Rube" Foster, or Paul Robeson, the problem is that not enough contemporary athletes display subservience or humility. Although largely apolitical, modern athletes, whom I call Ballers of the New School (BNS), are trouble because they do not "know their place." The contemporary Black athlete—represented by an impressive, mostly White armada of advisers—demands rather than asks. These Ballers of the New School use performance on and beyond fields of play to claim space in the American landscape, boldly asserting their own modern voice, style, rules, and values. What they assert is often limited personal concerns. BNS are complex because sometimes they transform and other times they reify the socially produced minstrel distortions of Black people. Athletes of the last three decades are problematic because they are not intimidated nor will they kowtow in front of a White presence. Athletes of this era demand as much respect and money as they can claim, without apology or overstated humility. Perhaps Latrell Sprewell's words in his famous AND 1 commercial best epitomize the complexity of sports culture, race, and BNS: "You say I'm an American nightmare; I say I'm the American Dream."

But long before Sprewell declared himself the American Dream, segregation in American sport gave rise to Black barnstorming teams forced to deploy clowning tactics in order to compete against their White peers. The unstated rule was to appeal to the White imagination of Black buffoonery (you can win if you make me laugh). Although integration in sports has existed for at least sixty years, there lingers a subconscious desire for the humble and funny. This generation refuses to play that game. Those who refuse to clown are routinely depicted as angry, full of rage, uppity, and ungrateful for their "opportunities." BNS who do not play by the rules of race (projecting the narrative of a happy, smiling, shuffling, high-fiving dude) are vilified for rejecting the old racial politics that America is fond of. To display discontent or seriousness and intelligence and introspection will quickly get one labeled formidable and threatening. Indeed, such behavior is certain to cast contemporary athletes as surly or get them thrown out of leagues as soon as their skills fade.

Modern athletes that are cast in this manner have committed a serious infraction: They have broken the racial covenant or racial contract, which according to Charles Mills in his book *The Racial Contract* "requires its own peculiar moral and empirical epistemology, its nouns and procedures for determining what counts as moral and factual knowledge of the world" (17). The contract is responsible for the tag of "bad" man of immoral stance that is often dumped on athletes of color. According to those who construct images of "good" and "bad" style, the White aesthetic is the only aesthetic of merit. Of course, the true problem with non-White sports stars is that they resist and shatter the invented and delusional racial mythologies that invented the Orients, Africas, and Americas. Mills argues that such constructions were achieved with a fabricated population: "inhabited by people who never were—Calibans and Tontos, Man Fridays and Sambos—but who attain a virtual reality through their existence in travelers' tales, folk myths, popular and highbrow fiction, colonial reports, scholarly theory, Hollywood cinema, living in the white imagination and determinedly imposed on their alarmed real-life counterparts." (18–19)

In the modern world of television, cable, and the Internet, images can work for or against the conjurer. The latter occurs when non-White athletes speak less affably to the media than their predecessors did and are unwilling to allow the White imagination to spin them in the simple image of the Calibans, Tontos, and Sambos. This is the crime that many contemporary athletes commit.

In their essay "The Uneven View of African American Ballers," Keith Harrison and Alicia Valdez explain that "Baller" is commonly a term that refers to the status of professional athletes, entertainers, or criminals.[1] Indeed, it is important to extend the scope of this term to include professionals who are doing their thing on their own terms. Yet what is germane to this generation of Ballers is that they enjoyed some real strides for the Black middle class, while also enduring severe hardships associated with the failures of post-industrial society (poverty, drugs, racial discrimination, unemployment) in predominately African American and Latino urban centers throughout America that increased the Black and Latino lower class. Theirs is also the culture of hip-hop, whose aesthetics and encouragement are founded on creativity, free self-expression, entrepreneurship, underground networks, the unconventional, and carving one's own space in a republic unwilling to provide equity and opportunity. Whether in the top strata or the bottom, BNS often reject the "model minority" role in America that is submissive, apologetic in speech, and willing to be put through the paces by White Americans to prove themselves worthy.

It is in sport culture that this rejection and White backlash is most pronounced. As we observe sport in America, race is a heightened and tense subject that many remain mute about. The BNS who reach hero status yet refuse to play the model minority to legitimize White racism often find themselves facing media campaigns that spin them as bad people. The dynamics of and response to this refusal are clear indicators of the racial state of our nation.

The fact that BNS like the "New Negroes" of the 1920s and 1930s must use sports to express defiance of Black servitude, dignity, and distinction from mainstream models of culture and conduct is a clear indication of how limited our racial progress has been. There are deep racial meanings and tensions entrenched in how athletes express themselves via language in the act of performance, celebrations, uniforms, the way they dress (NBA dress code), music, and personal affiliations, and the "mainstream" response to them. Because many BNS do not seek acceptance or approval, yet occupy hero status, they are deemed a threat. What they threaten with their popularity is to redefine cultural "norms" and values that are foreign to the ruling White class. This is at the core of the racial conflict between BNS, professional sports leagues, fans, and other powerful entities that control sport culture in our society. The myth of athletics as a level playing field that subordinates all ethnic, gender, and class identities has been well preserved in America. But it is more myth than reality. Closer scrutiny of the response to BNS reveals war waged on racialized fields of play.

BNS are often very much connected to the hip-hop music and culture—a principal medium for these youth to express their views of the world, the turbulence and chaos in their lives. Kevin Powell explains himself as a member of this generation: "I am very much like a lot of heads in the hip-hop generation: I am not going to smile, shuffle, or give a good goddamn what anyone thinks about me, and that most assuredly includes White folks. . . . I say what I feel, when I feel it, and exactly how I feel it. . . . I have no doubt that the outspokenness—be it political or apolitical— that is so discernible in hip-hop today is the residual effect of the bluntness of the later part of the Civil Rights Movement" (Powell 7). This is the sentiment of BNS in sports and other sectors of contemporary American culture.

Understanding hip-hop attitude helps us to understand modern athletes who openly signify on coaches, media, fans, and owners and who are willing to target their oppressors with parody that does not follow traditional rituals. To understand hip-hop as an alternative institution is to understand BNS as an alternative generation intent on existing on its on terms. Also, BNS have a sense of self-determination, independence, and freedom that grew out of Black Nationalism and the Black Power generation. If storied former heavyweight champion Jack Johnson "represented a new modern position on race manhood somewhere between the archetypes of Booker T. Washington's skilled trade laborer and W. E. B. DuBois's 'talented tenth' professional/intellectual" (Baldwin 196), BNS represent post–civil rights expectations of equality, opportunity, and hope without any compromise or displays of public humility.

BNS are somewhere between a young Muhammad Ali, Michael Jordan (particularly the young Jordan), and Allen Iverson. While many BNS are very individualistic, some of poor moral character and perhaps ungrateful to the civil rights generation for their good fortune, they do know poverty and the failed promises of "the Dream." I think that their general determination to maintain control of their bodies is their way of expressing freedom and agency in opposition to mainstream Anglo cultural ideology and morality.

Imagine being young (19–26 years old), rich, famous, and very good at your chosen profession. Imagine such a person often being nearly perfect at what they do. Dwyane Wade of the Miami Heat basketball team is an iteration of a BNS. Why? He enjoys playing basketball professionally, but his sights are also set on capitalizing his basketball star status, parlaying it into acting, modeling, owning a clothing line, restaurants, and other business ventures, and having real power beyond the basketball court. BNS strive to become brands that can achieve commercial success and call shots. They understand that the opportunity to do so is linked to how they perform and that those opportunities must be accessed now. The perception is that the peripheral business ventures are distractions; that BNS do not work hard enough or lack the requisite hunger for success.

The persona and style that BNS embody in view of mainstream America is a reminder of those harsh realities in the non-White inner cities of America, but contemporary sports institutions want them to bury this in the background. The mantra of most BNS is being true to who they are as a person and as a player. They seem unwilling to allow America to use them as standards of hard work and of the American meritocracy narrative. Not all BNS aspire for acceptance from White people or mainstream institutions. This is what creates problems. The independence and belief in doing things their own way give rise to tensions that earn such BNS unflattering media coverage.

What is omitted in this media coverage is that BNS work to live and earn their living by making athletics look more like play than work, effectively turning it into a career (Kelley, *Race Rebels* 173). They are "these niggaz straight off the street talking shit and not only are they making money, but they're influencing the culture at large . . . [saying] look, this is who we are, take it or leave it" (Nuruddin interview with Boyd 59). Ballers defiantly reject century-old postures and expectations of being temperate, peaceful, and pious to "prove" to the world they are good and should be accepted. Fans and the media loathe them taking a stance that eschews racial humility. Hence, fans and the media deride BNS who refuse to display humility. And if fans or the media step beyond the boundaries of respectfulness, BNS will retaliate (with a choke hold or even a punch in the face).

BNS reject such double standards that demand better behavior than Whites and higher performance for the same rewards. BNS remind America of the asymmetries of the present, the failures of civil rights, the limited change; their histories and narratives make it difficult for media to elude the issue of race. BNS are perceived to "not give a fuck" because their ethos is deemed a challenge to the propaganda of America, "which is always articulated by those in power and seldom applicable to those who live on society's margins" (Boyd, *Basketball Jones* 66). Perhaps merely saying "I don't give a f**k" does not effectively challenge true power or liberty as Boyd suggests, but it does indicate the determination of this generation to forge their own destinies, carve out space on their own terms, or, to paraphrase the rapper Jay-Z, when facing the fork in the road, choose to go straight. Like Jack Johnson, Ali, and other pioneers, BNS aim to be their natural selves—unconcerned with the approval of mainstream Americans. By confidently engaging Afro-diasporic cultural traditions, Black celebration, and style, they stamp themselves worthy.[2]

While one flaw of many BNS is limited political focus or activism, like the zoot suiters of the 1940s, the social context of baggy pants, attitude, braids, locks, platinum chains, and other aesthetics associated with hip-hop fashion lends implicit oppositional meaning. Still, there is something subversive about many BNS refusing to "play ball" in the expected manner. In many ways, the insistence on evoking hip-hop style and attitude is their unconscious way of reminding the world that their success is an exception and that the norm plaguing urban communities of color is a lack of resources along with poverty and nihilism.

Of course, my ideal model of a Baller is one who calls shots without being led by the nose or limited because of race, embraces intellectualism, and is conscious of their responsibility to their community. The term "Baller" has a wider reach than sports figures. In Black popular culture, particularly a post–civil rights generation intent on resisting subservience, a true Baller transcends the role of trickster figure, second-class deferential citizenship, cultural inferiority, or less than full rights as American citizens. Thus like the hip-hop, post-industrial, post–civil rights generation that spawned them, BNS are, when necessary, abrasive, confrontational voices amplified to challenge the marginalization, racism, hypocrisy, and class complacency that has long been muted.

BNS—the majority of whom come from the urban underclass or the subaltern culture embracing hip-hop that insist on being themselves and assuming equal socioeconomic opportunity—are chastised in the media. The main reason they are attacked is because their posture, behavior—being "real niggaz"—is an affront to dominant meanings ascribed to their experiences (Kelley 180) or to the racial contract. A cursory glimpse at the history of the racial contract reveals how society is structured to generate judgments about good and bad or justice and injustice that privilege Whiteness and defend all associated with it as normative and those that are not White as grotesque or uncultured. It explains the actual "genesis of the society and state, the way society is structured, the government functions, and people's moral psychology" (Mills 5). In our culture, we believe sports transcend these structures, but Ballers remind us that this warped moral psychology thrives in sports culture. If you watch closely as athletes of color struggle with coaches, owners, and media over rules, inclusion, and self-expression, what you will see are the following: the borders of racial privilege; the constructed law or contract; the contract of formal legal controls over entry and exit; rights of citizenship or non-citizenship.

Visibly defiant, Ballers reject and respond to the notion of privilege that makes all Whites beneficiaries of this contract. However, the trick is that not all Whites are signatories. Ballers acknowledge constructions of racial borders that have drawn dividing lines between Americans, and they push past them, navigating their own unique routes around, over, and through them. Relying on the ideology and aesthetics of the post–civil rights era, which include Black Power and hip-hop, Ballers negotiate an identity that resists "the hegemonic culture and its attendant racism and patriotism ... and the class conscious, integrationist attitudes of middle class blacks" (Kelley, *Race Rebels* 165). They are also in a better position to move forward and capitalize on the gains or promise of previous generations.

The post–civil rights Ballers attempt to transcend the trappings, or the fee of crossing over to "make it," as outsiders in America. Ballers are unwilling to negotiate with their own authentic self or risk betraying who they are for "acceptance," as previous generations had to. As post–civil rights products, their "social locations have allowed them [urban youth who comprise the bulk of Ballers] to demystify aspects of hegemonic ideology while reinforcing their ties to it" (Kelley, 181).[3] In the tradition of bad men and tricksters, they embody signifying and irreverence that challenge power relations in subtle and overt ways. Also, the dress, style, and other symbols associated with BNS serve as reminders to media and fans that the athletes before them are aberrations; sports are limited upward mobility tools, and BNS represent the vast majority of their peers who are forced into low-wage labor and who face increased economic displacement, a paucity of job prospects, and unprecedented poverty. Consciously and unconsciously, BNS carry themselves so that they "keep it real," are unapologetic about maintaining connections to their roots, reminding America of the oppressive policies and racist neglect that produced them.

*Personal Reflection on Race, Sports, and Racism*
In the post–civil rights era, non-Whites still suffer racial indignities or insults in schools, and in sophisticated, subtle ways. The truth is that over the past thirty years my generation has been beset with economic dislocation, environmental racism, inner-city divestment, inadequate schooling, and numerous other misfortunes. My first social indignity occurred when I was ten years old. Sadly, it happened in the space where America mythically prides itself on making racial strides—sports. Although I experienced several such incidents over the years, I can still vividly recall one incident that will forever remind me that sports have the same propensity for racism as any other component of American culture. My feelings and response were in line with BNS.

My Mathews-Dickey Boys Club (in 1986 it became Boys' and Girls' Club) football team from North St. Louis traveled far out to the suburbs to play a team from a town called Crystal City. They were an all-White team, while we were all Black. We dominated from the opening whistle. At one point late in the second quarter, I had just scored my second touchdown, putting the game completely out of hand, and as I jogged to the referee to give him the ball, one of the White kids crossed my path, blurting through his mouthpiece, "You little damn nigger." I was immediately in shock, stopping as though tackled by the force of his words. Did he just call me what I thought he did? On that football field, while I was standing in the end zone, waiting to hand the ball to the referee, it marked the first time in my life anyone had called me such a thing. At that moment, I really became aware of my Blackness and an alternative perception of it by Whites. Not in the sense that for the first time I learned that I was Black, but that in America it represented something negative. The touchdown that I had just scored did little to absolve the pain or anger of him calling me a "nigger." It is a memory that, try as I might, I cannot erase from my mind.

Where does a ten-year-old learn to call another ten-year-old a "nigger?" Who teaches that? What makes him think I am an "inferior" nigger and that he, in his Whiteness, is "superior?" Once I got to our sideline and reported the awful incident that had just occurred, Mr. Coleman, our assistant coach, hit me with a much more stunning if not injurious rebuttal. When I told him what the kid had just called me, he was disgusted with my preoccupation with meaningless words. "Look at the scoreboard and tell me who is winning," Mr. Coleman demanded of me, pointing to the beautiful electronic scoreboard that showed: Visitors, 42, and Home, 0.

"We are," I replied.

"All right, then," Coleman said. "They want you to fight them so you can get tossed from the game or we will be disqualified. Just win the battle on the football field. Now get over there and sit down." I looked at him stunned. My feelings hurt. I turned away toward the bench. Still, what he said was not enough. If I scored three more touchdowns and we thoroughly humiliated them, it would not erase the sting of being called a "nigger." The silent, nonviolent pleasure of winning the game did not satiate my appetite for revenge, blood, or a sincere apology. This is how Jackie Robinson must have felt—the pain of their racist ignorance negating the joys of playing the game well.

As the game progressed, my teammates came to the sidelines with similar reports, only to have Mr. Coleman instruct them to find solace in winning the battle on "the scoreboard." I realize now that Mr. Coleman came from an era that watched Black pioneers in sports suffer through verbal abuse and even physical humiliations to prove that they were equal to Whites. Sports were embraced because dominance in them was a safer zone for cutting the myth of White supremacy down to size. They were proud of these achievements, the opportunity to prove one's worth, equality, and humanity on par with Whites. However, my teammates and I were not of Mr. Coleman's or Jackie Robinson's era. We were definitely cut from the cloth of Jack Johnson and more akin to Curt Flood and Muhammad Ali. As BNS, we found it unnecessary to measure ourselves against Whites or to seek their approval. We took for granted that we were at worst just as good, if not better than them. In fact, we were of the opinion that they needed to prove their worth to us! And judging from the score that day, they had failed miserably in this task. Thus, suffering a racial indignity to prove we were better was crazy to us. However, kicking the racist's ass for stepping out of line made sense to us. Although I could not articulate it effectively at the time, I was not feeling Mr. Coleman's philosophy—nor were my teammates. As a member of the hip-hop generation, as a post–civil rights, post–Black Power BNS, I wanted to kick that kid's ass for calling me a "nigger"—in fact, my boy Ossie Jenkins bit him on the leg in a subsequent pileup while my boy Boo kicked and punched random players who made racial remarks. Up by six touchdowns, the penalties were harmless.

Like modern sports stars, I hail from a generation whose nomenclature varies from "Hip-Hop" to "New H.N.I.C. (Head Niggers in Charge)," but whatever you call us, we believe in demanding respect, embracing our own culture, among other things, and checking a cat's collar at the door if she/he steps incorrectly. Ballers also understand (some can articulate it better than others) that as a non-White there are limited privileges, few opportunities, and many failed promises of post–civil rights progress. Anyone looking at society with honest eyes must agree that this generation has experienced up-close community drug trafficking, police and neighborhood violence, political and police corruption, abhorrent educational systems, mass imprisonment (primarily Black and Latino males and females), widespread unemployment, and meager economic opportunities. These bleak realities engender a Baller mentality that requires people of color to find creative ways to construct opportunity for themselves (historically this has been the case). While seeking and constructing creative avenues of success, Ballers step outside of the norm because the norm does not allow entry. Ballers stare at the proverbial fork in the road, seeing it for all of its racial limitations in both directions, and are unafraid to forge straight ahead without veering left or right. We see much of this mentality revealed in hip-hop and sports as an empowering entity for people of color.

What Ballers have in common is that they demand, break, or at least trouble the racial contract concept that is central to my discussion of sports and American culture. Unfortunately, many Ballers are without a mission, a commitment to community, or a sense of responsibility to the struggle against racism. Many are well versed in the language of "giving something back to the community" but lack a true understanding of what this means. Ashe, Flood, Brown, and Russell understood and were driven by the symbolic weight of race—that what they represented was larger than them. Post–civil rights America, for all its failed promise, has created some gains and a false sense of comfort that occludes an understanding of what has been achieved and what still needs to be done. As a result, misdirected demands and individualism reign among many but not all Ballers of the New School, who exist on two levels: conscious and self-conscious. In the view of many White Americans, the problem with both categories of Ballers is that they are not grateful enough for being allowed to participate, they lack the outward humility of previous athletes, and they are more concerned with appeasing themselves than garnering White acceptance.

The street definition for "ballin'" means to exhibit a high-rolling or flamboyant lifestyle or to display one's wealth while having fun. It also implies finding alternative means toward success. However, in this book the term "Baller" is not exclusive to sports, or to displays of wealth, nor is it to be mistaken with drug culture, although drug dealers share a similar impulse that is focused on getting paid in a limited racial economy whose avenues to social mobility are often restricted for non-Whites. Baller is a term meant to capture the ethos of members of the previous generations and this (hip-hop) generation of athletes and professionals insistent on making their mark, challenging norms, doing things on their own terms, with their own style or flamboyance, prideful of their ethnicity or race, while, as we like to say, "making a come-up." Like early hip hop artists who maintained a street-level approach in the creation, shaping, and control of their product without sacrificing creativity, being a Baller is about the politics of power on aesthetic, intellectual, creative, and political levels. Because White supremacy demands hegemony and subservience for success, BNS are always in conflict with the dominant cultural values and aesthetics as they situate themselves at the forefront of the American reality on their own terms, in their own image.

Furthermore, the term "Baller" reflects generations past and present willing to take matters in their own hands and control situations, "call shots" as we say, so they can be the best. It also is an appropriate term for the athletes of this, generation, who are consumed with "ballin'" and controlling their own destinies. NBA all-star Ron Artest explained what being a Baller means in a November 2004 interview with *Slam* magazine, "I just try to be myself, try to do things that I want to do." Indeed, the NFL perennial Pro Bowl wide receiver Terrell Owens would concur with Artest. Owens has for years been criticized for his talk and showboating after scoring touchdowns. But Owens, in Baller spirit, insists he will "still go out there and do it [his post-touchdown antics] and still have fun" because that is the way he plays the game. Artest and Owens, Bonds, and Serena and Venus Williams are examples of BNS who do not try to fit any molds that satisfy the dominant culture's racial or moral assumptions of superiority.

On one level, Ballers are leaders, confident in themselves; people who get paid based on leisure work. Thus, executives and various other professionals fit this description. Todd Boyd uses the term H.N.I.C. (Head Niggers in Charge) to define this generation, but the term "Baller" more poignantly captures the essence or ethos of modern youth, professionals, or athletes of different backgrounds. It is a term that clearly reflects the capitalist ideals of American culture. For example, a friend of mine uses the term "Baby Baller" to describe young academics making their way through the ranks, suggesting a wider connotation for describing one who is making their mark. But in essence the constant for all Ballers is battling racial hegemony to develop things on one's own terms, without the ticket of subservience for success. Again, BNS are often in conflict with the dominant cultural values and aesthetics as they situate themselves at the forefront of American reality in their own image.

In a broader sense, a Baller is a person doing their thing in their profession (be it a musician, lawyer, businessman, academic or, athlete) and getting properly treated and compensated. Take, for example, Michael Jordan, the king of marketing sports apparel. People forget that the NBA fined him for wearing his own "colored" shoe. Shortly thereafter he distanced himself from his early commercial director Spike Lee and B-boy hip-hop connections he initially forged to make Air Jordan the most popular brand of basketball shoe in the world. This was symbolically outlined in the commercial where Jordan leaves Mars Blackmon, the ultimate B-boy, behind hanging on the rim of a basketball net at the end of one Nike commercial. While Nike and Jordan engendered a Baller spirit for daring to market a Black hero/icon in Jordan, his shift to appeal to a more mainstream conservative market (perhaps fearful of being thought of as too Black) contradicts his early Baller status. In the end, some of his Baller status (despite his Brand Jordan line of athletic apparel) is revoked because he decided to take a fork in the road instead of continuing to forge a path unafraid of openly reflecting Black culture. The Jordan situation epitomizes the conundrum for modern athletes in a multibillion-dollar sports industry. Many of them want to make money and be themselves, while also controlling market shares and gaining leverage for higher salaries and endorsements.

The real powerbrokers or shot callers are team owners and league officials (the NBA is a classic example). In our culture the racial contract shields team owners and league officials from confronting choices between their personal or financial well-being and the integrity of the games. Indeed, no one complains that baseball and basketball league commissioners Bud Selig and David Stern are paid too much or should sacrifice some of their package perks for love of the game or loyalty to fans. Certainly one must wonder if their White male status validates their worth according to the rules of the racial contract. For non-White athletes, the absence of White privilege summons a persistent barrage of questions regarding their morality and true worth.

The term "Baller" also captures the capitalist ideals of American society—a desire to control situations and do well financially. Thus, Ballers do their thing in their profession and get properly compensated. A critique of Ballers like Jordan or say Russell Simmons is that individualist pursuits compromise the common good of the community. Phil Knight—the Nike sports apparel king who began in the early 1970s selling track shoes out of the trunk of his car as a company called Blue Ribbon Sports, then went on to revolutionize the shoe, marketing, and sports apparel industry— definitely has Baller spirit. He took chances, switching from solely focusing on running shoes to taking a chance in the basketball shoe market, hedging his bets on bold ads and endorsements from African American athletes when Madison Avenue thought Nike was crazy. Now Nike owns the basketball shoe market, claiming among its subsidiaries Converse (the original king of the basketball shoe market). But his White privilege allowed him easier access to avenues of opportunity and to resources that post-hip-hop generation non-White Ballers often found and find difficult. While the successful Nike subsidiary Brand Jordan is one argument against this assertion, it is important to note that Jordan's neutral and apolitical persona play a profound role in his popularity and this opportunity.

African American sports performers are indeed in a conflicted space. While somewhat embraced and adored on the courts and fields of play, they are despised, feared, and distasteful once they step outside the lines or off the courts. As a Portland sportswriter intimated to me at a luncheon a few years ago: "Allen Iverson is a great player, but I don't want my son wearing his jersey because I don't like him as a person; his work ethics are not something I want my son admiring." I looked at him, a very pleasant member of my table up to this point, and asked him why. He said: "Because he has a penchant for having conflict with his coach and missing practices, dressing inappropriately, and wearing tattoos." Then I asked him: "What are your feelings regarding a journalist who does not dress very well, but is talented enough to get away with working from home, occasionally comes to the office, yet always meets his deadline, while winning awards for his performance? Are his ethics immoral or unsavory? Is he lazy?" He looked at me for a moment. I knew he was puzzled, for he knew I was speaking of him, but he never expected the question to be framed in such a way. "That is different; it's not a sport" he responded. His initial comment and lack of response speaks volumes about our culture and race. Although he was unable to muster a coherent response, what he meant was that he was protected by his racial contract. The rules of the game change along with one's hue. Silence ensued at our table. I let the conversation drop but could not stop thinking about why BNS are so despised and why there is so much fear that White children will embrace and emulate them.

Perhaps my newspaper friend is enslaved by a pathology of epidemic proportions that deems all Iverson-like athletes (Black) lazy and unprofessional. Now, the Iversons of the world are not without flaws; they should be more accountable. But since American culture measures athletes' successes by their individual production, missing practice or refusing to wear a tie shouldn't matter; instead, leading one's team and the league in scoring and steals (defense) and producing victories should earn him great favor in a culture that values meritocracy.

Suddenly the earlier banter and chatter at the table had spiraled into the dark clouds of race. Still, I decided I had nothing to lose by pushing a bit further: "So tell me," I politely queried, "how come those involved in or who view sports, especially White sports journalists, skirt racism in sports, which is replete with examples of racial bias and inequalities reflective of the nature of American culture? For example, why is it that professional hockey (which is at essence violent, brutal, and encourages immoral behavior) and its participants are rarely critiqued at the same level as football, baseball, and especially basketball players for being bad role models?" More silence. So I pressed on: "I mean, how come nobody talks greed about hockey players, who, during the 2004 lockout, left to sign contracts (over one-third of the league) in other countries until the NHL matter was settled?" Even more silence coupled with a stupid look. He had nothing to say, and I was not surprised. I am bothered that people will read sports news stories judging Iverson and others like him based on biased analysis from people like this sportswriter. Meanwhile, the absence of criticism directed at hockey players' team fidelity speaks volumes about the privilege of race in America. The intellectual Baller in me refused to remain silent without challenging what I felt was a racially charged morality judgment on the part of my new sportswriter friend. His silence to my queries spoke volumes.

## Who Can Be Ballers?

The previous generation had fought hard and suffered indignities that my generation would deem unacceptable, to provide us with the opportunities they never had. We are the beneficiaries of their struggles. The reality is that numerous laws were passed to end discrimination and racism in the areas of housing, politics, education, and employment. Unlike our elders, we could go to school (if we were willing to take the forty-minute bus rides to the suburbs or across town) with Whites (who had now fled to suburbia), use the same bathroom, eat in the same restaurants, and compete with and against them in sports. But to paraphrase Malcolm X, changing laws is meaningless unless the hearts and minds of Whites change with those laws.

BNS represent a generation engaging American society post–civil rights, expecting that the hearts and minds of the country embrace difference. BNS, while expressing the agony of life and transcending it via toughness of spirit, demand the right to coexist equally, if not always peacefully. BNS are hesitant toward nonviolent tactics or humility as a viable strategy. BNS are a generation raised on hip-hop, which fosters ethnic pride and expresses the political and economic disenfranchisement of Black and Latino youth and other groups and yet continues the dreams of instant gratification, wealth, and success endemic of American culture. But hip-hop also reflects a character, attitude, thinking, style, way of viewing the world—strategies of freeing oneself from the struggles of inner-city life that truly impact BNS. The true BNS understands that what one thinks and does is who they are.

As a result, BNS are influenced by hip-hop's credo, according to rapper KRS-One, of rethinking and challenging norms or foundations of society or going against the grain. At times it has led to BNS confronting racism, but always, like the blues, engaging the impulse of self-confrontation. Like hip-hop, BNS do not fear displaying their own cultural aesthetics and ethnic values (keeping it "real," so to speak). Like the blues, soul, and funk upon whose shoulders hip-hop stands, hip-hop encompasses African American folk expressions and attitude via language, posture, and stylized dress culled from street culture. The values that underpin so much of hip-hop culture—the materialism, brand consciousness, gun iconography, anti-intellectualism—are very much by-products of the larger American culture. The genesis of this attitude should not be dumped in the lap of Black American youth culture or its athletes as validation of immoral pathology systemic among this group of people—which is often the case in media depictions.

This was definitely the case during the Ron Artest and Detroit Piston fans melee in 2004. Artest was known for his embrace of rap and hip-hop music. As hip-hop activist Davey D explains, hip-hop attitude found itself at the forefront for another menacing societal ill—sporting violence. But how can we attach such blame to hip-hop regarding something as violent as sports? Nobody assumed that the White fan who threw a full cup of beer on Artest as he lay on top of the scorers' tables trying to avoid a fight acted because of country music or rock 'n' roll attitude. Davey D wondered if the White fan or Artest had been listening to Guns N' Roses before the game, would people assume that they had a rock 'n' roll attitude as opposed to a hip-hop attitude? Such cultural imperialism and assumptions frame the racial tensions in our culture. Few want to accept that violence at sporting events has nothing to do with hip-hop, but everything to do with a culture with a history of violent racism.

Hip-hop realness, gritty urban flavor, post–civil rights resolve to make one's own way without humility or concessions bubbles into modern boardrooms, university classroom lectures, books, marketing, film, and other venues where Ballers are present. In sports culture, it is visible in the locker rooms, playing styles, interview transcripts—the cause for conflict between modern media, fans, and coaches. Hip-hop's influence upon youth music, marketing, language, clothing, and sports is pervasive.

Who can downplay the role of race in the hip-hop generation's widespread jailing and police profiling, inadequate education, and renewed segregation along with disparate economic opportunity? In poor urban communities, the mantra is that unless one has a "wicked jump-shot," can run a sub-4.4 forty-yard dash, has at least a forty-inch vertical leap, is close to seven feet tall, or can spit wicked rhymes, the outlook is bleak. Not only are twentieth- and twenty-first-century athletes unafraid of White people and uninterested in proving their worth to them; they are disgruntled that the promises of the civil rights movement are empty—even if they are not conversant in the specifics of those promises. Thus, the ethos, the aesthetics, the music, and the attitude of this generation are far from attempting to make concessions or taking shit quietly. The response to this hip-hop generation of sports stars is similar to that of the Portland Trail Blazers of the NBA, who in 2003 cleaned house, including its marquee player Rasheed Wallace, in hopes of projecting a positive perception of a team that everybody in Portland could be proud of again (the 2010 Blazers is filled with young players with a "clean" image).

But who can be proud of a past that mistreated Black athletes or a contemporary era that continues to snub them when they show too much pride? Sports media romanticize the past. For example, pimps like Harlem Globetrotters owner Abe Saperstein undercut Black-owned teams like the Rens for the best players (whom he often underpaid) because he knew the Globetrotters, along with the New York Renaissance (from 1920 to 1950), was the only show in town for African American players. Instead history paints him a savior or ignores this fact completely. The Globetrotters is forever a reminder that serious athletes were reduced to clown ball (the same was true of most barnstorming Negro League baseball teams) because of racism in America. And by the mid-1950s when African Americans made their way into the NBA, players like Woody Sauldsberry and Bill Russell were often at odds with racial politics of the time. Things were so bad that Sauldsberry, a former Rookie of the Year (1957–58), became so frustrated from fighting racial battles in the NBA that he quit in 1966.

Although BNS are likely not well schooled in the history of pioneers like Sauldsberry, they do know about racial battles. As post–civil rights products, they give voice to their disillusionment. How players play, celebrate, and respond to authority reflect a subtle protest against White power and dominance in all aspects of American society. In the same way that break-dancing, deejaying, and graffiti art have come to encompass the essential elements of hip-hop, so have the attitude, style of play, and other elements defined BNS in American sports culture. BNS represent a rejection of bourgeois and dominant culture and an embrace of being true to one's self, working for one's self, and making opportunities where none exist. To understand hip-hop is to begin to understand the modern athlete in American sports culture—a truth that American media and image-makers loathe.

Make no mistake that race is real. It lives and breathes in sports culture, but BNS emerged onto the scene as beneficiaries of a previous generation that bravely confronted many explosive issues that continue to plague contemporary society: namely, racial hierarchy and imbalanced distribution of wealth, education, and power. BNS have endured the recent escalation in the last two decades of Black rage and White backlash that culminated in wage declines, renewed racial divides, and, as Cornell West has suggested, "a massive transfer of wealth from working people to the well-to-do, and an increase in drugs and guns in American life" (*Race Matters*, 157). Yet media and others insist on attacking BNS, who are shaped by a society driven by money, a society whose massive racial divide often translates into huge gaps between rich and poor along color lines. Curt Flood of the St. Louis Cardinals (discussed more in chapter three) is a shining example of what it means to be a Baller. He fought being traded on the grounds of the reserve clause violating federal antitrust laws (Ashe 21–22). Flood opposed baseball's reserve clause, which bound all players, for life, to the first club that signed them. In 1970, with the support of the Players Association, Flood filed suit in United States District Court for the Southern District of New York against the National and American League presidents and all twenty-four Major League teams, asking for $4.1 million in damages (21). Flood, a pioneer BNS, was in fact demanding the right to negotiate. Flood's "Balleresque" boldness resulted in a double victory for players facing bondage on the grounds of their status as players with the first team that signed them and for Black players being discriminated against financially because of their race.

The irony of sport is that although it is applauded for crossing racial lines or making significant social strides, it literally keeps us divided along racial lines by both the line of scrimmage and opposing sidelines, as my own personal football story revealed. Football managed to introduce a group of ten-year-olds to racial conflict instead of uniting us as human beings. I am unable to ignore the reality that much more than a simple football game had ensued that Sunday afternoon over twenty-five years ago. What had occurred was a race war between ten-year-olds. The opposing team's objective was to beat us and prove our inferiority or, worse, their supremacy. And our objective was to, as Mr. Coleman suggested, embarrass them such that they knew that White supremacy was a fallacy. The game was a symbol or marker upon which they could test the myth of White supremacy that their social world had taught them. They were angry because our convincing victory proved it false. For us, it was supposed to be an opportunity to feel good about ourselves, to graciously smash the myth, even in the face of being called "niggers."

So racism is nothing new in sports. My being called a name while playing football as a ten-year-old is similar to what the great Fritz Pollard, who played for Brown University in 1915, endured after a stellar performance against Yale. In a backhanded compliment after a game, an opposing player told Pollard: "You're a nigger, but you're the best goddamn football player I ever saw" (102). What appears to be a situation where Pollard's performance transcended his race was really an acknowledgment that despite how well he played, he was still a "nigger." Indeed, racism dies hard—even on fields of play.

*Two Minute Drill on Race and Sport*
Reflecting again on my childhood racial sport incident reminds me of what the writer James Baldwin said about the conundrum of racism and White supremacy in America. According to Baldwin, racism exists because many Whites have unfortunately been raised and acculturated to believe in their supremacy as Whites, only to grow up and discover that this is a myth and a fallacy. Now that I am an adult, I have more pity than hate for the boy who called me a "nigger"—who felt I was somehow inferior to him. Yet I reserve my anger for his parents and coaches, who

were responsible for his behavior. I am equally critical of my own coaches, who demanded we suffer this verbal indignity in exchange for an opportunity to display supremacy on the field of play. New School Ballers are not "feeling" this.

However, in fairness to our coaches, our victory that day was a small victory for them because they placed racial stakes on our game. Their generation did not have that opportunity. But moral victories or winning the battle on the field is not enough for me, or my generation. As BNS, we feel entitled to political, economic, and social privilege—alas, the racial conflict in the modern world is a conflict amplified in the world of sports. That incident and similar ones against other White teams have aided my understanding of the pain that Larry Doby, Jackie Robinson, Bill Russell, Jim Brown, and others endured as mid-twentieth-century sports pioneers.

My incident occurred nearly thirty years after Robinson, Doby, and others made "racial strides." Those who say race is void in sports are lying or closing their eyes to the truth of racism in American culture. Sports reflect the racial trials and tribulations in our society—a fact that is uncontestable given the controversy surrounding the ongoing biases against Black coaches, quarterbacks, front-office personnel, and BNS like Barry Bonds, Floyd Mayweather, and Allen Iverson. These athletes do things their own way, opting not to seek approval; they insist that fans and media take them as they are.

Our contemporary society remains driven by assumptions of White supremacy as an accepted state of affairs; since it is not frank or overt, few discuss it. It is a delicate subject. Even despite the election of America's first Black president. And when it is prevalent, the past is rewritten so as to deny or minimize the obvious fact of global White domination and discrimination. So, in the sports world, rather than openly discuss the discomfort with Black heroism in American society or the true currents of racism, we shrug it off, allowing the subtle negative messages to blare away in our ears. The media display, report, regard, and present to the world information and images void of these truths that I hold to be self-evident: What we receive daily are doses of a colonial construct that conveys a hierarchy of races and civilizations suggesting that Whites belong to the superior race and civilization and that non-Whites are immoral and inferior.

Racism continues to haunt modern sports professionals, amateurs, fans, and American culture. Therefore our society needs Ballers that are as concerned with the final score as they are with imposing their own styles and aesthetic conventions without fear of banishment, while forcing the world to contend with them on different terms. The real problem with athletes like Rasheed Wallace, Curt Flood, Barry Bonds, and other BNS is that they reflect some aspect of what poet Quincy Troupe calls "unreconstructed Black men." Such men and women, despite newfound privilege or wealth, continue being themselves (they keep it real) and are unwilling to turn a blind eye to their roots, social inequities, impropriety, exploitation, or racism. Real Ballers are never muted or blinded by their own good fortune. True Ballers see their good fortune for the aberration it is in a climate of heightened racial hostility and regressive legal policies. Hopefully more modern athletes can follow the footsteps of the previous generation and aspire to be Ballers or individuals who call shots on their own terms, embrace leadership, intellectualism, and their ethnic identity without excessive humility or apology. Those capable and willing to claim space beyond what the racial contract designates for them are truly Ballers, in any era.

# CHAPTER THREE

## ORIGINAL BALLERS AND NEW SCHOOL BALLERS

*Racism systematically verifies itself when the slaves can only break free by imitating the master: by contradicting his own reality.*

—John O'Neal

*Some say I'm what's wrong with sports today. I say, I'm the American Dream.*

—Latrell Sprewell

*I am not a role model.*

—Charles Barkley

As I listen to reporters and commentators and read sports columns, I have one question to ask: "Why isn't it okay to be Black?" Any aesthetic or cultural values that are non-White are condemned as immoral or negative—until appropriated by the dominant culture. The athletes whose on- and off-court styles or values reflect those of White American culture are embraced. All "others" are labeled outlaws, criminalized, their bodies a fetish or engrossment, the subject of ridicule and gaze. In his political autobiography *Die Nigger Die!* H. Rap Brown explains the phenomenon of Black pride, acceptance, and success in America this way: "When a

Black man looks at Black people with a Black mind and a Black soul, it is immediately apparent that Black people possess certain unique characteristics that not only distinguish them from Whites and Negroes, but that have greatly contributed to the survival of Blacks. Whites recognize this and have always attempted to eradicate these characteristics or discredit them. In instances where they have succeeded, Negroes have been created."[1] Brown characterizes American culture in the twenty-first century. Of course, the true problem that non-White sports stars present is that they sometimes resist the invented; they resist being made "Negroes." The response to BNS who reject these expectations is an indication that we still inhabit a world that is threatened by and does not respect the cultural values of "others." The expressive Black youth culture that BNS represent is thought to be threatening and detrimentally different from the dominant culture.

In fact, a closer examination of the corporate embrace of Michael Jordan, the modern symbol of racial progress, reveals that its okay be "like Mike" as long as one embraces a nonracial persona deemed "acceptable." But people get a case of selective amnesia when it comes to remembering the young Jordan with his New School swagger, big diamond earring, outlaw red-and-black shoe with his name on it, gold chains, baggy shorts, and fat rides as a representative of the new culture of basketball, even sports. Young Money (Jordan) was as counterculture and trendy as some of the most hated BNS (which earned him the ire of some veterans during his first NBA All-Star appearance). But over time Jordan was embraced, partly because he shaped his persona in ways that appealed to the majority (rejecting hip-hop, always saying the right thing, never touching any politics). The harsh response to BNS who fail to follow the revised Jordan formula confirms that cultural "otherness" is unacceptable because it challenges notions of Whiteness as the norm.

The normalization of Whiteness as rightness is masked in the racial transcendence of a Jordan, a Tiger Woods, and other successful "crossover" star athletes. If only palatable identities that make you forget they are Black are acceptable, then we have not progressed very far.

This is why modern stars that leave their hip-hop culture and attitude at home in favor of an altered personal style are rewarded with good press coverage and endorsement deals. Athletes' cultural presence positions them as leaders and trendsetters, which in turn empowers them as perhaps the most effective endorsers of products from beer and razors to cars. They shape images, culture standards, and attitudes in the younger sector of the viewing public. Nobody wants to admit the contempt that the media and corporate entities have for contemporary athletes with their tattoos, cornrows, Black self-expression, and style that is not the "norm." How else do we explain why media often depict them as egomaniacs or villains, instead of the heroes that sportswriters envision from their boyhood?

These hip-hop generation-bred BNS see disparities in their workplace—they say what they feel; they are unwilling to alter their images to appease a public, and will not accept anything less than full respect. The racial contract that fuels or expects feelings of non-White cultural inferiority contributes significantly to why BNS are marketed as aggressive and violent for profit, then judged immoral cultural outlaws who do not know their place. It is also the reason why athletes like Tiger Woods and Grant Hill are considered "nonthreatening" Black men, palatable to an American public, while "philistines" such as Mike Vick, Allen Iverson, Terrell Owens, and Randy Moss have jerseys that outsell most other players' in their respective leagues. Popular culture embraces the latter, while the "tail wagging the dog" refuses to acknowledge the public support of them. The rejection of clearly expressed Blackness and the embrace of neutral images inform us that America is not as "post-race" as we want to hope it is.

BNS are a problem because they are uninterested in changing who they are or participating fully in the charade that teams and corporations have set up to control their images. Many are conflicted by what it means to gain "mainstream" acceptance. There is indeed a problem with being asked to reject one's natural self and put on airs to gain "mainstream" appeal, especially when your jersey sales indicate the fan base loves you. It is even more problematic when the "mainstream" uses or pimps elements of the very culture modern athletes are asked to abandon and then begins to ascribe new meanings to Black cultural representations in its marketing of athletes (for example, the hip-hop music played during NBA games). In the modern sports culture, many of the most visible athletes in the most popular sports are Black and Latino. And more often than not, these athletes' aesthetics do not reflect "mainstream" culture. Athletes of the 1960s and 1970s reflected the style and sentiments of soul, funk, and jazz culture. Hip-Hop culture is the driving force of this generation of athletes. As cultural critic and anthropologist Cheryl Keyes points out about hip-hop, coolness is important because it "enhances one's social competence, pride, dignity, self-esteem, and respect. Cool posing [is a way of] exhibiting grace under pressure" (153). Hip-hop culture is about one's style during performance: it allows empowerment of voice; it is inspired art without any nurturing; it is lived and performed daily; it is about doing what feels natural. Modern athletes bring this inspired art on to playing fields and courts. BNS do what feels natural.

As popular culture's greatest heroes—a vital and unique component of our culture—athletes possess enormous potential to influence people and perhaps even create change in the world. Although many athletes (rightly so) do not feel they should be burdened with the responsibility of being role models (see Charles Barkley's "I am not a role model" commercial), the media, some fans, and parents see them as such. However, the rebellion of the hip-hop-influenced BNS must be examined with early pioneers, whom I call the Original New School, in mind. These individuals have exhibited far more courage, been more daring, risked more financially, and made greater social and political statements than most contemporary BNS combined. Despite all the "hip-hop grace under pressure" personas, coolness, and hypermasculine resistance, BNS must recognize the examples and courage of their predecessors. These trailblazers have paved the way, often risking much while realizing less financial return than contemporary athletes.


*Talking about Old School*
BNS are direct descendants of a previous generation that faced more overt struggles and whose actions required more courageous acts of opposition and sacrifice than BNS experience themselves. They often endured overt hate and anger from the American public. Although some BNS are similar to early rebels, (Original Ballers like Jim Brown, Althea Gibson, Jack Johnson, or Muhammad Ali), they have not made nearly the same sorts of sacrifices. Also their cocksure sway of "realness" and brashness and their opposition to discrimination set them apart from modern BNS. The Original Ballers were far more "real," political, daring, and provocative.

In the face of overt racial strife five decades ago, these pioneers made significant strides in boxing, baseball, tennis, basketball, and football that have changed people's attitudes throughout the world. They definitely fit the description of folk heroes: bad men and women who fought back against their oppressors, creatively disdained social conventions, and stood up unselfishly to hegemony, performing acts of "badness" in the face of racial oppression. The athletes of the earlier era were inspired by blues and jazz ideals, and the aesthetics of outlaw figures common in African American folk culture.

Blues, which emerged in the early twentieth century in New Orleans and other areas of the South, borrows from the structural devices and harmonic technique of the work songs and spirituals, but is without a chorus. The athletes of the first half of the twentieth century are most influenced by the blues and reflect it. Like the blues, which relies on call and response and exposes life's trials and troubles without waiting for heaven for justice, they spoke out and took action.

And athletes from the early twentieth century to the late 1980s personify more of a jazz persona that cultivated the emergence of hip-hop and BNS. I say this because jazz is comprised of disparate, divergent elements, a conglomeration of rural, urban, inland, portside, established, and new. It is a city phenomenon. As such it uniquely captures the cadences, voices, and emerging new physical identity of modern cities in America. Original Ballers like Jack Johnson, Satchel Paige, Jim Brown, and Curt Flood certainly fit this description and echoed their sentiments. Like the train, which is associated with the blues, they represented a shift away from the land where their parents and grandparents had been slaves, along with the conditions that threatened to continue this legacy. Unlike in the spirituals of their forebearers, their generation was uninterested in trains taking people to heaven or the underground railroads to freedom. They were the first generation to really pressure America to abide by that promise of equality in freedom. They forced America's contradictions into the public sphere, where they had to be dealt with like never before.

Unfortunately many of the contemporary Ballers are unwilling to make the same sacrifices. They do not really believe they have the power to determine the course of the war, education, or politics. And, many fear that an unpopular position could lead to an exit from the sports world or a loss of financial rewards. Although there are some modern sports figures in the spirit of those outlined below, not enough of the New School Ballers are following in the footsteps of the Original Ballers—true athlete/rebels.

*John Arthur "Jack" Johnson (The Original Baller)*
No discussion of the New School can commence without mentioning Jack Johnson, who in 1908 became the first Black heavyweight champion of the world. Born in 1878 in Galveston, Texas, he was perhaps the most famous, outspoken, cocky, brash, flashy, masculine to a fault, and resistant to White supremacy athlete of the twentieth century. He was also perhaps the most publicly and financially persecuted for these very same reasons. Johnson's career was one spent being hunted by the police and chased out of the country for his defiance of cultural codes that dictated that Black men act subservient and restrain from public displays of self-confidence—

and stayed away from White women.

Johnson was an interesting and quite entertaining fellow whose greatness was his ability to convince Tommy Burns, then the champ, to cross the color line that barred giving a Black fighter a shot at the title. (Johnson agreed to fight for a purse of $5,000 while Burns was to receive $35,000.) Johnson chased Burns around the world until he finally relented and agreed to fight him. Johnson spent his entire career punching myths of White supremacy and its false power squarely in the jaw. For example, he queried Tommy Burns while thrashing him: "Who told you I was yellow? You're white, Tommy—white as the flag of surrender!" (Ashe 34). Johnson went on to rule the heavyweight division for six tumultuous, yet colorful years, calling shots, doing things his way, seeing whatever women he chose—White or Black. The only thing that beat him was a system of institutional racism and hate. The American government fabricated an indictment under the Mann Act (White-Slave Traffic Act) for taking a woman across state lines to halt Johnson's career.

Johnson finally tired of running and allegedly struck a deal in 1914 to fight in 1915 in order to "give" the title back to the new "Great White Hope" Jess Willard in a fight in Havana, Cuba, for $30,000 and a chance to return home to see his mother. In the end he served time in Leavenworth, Kansas, in 1920 for violating the Mann Act, a charge to which he entered a plea of not guilty.

Most of Johnson's troubles, including the falsified Mann Act that literally placed him on the run (he spent several years jumping from Paris, Russia, and England looking for fights), stemmed from his being a Black heavyweight champion and refusing to show humility in the face of White supremacy. Jack could have "known his place," refused to date or marry White women, and followed the rules of the racial contract for the sake of wealth, but he did not. In fact, he earned enormous wealth (although he squandered much of it on clothes, jewels, and cars) while insisting on being Jack Johnson. Indeed, his crimes were none other than holding the title, refusing to defer to authority, and his unforgivable Blackness.

*Muhammad Ali*

Muhammad Ali once remarked to James Earl Jones after seeing the 1968 play *The Great White Hope*, which was inspired by the struggles of Jack Johnson, "You take out the issue of the white women and replace that with the issue of religion. That's my story." Like Johnson, Ali was maligned during his career, forced to abandon the title because of his principles and lack of humility. Ali's principles, of course, revolved around his religion. But both men were brash, outspoken symbols of Black masculinity, and this is what caused trouble.

Ali, who became the undisputed heavyweight champion in 1964, was among the first twentieth-century athletes to understand the power of the camera. He loved it and it seemed to love him. Like Jack Johnson nearly fifty years earlier, he represented a new kind of Black man whose confidence, assertiveness, playfulness, and introspection both delighted and horrified his audience. He was also able to transcend the confines of boxing, emerging as a media celebrity because of his words and deeds.

The irony with Ali is that today he is embraced worldwide as a hero, but during his prime he paid a heavy price for standing up for what he believed in with much less public support. Unfortunately, Ali was not much embraced when he changed his name from Cassius Clay to Ali and announced after defeating Sonny Liston for the heavyweight title that he was a Muslim. He was hated more for his mouth, his self-confidence, and his outspokenness against American racism and hypocrisy. At the peak of his career, Ali lost millions in purses and endorsement opportunities because of his religious and political beliefs. The most damaging was his stance against the Vietnam War. His conscientious objection to the war got him banned from professional boxing and labeled unpatriotic. Although the FBI conducted a hearing that determined Ali was sincere in his religious objections to joining the U.S. Army, the Department of Justice and Selective Service Board decided to make an example of him—a form of systemic racial bias. Ali could have taken the easy path. He could have apologized for his views and accepted the promise of a noncombat appointment, but his principles would not allow him to do so. Instead he endured being stripped of his heavyweight championship title, his passport, and the ability to earn a living boxing for nearly four years.

As much as Ali, who is currently far less verbal due to Parkinson's disease, is revered in the memory and minds of modern fans, people selectively forget he was enemy number one for his outspokenness. Ali was everything Madison Avenue sought: smart, attractive, articulate, charismatic, with a great sense of humor—and he won. However, he was also Muslim, refused to join an immoral and losing war, and made it quite clear that he was an unreconstructed Black man. Although this did not endear him to corporate America (he only got a D-Con roach killer endorsement deal), he was everything that BNS wish they could be or should at least strive to become—a standard-bearer for the modern athlete.

## Leroy "Satchel" Paige

Born in Mobile, Alabama, in 1906, Leroy "Satchel" Paige was the colorful pitcher who dominated the Negro Leagues for many years. He had to wait until he was in his forties to get a chance to pitch for the Cleveland Indians. As a forty-something player, he won Rookie of the Year. Paige was a pioneer who often dictated whom he would play for, how many innings he would pitch, and for how much. He was a rare blend of unbelievable talent and unending charisma. The man was infamously credited with almost destroying the Negro Leagues because he formed a team of all-stars that played in Cuba for lots of money.

Paige was flashy, dressed extremely well, drove a bright red convertible, was friendly and charismatic, and insisted on doing things his way. The latter of these attributes is precisely what kept him from being picked first to play in Major League Baseball before Jackie Robinson, his Kansas City Monarch teammate. While in Major League Baseball, his innovative "Hesitation Pitch" was so baffling to batters that it was ruled illegal by the American League. Paige, truly an Original Baller, refused to let racism or age keep him out of Major League Baseball.

## Andrew "Rube" Foster

Andrew "Rube" Foster, was a visionary in his own right. He responded to the White baseball league's segregation policy by spearheading the founding of the Negro National League, which flourished from 1920 to 1931, operating in the Midwest and South. Foster was a great player, manager, and league president whose BNS spirit led him to form a partnership with John Schorling in 1910 to organize one of the best Black teams in history, the Chicago American Giants. The American Giants dominated all other competition, winning roughly eleven championships. Next his vision led him to form the Negro National League, which had some teams that could compete with the very best Major League teams of his era. He increased interest in baseball, specifically the Negro League, with innovations such as All-Star Games and night games.

Rube was indeed a "Baller" in the true sense of the word. He was an awesome pitcher, revolutionary manager (his teams won the first three Negro National League pennants via his revolutionary strategies that utilized speed, psychology, and the bunt-and-run), and president of the Negro National League. As a pitcher (he compiled a record of 54–1 his second season with the Cuban X-Giants), manager, and executive, the man exhibited total control, calling the right shots. Unfortunately, Foster is not often remembered for his contributions to moving America closer to equality. Many forget that the Negro National League played a key role in contributing to economic development in Black communities. Foster's league faltered mainly because of racial stresses, the Great Depression, and his own untimely nervous breakdown in 1926 that led to his death in 1930. However, he did not let American racism and prejudice deter him from playing the game he loved on his own terms.

## Curtis Charles Flood

Curt Flood is perhaps the most famous yet underappreciated Baller of them all. He paved the way for what we know now as free agency in professional sports, because he was courageous enough to challenge the

Major League Baseball's "reserve clause" system. Flood—a star who had earned three All-Star appearances, seven Gold Gloves, a pair of World Series championships, and $90,000 a year—risked it all when he accused baseball of violating the Thirteenth Amendment, barring slavery and involuntary servitude. Flood's public stand against the reserve clause argued that the clause violated antitrust laws by depressing wages and limiting a player to a single team, as well as violating the Thirteenth Amendment. Born in Houston, Texas, and raised in Oakland, California, Flood single-handedly brought about free agency but never benefited from it.

Curt Flood epitomized what it means to be a Baller in his 1969 refusal to be traded from the St. Louis Cardinals to the Philadelphia Phillies without his consent. Thus when the Cardinals attempted to trade him, he did the unheard-of and sent a letter to Commissioner Bowie Kuhn stating his refusal to exist as property, that he wanted the freedom to play for other clubs the next season, and that the clause was unconstitutional. Then he shocked the baseball world in 1970 when he filed a suit against Major League Baseball and its reserve clause. He argued for free agency and the right to choose his team and negotiate his salary. The public and the media initially reacted to Flood's action negatively, branding the outfielder an ingrate, a destroyer, even a blasphemer. Despite negative public sentiments, Flood simply decided it was time to tear up the racial contract, for his principled stand dually challenged baseball and race.

Flood's case eventually climbed all the way to the Supreme Court, where his lawyer, former Supreme Court Justice Arthur Goldberg, put forth evidence that baseball's reserve clause violated the antitrust laws by depressing wages and limiting a player to one team. Baseball's defense team attempted to counter Goldberg's broad arguments for human and labor rights point by point, but the crux of baseball's argument dealt with such ideas as tradition and "the Good of the Game." Despite gaining some public sympathy as the truly antiquarian nature of the reserve clause became known, Flood still lost the case. The Supreme Court ruled in favor of baseball 5 to 3, using a "logic" that combined a liberal use of *stare decisis* with a belief that baseball simply should stay the way it is.

Flood's decision to fight Major League Baseball, to attack its myths of meritocracy and fairness, effectively cleared the way for modern free agency. Unfortunately, it destroyed his career in the process. What makes Flood so amazing is that he left a lot of money on the table to fight for a principle. Few players were willing to take the stand he took; in fact, despite financial backing from the Players Association, few players were willing to risk being "whitelisted" to testify on Flood's behalf. He also realized he would very well never play again (which happened). However, he was unwilling to drop the case and settle for a better contract for himself. He also knew the magnitude of his act for future players (who now earn on the average of $1–2 million as opposed to the $25,000 salary when Flood launched his case in 1969).

Flood is an ultimate Baller because his challenge merged the fights for racial justice with the rights of all baseball players. His goal was to make an impact on his "corner of society," to challenge America to fulfill the values it long championed. What is honorable is that Flood was willing to do this at his own detriment, sacrificing his place in the Hall of Fame (which he has yet to achieve but deserves) and his ability to play the game he loved because of a principled stand that has reaped huge dividends for modern players. Like former tennis star Billie Jean King, he fought so that he and his peers could be compensated fairly. He should forever be recognized for his courage, commitment, and enormous baseball talent.

*Jim Brown*

When the great Jim Brown walked away from football after nine years, he owned the rushing title and was the best player in the NFL at the time. The world was shocked. During his career he led the fight on and off the field against racism and bigotry. Brown was a true Baller; he was brash, bold, confident, proud, and determined to receive equal treatment. On the field he was a team leader, helping to design and call plays for a few seasons. Known as an activist, he was outspoken. Refusing to leave the set of the film he was shooting at the time (or endure the daily fines team owner Art Modell imposed on him), Brown stood at the fork in the road and headed straight for a career as a movie star. After nine years he suddenly retired on his own terms during this disagreement. He has a true Baller spirit. He went on to become an early Black leading man in Hollywood, making a new way for himself, on his own terms.

Despite football and acting success, Brown has never shied away from political concerns. In the 1960s he was one of several prominent athletes that founded the Negro Industrial and Economic Union (NIEU). The goal of this organization was aimed at working with Black businessmen and -women from around the nation to provide financial backing for Black-owned businesses. In the 1990s he started a nonprofit foundation committed to changing the lives of youth, particularly those trapped in the clutches of gang culture. Among his achievements with this organization has been his ability to get members of the Crips and Bloods gangs to his house to start a summit to quell violence. As part of his program, he goes into prisons and encourages youth to study and get themselves together. Always determined to maintain a sense of self, he has been known to say: "I am not a slave, I am not a slave mentality." He openly protests discrimination and oppression, using his high-profile position as an athlete to challenge racism in America.

*Althea Gibson and Dr. Robert Walter Johnson*
Born in Harlem and shy, Althea Gibson began in the Negro Tennis Association but wanted an opportunity to play in the all-White United States Tennis Association (USTA). With a little help from Alice Marble, who wrote a public letter embarrassing the USTA for refusing to allow Gibson to compete, Gibson became the first Black to play at Forest Hills in the American Tennis Championship. Gibson, like Robinson, was treated very badly as she forged new ground. She even had to undergo the

humiliation of a physical examination to confirm she was a woman! Although she did not win that tournament, she did win the battle of opening the door of opportunity. Gibson's Baller spirit is all the more impressive because she endured psychological cruelties and inequities in her quest to play in the USTA as the lone pioneer and without the nation watching closely. She did not have the same audience of the major sports like football, baseball, and basketball. There was not a throng of people following Althea Gibson as she blazed a new trail—she had to go it alone.

Although she went six years without winning a major tournament, in 1957 she became the first Black to win Wimbledon. Anyone familiar with the isolation and segregation of tennis understands the significance of her achievement. Venus and Serena Williams had each other but Gibson was alone. Despite the obstacles of racism and isolation, Gibson did not give up and managed to dominate women's tennis from 1956–58. Several obstacles made it difficult for her to truly develop her career: her gender, lack of sponsors, and her race. Without sponsors she could not make a living playing tennis.

It is important to point out that pioneering Black tennis players like Gibson and Arthur Ashe were aided by important mentors and visionaries such as Dr. Robert Walter Johnson who for over twenty summers took young Black American tennis players into his home, and fed, clothed and trained them out of his own pocket on the clay court in his backyard. He helped to cultivate and support champions like Gibson in hopes that change would be lasting. Monday through Thursday, morning to night he worked with youngsters on his court, drilling them on fundamentals of the game and on comportment. He emphasized calm intellect, demanding that they conduct themselves in a way that honored Black people from how they dressed to how they played. Although Dr. Johnson did not personally break barriers or win championships, he did play an important role in the success of pioneers like Ashe and Gibson.

*Wilma Rudolph*
Wilma Rudolph was the first of many Black women track stars from Tennessee State. She won the bronze medal in the 100-yard dash in the 1956 Olympic Games, then won three gold medals in the 1960 Olympic Games in Rome. Her success not only opened the door for Black women athletes, but for White women athletes as well. Suddenly women in track received more attention and respect. A true Baller, Rudolph used her stardom to make changes. For example, she refused to be honored in a parade in her hometown of Clarksville, Tennessee, because the parade was segregated. In 1960 she stood her ground and used her influence to make things different—if only for a day. The mayor relented and made the parade integrated. Her stance compelled him to make a speech using the analogy of the white and black keys on the piano having to work together to make good music. This was a huge breakthrough in the previously segregated town.

*Bill Russell*
Equally as important was William Felton "Bill" Russell from Monroe, Louisiana, who joined Jim Brown as a member of the Negro Industrial and Economic Union and resisted prejudice throughout his magnificent NBA career. As *the* leader of the most dominant dynasty (eleven titles in thirteen years—including eight straight), the Boston Celtics, Russell changed the game of basketball and the role of Black men in sports. He is most famous for becoming the first Black coach in the NBA and the first one to win an NBA title (as player-coach). Russell was a true leader who, like Brown, was outspoken regarding social injustice. Playing in Boston, a notoriously racist city, Russell never backed down from a challenge or unfair treatment. When he purchased a home in a white neighborhood, trash was thrown in his yard and neighbors wanted him to move until they learned he was a Celtics star. He made it known he resented being accepted only as a basketball player. Once when he was denied admission to a Kentucky coffee shop, he led a boycott of the Lexington game to bring attention to this bigotry.

Never one to follow, he called his own shots on the court, as well as off. In the 1960s Russell once declared that a major problem for Blacks in America was that they lacked race pride and had too long been victims of psychological warfare. In fact, he never signed the racial contract and has been unforgiving regarding the racism he was forced to endure. In 1974 when he became the first Black elected to the Hall of Fame, his absence at the event made a huge statement, a bigger statement than his failure in 1972 to attend the Celtics' ceremony retiring his jersey. Indeed, Russell was a trailblazer, a maverick in his own right—an original BNS—a model of dignity and pride.

### Frederick "Fritz" Douglass Pollard

Fritz Pollard was the first Black player in the Rose Bowl (1916) and the first Black head coach in NFL history (1921). After World War I, he joined the Akron Professionals, remaining in the American Football League with four different teams as a player or player-coach until 1926. The wiry elusive running back was indeed a pioneer of racial advancement—evident from his post-playing days when he organized all-Black teams to play exhibition games all over the country in an effort to force the NFL to sign more Black players. The Black Coaches Association pays tribute to his efforts as an original or pioneer New School leader through its Fritz Pollard Alliance, which promotes minority hiring.

### Ralph Wiley

Ralph Wiley was perhaps the most famous African American sportswriter to emerge in a long time. Wiley never pulled any punches; he always challenged the norm, always insisted on telling the truth, and was never afraid to mix talk of sports with race. As a writer and social critic, he is a hero to me. His death 13 June 2004 was a difficult loss. Contemporary New School sportswriters like Scoop Jackson, Stephen A. Smith, and Michael Wilbon owe a huge debt to Wiley—we all do. He was not afraid to speak the truth, no matter whom it angered, made uncomfortable, or offended. The author of books like *Why Black People Tend to Shout* and *What Black People Should Do Now*, he was an inspiration for the type of work I am doing and aspire to do in the future. His body of work is serious, captivating, and necessary. He never shied away from tough subjects. He is a modern standard-bearer of sports journalism.

*Tommy Smith, John Carlos, and Dr. Harry Edwards*
As the 1968 Olympic Games in Mexico City were approaching, Black athletes were mulling whether to take a political stand and boycott the games, or to run and jump for medals. Under the tutelage and leadership of Harry Edwards, a professor at San Jose State, Black athletes decided to run, win, then make the ultimate stand. Harry Edwards made the famous statement, "We need to say more than our athletic feats." Many prominent figures such as Jesse Owens and Jackie Robinson were divided regarding the best course of action. Owens was against the boycott, while Jackie Robinson was for it. Even the athletes could not agree. In the end they decided to compete in the Olympic Games, and each Black athlete was free to do what ever he/she pleased. Two runners, Tommy Smith and John Carlos, placed taking first and second in the 200 meters. On the medal podium, they decided to each raise a fisted, black-gloved hand during the playing of the National Anthem at the medal ceremony. Such a daring show of political expression and cultural pride had never before been seen.

The U.S. Olympic Committee was outraged at Carlos and Smith's display, but the message or gesture will never be forgotten. The point had been made with the image of the two Black American Olympic medal winners standing before the world; silent, black-fisted gloves raised. It is perhaps one of the most famous and recognizable sports photos ever.

The leadership of sociology professor Harry Edwards helped focus the consciousness of Tommy Smith and John Carlos, who at the time became villains but have since been raised to hero status in the contemporary imagination. Thanks to the encouragement of Dr. Edwards, their silent act of protest came to symbolize the injustice in the United States of America toward Blacks. Dr. Edwards represents an era of university professors who actively pushed for change; he also pioneered the serious study of issues of race in sports sociology. His impact and influence was so great that Hall of Fame coach Bill Walsh hired him as a consultant for his great San Francisco 49ers teams that dominated football in the 1980s and early 1990s. Walsh knew there was a cultural void and hired Dr. Edwards to help him understand and relate to his growing roster of Black players.

* * *

It is clear from examining this short list that BNS are merely the second coming of earlier mavericks or "Original Ballers," whose style, spirit, politics, and courage dangled fearlessly from their sleeves in openly hostile times. And although this list is male-heavy, women are not to be excluded. For example, Billie Jean King is a Baller because she made it clear to the world that women are indeed equal to men, if not better than men in sports. Martina Navratilova fearlessly stood up and stepped out against anti-gay sentiments in declaring to the world that she is a lesbian. She marked the first time that a professional athlete had the courage during the prime of their career to be openly gay. The list goes on and on, but King and Navratilova are mentioned because they are exceptional individuals that stood tall in the face of gender and sexuality discrimination and created true change.

Most modern athletes are without the "benefit" of the political climate of the civil rights movement and Jim Crow. Moreover, the post-civil rights-era generation lacks the clear engine of discrimination that propelled their foremothers and forefathers into action. But modern players are influenced in some sense by expressive hip-hop culture, which values expressiveness and creativeness and honesty to one's roots—using the mantra "Keepin' it real"; however, this hip-hop culture is bankrupt of its original post–Black Power consciousness and spirit of sacrifice. The lack of focused political consciousness in this generation of athletes at a time when social, economic, political, and educational opportunities have deteriorated is unacceptable. So despite the majority of Black sports stars' resistance to "proper" cultural etiquette in favor of personal creativity and street personas, the threat they represent is hollow compared to a Jim Brown, a Curt Flood, or a Muhammad Ali.

*Rejection and Embrace of Black Style*

*Los Angeles Times* reporter David Wharton correctly suggested that America and sports have made minimal strides in the way of cultural pluralism and racial equality. Wharton reveals in his article the fear of leagues like the NBA, which while creating an environment that entices young people, risks alienating it core customers—wealthy, older White males and females. The NBA wants to juice hip-hop's popularity for all it is worth without honestly embracing the cultural connections that gave it birth. However, the flip side of this fear is that hip-hop is very much a part of the modern NBA game. Its core customers seem to embrace it. They move to the hip-hop-infused beats that blast during time-outs, commercial breaks, and halftime.

An appropriate discussion of the psychology of "outlaw" culture attributed to the rap music of the Ballers of the New School warrants a brief comparison to historian Robin D. G. Kelley's explanation of the hep cats (as they were called) in his book *Yo' Mama's Disfunktional!* who donned zoot suits during the Second World War. These men were indifferent to the war and defiant toward Whites in general and servicemen in particular, but they also placed a premium on the "pursuit of leisure and pleasure; they possessed a laid-back attitude toward work." The repercussions for such defiant behavior were "ridicule, severe punishment, and even beatings" (173). Similar to the media snipes at BNS, the "white soldiers engaged in what amounted to a ritualized stripping of the zoot" (172–73). However, this was a popular form of dress among African American and Latino youth at the time, just as hoodies, baggy pants, Raiders caps, braids, gold teeth, cornrows, stocking caps, and boots are the "outlaw" gear of today. Just as the zoot suit reflected the style politics of the 1940s, in a similar manner hip-hop clothing and aesthetics mirror the politics of the current generation of youth.

Both styles represent what Kelley refers to as large bodies of the Black working-class youth in urban America "whose social locations have allowed them to demystify aspects of the hegemonic ideology while reinforcing their ties to it" (181). The New School Ballers mostly follow the credo of hip-hop culture, which is about being "real niggaz," refusing to fake it for the public. They ain't about to smile for "massa." No, for them playing ball translates into being modern hustlers, hipsters who migrate from the blacktops and sandlots of urban working-class (or not) Black America, seizing "spaces for leisure, pleasure, and recuperation" (180). And, much like the zoot suiters, who were hostile to wage labor and refused to have a "slave" (job), New Schoolers display equal resistance to allowing "work to become a primary signifier of identity" (174). Instead of accepting the posture that they should be happy to have a job as a professional athlete, they flip the script—the teams should be happy to have the New Schoolers playing for them. The rejection of the traditional work ethic and the privileging of leisure erupt the divide between Ballers of the New School, coaches, the media, and fans. It also drudges up myths and not-so-subtle suggestions of Blacks as lazy.

The message sent repeatedly to Black style trendsetters is that sport is universal and race is not a factor—as long as participants leave their personal styles back in the ghettos where they got them. Meanwhile, sports journalists forget that America is a country notorious for its emphasis on individualism, rooted in capitalism—the antithesis of the teamwork, socialist, and self-sacrificing ideas championed in the media. Hell, the very career of sports journalism is the ultimate expression of individualism. America is a "Me Generation," founded on individual expression and concern with self. Upon hearing references to race, sports pundits often respond in heated denial, claiming that "there is no way you can talk about race because sports has been the leader in altering race relations in America." However, the truth be told, the racial contract is alive and well in sports as well as all other facets of society. Claiming that these athletes are models of success and universal acceptance is deceiving because many Whites embrace them only as long as they agree to fit in and leave most of their "Black" style at home where it belongs.

*AND 1 Keeps It Real*

Perhaps the best proof of the marketability of BNS is the AND 1 sports apparel company and its Street Ball team that travels the country Globetrotters style, taking runs at the best each city in the United States has to offer. The AND 1 Street Ball team is very similar yet divergent from the Globetrotters of 1926, who despite fielding the very best players in the country, became sports minstrels because there were no opportunities for Blacks in White-owned professional sports. They opened with their famous "Magic Circle" to the tune of "Sweet Georgia Brown," throwing the ball behind their backs, bouncing it off their heads, kicking it to players in the circle from behind. They were international ambassadors of goodwill.

That was then and this is now. Using a Street Ball team that has been represented by players like Skip To My Lou, Hot Sauce, Escalade, Main Event, Spyda, the Pharmacist, Baby Shaq, Sik Wit It, and The Professor—players whose style, attitude, and luck might have kept them from an NBA team—AND 1 has emerged as a leading basketball-exclusive footwear and apparel brand in the world. They are the BNS of the basketball apparel business. Funny how a company that is headquartered in Paoli, Pennsylvania, and began by selling T-shirts out of the trunk of a car has risen near the top of the basketball apparel ranks. By pushing the AND 1 Mix Tape Tours, they create opportunities besides the NBA where ballers can strut their stuff. The company goes out of its way to identify with the grit, fearlessness, and the bravado of the playground and street ball.

Gritty is what AND 1 represents. It embraces street, street ball, and hip-hop, turning outlaws into marketable products. Perhaps it is fitting that a company whose T-shirts are printed with trash-talk like: "Pass. Save Yourself the Embarrassment" and "I'm the Bus Driver. I Take Everyone to School" could rank second only to Nike in NBA endorsees. It is also famous for its Latrell Sprewell commercial (after Sprewell was suspended by the NBA for choking his coach during a dispute). With Jimi Hendrix's version of the "Star-Spangled Banner" playing in the background, Spree, while getting his hair braided (doing what he does, being himself), uttered, "I am the American dream." The company at least embraces the reality that there is an alternative reality that the mainstream is willing to receive.

Using hip-hop marketing and promotion tactics, a mixed tape, the 1994 And 1 Mix Tape Tour took the discreet Pennsylvania shoe company toward the top of the basketball sports apparel world (as of 2005, annual sales topped at $180 million). But the company's meal ticket is undeniably the street ball Mix Tape Tour. So popular has the tour become that Nike had to keep it real by starting a Battlegrounds Tour in 2002 to keep from losing further ground to the upstart AND 1.

The company has risen so far and fast largely because of the 1994 volume 1 tape that was broadcast in sneaker stores featuring Skip To My Lou (Rafer Alston), making crazy move after move. Their ESPN2 street-ball reality series airs segments from Mix Tape Tours each year as they travel the country from city to city holding open runs, trying to find the next unknown talent to join the AND 1 tour team. Not only does AND 1 keep it real, but it has found a way to tap a new market of talent and fans who believe they can make the tour or be like Skip, Hot Sauce, or The Professor. Talk about being a BNS, proof that AND 1 represents the next wave, in a June 2005 *Sports Illustrated* feature story, Ron Skotarczak, vice president for marketing and entertainment, revealed that AND 1 holds over 20 percent of the NBA players under contract because of the company's street credibility (Nike still has over half of all NBA players).

*Mike and Nike*

Although AND 1 has gained a toehold in the basketball market, it is still impossible to discuss revolutionary Ballers or BNS in any manner without discussing Phil Knight, his Nike sports apparel empire, and sports icon Michael Jordan. Together they revolutionized sports marketing and, to some extent, America. No company was willing to risk naming a shoe after an athlete—Phil and Nike were. In fact, they gave Jordan one of the largest contracts ever, with a huge marketing budget to boot. They were Ballers calling shots, willing to go against the wind.

Again, I turn to Phil Knight or Nike because of his Baller spirit and company that uses so many contemporary athletes to promote sports apparel. Many of its athletes are rebels. As one strolls the beautifully manicured Nike campus grounds filled with state-of-the-art sports facilities, and buildings named after its most famous athletes (the most recent being the Tiger Woods building with its impressive spinning ball in a pool of water), it is easy to forget that New School hustle spirit, mixed with a hefty dose of Black culture, created the Nike sports dynasty—and made Knight a billionaire. It is also easy to forget Knight's humble beginning with Blue Ribbon Sports in 1964. Or that he and his former track coach started it all with a $1,000 investment split between them. Knight launched the company from his home, selling shoes, made with a waffle iron, out of his car at track meets. He once was the David taking on the Goliaths—philistines of the sports shoe and apparel world. Nike earned its status with a gritty risky attitude that led it to revolutionize sports marketing by attaching personalities to products. (Its first big star was Steve Prefontaine—tough, gritty, shot-caller.) A true hustler maverick, Knight is similar to underground rappers and deejays hustling their records on the streets out of their cars at events. Race is perhaps the only and most distinctive difference between them.

It was a maverick spirit that compelled Knight and his Nike company to lay much on the line (thanks to former Nike executive Rob Strasser and current creative geniuses like Tinker Hatfield and Trevor

Edwards) to lure a young Michael Jordan out to Portland to sign with their company (beating out then giants like Converse, Adidas, and Reebok). Eschewing race, they were willing to invest in an unproven Black basketball player at a time when the world was unwilling to go near the color line. One has to respect Nike's gangsta spirit, because just over twenty-five years ago Converse (which they now own!) *was* what Nike is now. When I was a kid Converse was the shoe to wear. Besides, they had all the top NBA stars under contract with them at the time (Magic Johnson, Isiah Thomas, Larry Bird, and Dr. J).

Indeed, one also must respect Nike's Baller spirit for hiring a young Black filmmaker named Spike Lee to direct the early Air Jordan commercials in the 1980s. They were the first to embrace street in the guise of Lee's alter-ego homeboy character Mars Blackmon. The commercials were a hit—Jordan was hip, and hip-hop embraced him because he was raw and defiant, setting trends as no athlete before or after him has ever quite equaled. But as much as I embrace this spirit, and give Jordan credit for scaling new heights, I cannot ignore the racial skid marks of Jordan's marketing shift later into his career. As his popularity grew, his marketing target audience changed. The construction of his image became more and more gray or vanilla, as he "successfully" crossed "traditional" cultural and social boundaries in America. I am not certain if Nike or Jordan is responsible for the shift but it certainly taints his Baller-status somewhat.

However, one thing his transition proves is that racial progress in sports is marginal. It revealed that the media's, the NBA's, and the public's lust for Jordan stemmed from his combination of extraordinary talent and savvy racial neutrality. White athletes are not asked to project racial neutrality. The ebullient personality Jordan projected and the fact that Nike seized upon his ability to compel people to focus on the *game* and not his Blackness suggest less racial progress than most want to admit. In truth, Nike and Jordan's willingness to give us a racially neutral icon that Whites could forget was Black and male speaks volumes regarding racial progress in the modern world (A point that was proven again during Barack Obama's campaign to become president).

However, whatever Jordan's shortcomings in the area of political consciousness, he must be commended for helping to alter the economics of sports for athletes, specifically athletes of color. His 1984 Nike deal was for the then unheard-of amount of $1 million annually (nearly ten times what the high profile NBA stars like Magic, Dr. J, and Bird were receiving at the time). When Jordan hit the Bulls up for $30 million-plus for his last three seasons, he again changed the game, escalating NBA salaries to what they are today. Despite taking the track of neutrality, he did, in all fairness, become the first Black pitchman to a predominately White America—even if he had to completely ignore race to achieve it. The achievement is bitter sweet.

*New School Ballers*

The pressures and expectations placed on Jackie Robinson and other Black pioneers in sports still hold true in the modern sporting world. America is a country that believes in assimilation rather than desegregation. Integration in America means we will allow you to play if you follow our rules, real and imagined, while trying to reconstruct yourself in our image. BNS choose between pursuing either the path of Jordan outlined above, or Stephon Marbury who started his own affordable line of sneakers, Starbury. Marbury, who is well paid, is less concerned with adoration of fans or image (his trade from the New York Knicks to the Boston Celtics in 2009 was a drama laden transaction) than his predecessor. Above all else he demands fairness and respect.

But I digress just a bit. The racial contract, as explained by Charles Mills, is directly responsible for the contradictions surrounding the rejection of the Marburys of the world versus the Jordans. And we see many clear examples of this rejection in sports culture as it changes rules to restrict BNS's forms of self-expression. According to Mills, the racial contract does not make it okay for New School Ballers to brag or talk trash because doing so marks them as immoral or uncivilized. Read the papers, watch sports television—the evidence is quite clear that Whiteness is deemed normal and all *other* cultural styles perverse. Over the years I have read and viewed countless news and journalistic critiques regarding how modern, mostly Black, athletes engage in behavior on and off playing fields that proves they are vicious, uncoachable, and immoral savages. These are the labels meted out. Their moral fiber is endlessly critiqued; their intellect constantly questioned. The subliminal—often overt message—the media sends to the public is basically: "See, we told you it was a mistake to bring these immoral animals into our civilized games because these people are dangerous."

The truth, however, is that the moral measurements leveled at Black athletes usually stem from the reality of their not being White or not trying to "act" White. They challenge issues of autonomy of space (public and personal). Their decision to uphold the hip-hop creed of "keepin' it real" is deemed by White fans, coaches, and the media as an affront and a challenge to Whiteness as normal.

The racial contract, which privileges Whites and Whiteness, does not respect the agency of ethnic minorities. This is problematic because the current crop of young stars—a post-civil rights, hip-hop generation—projects its own standard of what looks good, what feels good, what plays good on the field, and what doesn't. They do not adhere totally to the dominant culture's codes of correctness or humility. BNS look at Iverson in his sweats, retro hats, jewels, and other accessories and regard him as well dressed. In fact, Iverson's gear (clothing and accessories) costs as much as, sometimes more than, a traditional suit and tie. White supremacy—the racial contract or normalizations of Whiteness (whatever one wants to call it)—makes the media project White Anglo cultural standards as *the only acceptable standards.*

Even without the serious political stands or challenges to White supremacy their predecessors faced, BNS represent an affront to the racial contract—the source of tensions between the media, fans, and players in the modern era. Athletes of the New School understand their marketability in the modern world of sports. They understand that corporations market individual personalities, pitting them against one another; they understand that *Sports Center* is less likely to show highlights of a well-executed pick-and-roll, than of a high-flying dunk in someone's mug. BNS are not trying to leave the game broke and exploited like Joe Louis. No, they are "trying to get theirs"; they comprehend American capitalism, knowing full well that greed is at its core. They understand the parasitic nature of the sports industry and thus deal with their employers accordingly. Like hip-hop artists, BNS live by a creed of self-sufficiency, self-ownership, and self-validation expressing their ingenuity, innovation, and abilities in play, constantly reinventing themselves and the games they play.

Take, for example, LeBron James (2009 MVP), known to many as King James. He is considered the second coming of Michael Jordan on and off the court. James jumped straight to the NBA from high school. The Akron, Ohio native fired his agent at the time and formed his own company, which he runs with childhood friends. They secured an astonishing deal with Nike for $90 million even though James had yet to play a single game! The six-foot-eight-inch James, with the tattoo "Chosen 1" across his upper back, follows the mantra "be yourself." It is the mantra of BNS, yet for James it has netted the Cleveland Cavalier star 2007 endorsement earnings of $25 million. This same "self" has partnered with the likes of State Farm, Coca-Cola, Microsoft, Upper-Deck, Cub Cadet, and Bubblicious. A huge mural of James with his arms outstretched hung on a building in downtown Cleveland. The city had nestled its sports and economic hopes in the arms of this young man (2010 he joined the Miami Heat).

James is certainly not an aberration, but an example of BNS who are not the villains or one-dimensional characters that the mass media would have the world believe. We forget that we live in a hypermasculine American culture. Indeed, BNS are products of the tough, aggressive, strong, dominating, violent, and ultra-competitive culture they inhabit.

They carry onto fields of play an idealized model of masculinity—exaggerated hardness, icy cool, physical strength, the need for respect and power. The hostility to their refusal to convert their personas to appease the public, the media, teams, coaches, or fans is a constant reminder that America fails to fully embrace diversity, that change and equality remain an American dream.

On a minor level, BNS understand some of the oppositional meanings embedded in their earrings, tattoos, cornrows, style of dress, and other elements that comprise the expressive Black youth culture they mirror. Although rarely articulated with the clarity necessary to put critics on their heels, the insistence from many BNS to be themselves, for better or worse, is consistent with the ethos of Americans like Henry Thoreau. Unlike the original BNS, the world of the modern athlete is much more complex because of the corporate nature of sports. The current generation lacks a clear movement propelling it into political action in the same way that John Carlos, Tommy Smith, Jim Brown, Kareem Abdul Jabbar, and Ali were aided by an era of protest and activism. For BNS, the issues are complicated somewhat because although players do have greater opportunities and earn more, basic civil rights violations and discrimination do not exist in the same way. Certainly modern athletes' struggle to be true "unto thyself " is further complicated because not only are they employed by multibillion-dollar corporations, but many of them are multimillion-dollar corporations.

*Kobe Bryant*

Kobe Bryant of the Los Angeles Lakers has also been considered the heir apparent to the Jordan throne. Bryant was regarded as a model athlete, the perfect kid. He was smart, bilingual, well mannered, and marketable. All of that changed after the summer of 2003, when he was accused of raping a young White woman at a resort in Colorado. Suddenly Kobe, who received the media stamp of approval, garnered a questionable moral and ethical character because he had been acting "too Black." In addition to the rape charges (which he beat) he acquired a tattoo and an earring the size of a quarter, and began listening to rap music and allegedly had aspirations to be a rapper.

The damage to his image was severe. It was a divergence from the script he carefully followed during his emergence into the league straight from high school. Bryant followed a careful script planned out by his parents, sponsors, and advisers that placed him on the fast track to becoming the next Jordan. The Kobe Bryant image built on and off the court as clean-cut and well mannered made him a role model, while earning him millions in endorsements. However, his position as a role model and product pitchman suffocated some of his individual growth. While safe and palatable for companies he represents from the NBA to Spalding, it was far from *real*. The common misconception is that Bryant's change in appearance as well as persona, including him being charged with sexually assaulting a nineteen-year-old Colorado woman, are related to his embracing hip-hop culture. It was thought that all the hip-hop and flash—the "Black stuff" from his NBA peers—had finally rubbed off on him, fatally tainting the pure Kobe that America made and formerly embraced and adored with ease.

The Kobe once renowned for his ability to spit Italian and perfect diction, now spits game and Black idioms. The new Kobe keeps it real in what former teammate Rick Fox described as a "continual understanding of himself… and a willingness to be a little more true to himself" and less "concerned about what everyone else thinks." So what did Bryant do wrong besides get tattoos? Every true BNS knows that being true to self will earn one a drudging from the media, which despises contemporary athletes of color for such posturing.

While the emergence of the new Kobe best epitomizes Ralph Emerson's essay "Self-Reliance," which begins: "Man is his own star," it did not play well with the sports media. He was snubbed during MVP voting for two straight years (beaten out by Steve Nash of all people!). Emerson's popular mid-nineteenth-century transcendental idealism emphasizing self-reliance, self-culture, and individual expression are cornerstones of contemporary American thought and life, as well as hip-hop culture. African American athletes assert similar ideas in their dress, speech, and demeanor on and off the playing fields, becoming their "own stars," as Kobe has done, but they receive less than favorable receptions. It took the new Bryant several years to finally receive the Most Valuable Player Award (2008) because his image had been damaged. Part of his strategy was to pull back on connecting too openly with "Blackness" to regain some of his media-darling, good-guy status. If he continues to chill and keep things near "neutral," there is an outside chance that he can still claim the space Jordan once occupied.

*Flak Catchers*
Mahmoud Abdul-Rauf, Randy Moss, and Terrell Owens have caught more trouble, incited more ire than most contemporary athletes. The former was a phenomenal shooting guard before being run out of the NBA. The latter two are among the best receivers in football. Besides being adept at catching passes with great regularity, they catch a lot of flak on and off the field. They personify BNS-era athletes with their insistence on speaking their mind. Owens and Moss, for example, are the very best wide receivers that professional football has seen since Jerry Rice dazzled the NFL. Both athletes also say what is on their mind without pause or concern for what others think. Moss's most infamous comment, "I play when I want to play," has drawn the ire of the media since he arrived on the scene breaking rookie-receiving records that may never again be broken. He has been known to roll in a bright purple SUV with thirty-inch wheels and sparkling spinning rims, tinted windows, no door handles, and vanity plates that read: "Tipp Drill 84." Along with his statement to the media of self-determination, that was taken out of context, Moss has squirted an official with a water bottle, verbally abused corporate sponsors on a team bus, bumped a traffic controller with his car, and been fined for a retaliatory "mock" moon of Green Bay Packer fans after a game-sealing touchdown

in the 2005 playoffs. After much "drama," the Vikings traded their top player to the Raiders in the 2005 off-season, then he was traded to the Patriots in 2007, where he became a fan and media favorite again, setting records for touchdowns in a single season, while leading the Patriots to an undefeated regular season. Moss is clearly one of the top five players in the NFL, but the Vikings were willing to trade their brightest star because the organization was unwilling to cope with a Black male claiming too much ownership of his personal space. What is interesting is that since joining the Patriots Moss speaks less and is once again the best thing since vanilla ice cream.

Terrell Owens presents a similar problem. He corrects the way the media pronounce his name, giving it a distinctive sound from the common "Terrell." As a member of the 49ers, he was often outspoken in the media if he felt he did not receive the ball enough. He even infamously suggested that his then-quarterback (Jeff Garcia) might be gay. When the San Francisco 49ers traded him, he refused to be traded to the Baltimore Ravens, opting for the Philadelphia Eagles (then he was traded to the Cowboys. As an Eagle, he infused the team with the extra attitude on and off the field necessary to finally get them over the NFC Championship game and into the Super Bowl. He is best known and despised for his creative post-touchdown celebrations ranging from standing on the Dallas Cowboys' star at midfield, pulling a Sharpie out of his sock on *Monday Night Football* and signing a ball for a fan, grabbing pom-poms from a cheerleader and rooting for himself, or making the gesture of an eagle flying. During training camp in his second season with the Eagles, he made his disgruntlement with his contract public, and when he was sent home for a week, he worked out in his driveway for the media. This got him the money he felt he deserved and a fat new contract in Dallas where, after two up and down but very productive seasons, his mouth once again got him shipped out of town. (In 2009 Owens took his mouth and abilities to Buffalo.) He is not afraid to speak his mind nor do what he feels, no matter whom it upsets, or where it lands him.

Although these BNS upset the "norm," the situation is far less problematic because they exist in a post–civil rights era void of a clear political movement. However, the BNS that pose the greatest threat are athletes like Carlos Delgado or Rasheed Wallace, the latter challenging and critiquing the NBA for how it pimps young stars and turning public attention toward the $10 million eye-raising salary plus executive expenses of NBA commissioner David Stern. Then there is Carlos Delgado, who while a member of the Toronto Blue Jays refused to stand during the national anthem (There are also New School Ballers like Ethan Thomas of the NBA, who reads his slam poetry in protest of racism at anti–death penalty events). These incidents receive scant media attention; other political sorts of activity fall far below the radar.

## Mahmoud Abdul-Rauf

Perhaps the most famous BNS who paid the price for his political consciousness is Mahmoud Abdul-Rauf (born Chris Jackson). Abdul-Rauf was a star for the Denver Nuggets, leading the young team to the playoffs and toward a resurgence in the NBA. However, in 1996 Abdul-Rauf made headlines for refusing to stand during the national anthem because he believed the flag was "a symbol of oppression and tyranny." For this he became a pariah and this all-star player was systematically pushed out of the NBA. His story exposes the double standard in which players are expected to be apolitical unless a league or team gives them flags to wave and pro-war statements to deliver. But the politics behind his dismissal from the NBA are undeniable. He risked his young career for what he believed in, choosing to stand with his back to the flag as the national anthem took place prior to each game. He could have remained in the locker room, but America, we are told, is a free country where everyone is free to express her or his beliefs.

Abdul-Rauf was featured on Bryant Gumbel's HBO program *Real Sports* highlighting his mistreatment in the NBA for his political stance. Still a very capable scoring guard, he expressed interest in returning to the NBA, stunned that despite his great talent, no teams wanted to touch him. Before being traded, Abdul-Rauf was one of the leading scorers for the Denver Nuggets, a playoff contender. After he began his protests during the anthem, he was booed by his hometown fans and on the road, suspended from the team, then traded to the Vancouver Grizzlies, the Siberia of the NBA at the time (also coincidentally a team located in Canada), before finally being pushed out of the league altogether. It was a well-crafted exit that few paid attention to because the Grizzlies were perhaps the most ignored team in the NBA before moving to their current location in Memphis. Abdul-Rauf is among the few BNS to display a consciousness that challenges the contradictions of America. He is more of a threat than T.O., Randy Moss, or Allen Iverson because his act of resistance is of great substance—he is dangerous; he could have potentially awakened the slumbering Joes of the world.

## C. Vivian Stringer

C. Vivian Stringer is Rutgers University's women's basketball coach who is not well known despite being seventh on the all-time list of NCAA Division I men's and women's basketball coaches with over 800 victories. Throughout her thirty-eight-year career, which began at Cheyney State College in Pennsylvania, where she managed to lead her team to the 1982 title game (the first for women) without a salary, recruiting budget, or scholarships for her players. In 2008 Stringer became the first African American college basketball coach to obtain 800 victories and in 2009 whe was inducted into the Basketball Hall of Fame.

Unfortunately, what she will forever be most famous for is being at the center of the controversy involving Don Imus, who the day following her team's loss in the 2007 championship game leveled racially and sexually derisive comments at her players. Stringer led her team in a strong and dignified response to Imus's hateful racism and sexism. Despite losing her husband, a child, and having breast cancer, Stringer marches on. She has shown a willingness to speak out against a culture of casual vulgarity and hurtfulness, while constantly teaching the young ladies she coaches how to carry themselves with dignity and resolve.

*Allen Iverson*

Perhaps the most popular among modern Ballers is Allen Iverson. Iverson's battle against "White aesthetics" and hegemony are famous. As a member of the Philadelphia Sixers he feuded with his coach at the time, Larry Brown, because he refused to wear "acceptable" attire to games (a suit and tie like Brown). Now, I cite Iverson because his "attitude" personifies the hip-hop generation of New School Ballers. He is the biggest hero among basketball fans that never received a Madison Avenue deal. Tattooed from neck to torso, he is the antithesis of Jordan's and even Kobe's early iteration of "please everyone, smile, and assimilate" style. He does not try to be a problem; he just opts to wear what he wants, which is actually quite appropriate for the job he performs. Instead of wearing a suit and tie to go play ball, he wears throwback hats, expensive hoodies and sweats, and a little bit of "bling" (expensive jewelry) around his wrists, neck, and in his ears. A person whose aesthetics are centered in the hip-hop community compliments him for his choice of clothing, which rivals the cost of Larry Brown's suit and tie.

The widespread reaction to Iverson confirms that we inhabit a world that still does not respect the cultural values of others and where what is perceived acceptable moral, social, and ethical behavior is that of Whites. He is too outsized, off-putting and edgy; far from the benign image advertisers and the mainstream drool over. Thomas Kochman does a wonderful job of explaining such cultural and aesthetic differences in his book *Black and White Styles in Conflict*. His basic premise is that no style supersedes another, and that notions of White supremacy create style conflicts between Blacks and Whites. Although Iverson recently cut his braids, and the league forced a dress code, his feuds with Brown (as well as the new NBA dress code) epitomize where we are as a country in terms of cultural tolerance. After his third team in four years, he remained somewhat of a trendsetter. His popularity has not waned, and he still marches to his own beat. He earned roughly $30 million annually from his basketball salary, jersey revenues, shoe contract, and sports card and licensing revenues from video games without any Madison Avenue endorsements. Despite rebuking the mainstream game he managed to be one of the most popular and wealthy NBA players for over a decade.

*Venus and Serena Williams*
Male athletes alone have not posed a challenge to aesthetics or authority. The Williams sisters and their distinctive style have changed tennis forever, from their beads and Serena's blond hair to Venus's very short skirt and Serena's boots and Puma catsuit, which captured the unwavering gaze of the 2002 U.S. Open crowd and cameramen, who consistently zoomed-in on her from the rear. They not only have their own style—they design their own outfits. I have been a fan of Serena and Venus Williams since I read a newspaper article about them while living in St. Louis over a decade ago. They found their own unique path to the top of the tennis world, with their father, Richard Williams, carving that path, while taking the weight of the world onto his shoulders as he made good on his prediction that his daughters would be the two top-ranked players in the world and would routinely play one another for the major tennis championships.

Their route into tennis is new school in that they balked at the traditional tennis circuit. In isolation they perfected their games, practicing with each other. Once they both turned professional, they supported one another so they had to worry less about making friends and could focus on winning. Although the women's tennis circuit is notoriously unfriendly they were labeled anti-social. Meanwhile, their father assumes the duty of challenging racism in tennis. He regularly speaks out against perceived racial slights against Serena and Venus and those endemic in the culture of tennis. Journalists often made fodder of Serena and Venus, who hit the scene with beaded braids. This "nontraditional" adornment was deemed detrimental to their game as the beads clanged around their heads during play. But in the end both women carved images of beauty in the image of Black women that the public has slowly embraced. Still, Richard Williams danced on the heads of all doubters and haters as he strutted atop the press box at Wimbledon when Venus won the first of her many tournaments there in 2000. He caught flak for being unsportsmanlike and displaying poor taste. But he did not care; his daughters smugly smiled and basked in their rising dominance. Between 2001–2003 the Williams sisters were so dominant that they met in six of the eight Grand Slam title matches! As of 2009 they are once again in the top of women's tennis rankings.

These women have managed to situate Black women as both sexy and strong in their own unique brand of packaging. They have changed the women's tennis world, picking up where Flo Jo left off in reconstructing Black female sexuality in America. The Williams sisters, like many of the Ballers of the New School, bring an unmistakable style and attitude to tennis and to the American psyche, which was absent before, their combination of muscles, athleticism, style, intellect, defiance and progress, beauty and sexual appeal stormed the scene.

In 2000, 2002, and again in 2008, Venus and Serena Williams literally swept Wimbledon, the hallmark event of the season for professional tennis. They placed first and second in the singles and won the doubles championship for women, taking home most of the prize money. Speaking of money, in 2005 Venus Williams argued her case on the eve of winning the Wimbledon title that women should get equal pay. It generated a bit of bad publicity for Wimbledon, as she advocated equal pay for equal play, going so far as to offer to play five sets instead of the customary three to ensure equity of pay. She even wrote a strong editorial in the *London Times* addressing the issue. Like the great Billie Jean King before her, she was unafraid to take a stand for women's rights.

*Barry Bonds*

Barry Bonds is perhaps the most infamous of all the flak catchers previously mentioned. When I think about Barry Bonds, I cannot help but to recall the 1976 movie *The Bingo Long Traveling All-Stars and Motor Kings*—a comic, and somewhat inaccurate, depiction of the Negro Leagues and barnstorming before Jackie Robinson broke the color line. Bond's attitude reminds me of the conversation between Bingo and Leon when the All-Stars are playing a White team and humiliating them. As Leon is approaching the plate to hit what is certain to be another home run, Bingo pleads with Leon to ease the escalating racial tension by clowning around for the Whites. Leon angrily replies to Bingo, "I don't monkey shine for no White folks." Racial danger or no racial danger, Leon is a proud Black man and a ball player. In the end, Bingo tricks him into playing along, and they both have a good laugh at Leon's expense. Whenever I recall that scene, I think of Barry Bonds, who while playing the game of baseball refuses to play the game—he does not smile, grin, or dance to the media's tune, and for this stance he is branded the enemy. The hostility directed at Bonds stems from the racial contract that is disrupted when non-Whites refuse to know their place around Whites.

The problem with Bonds is that he does not fit any of the narratives that the sports world creates for Black athletes. First, he grew up during the 1960s a privileged son of San Francisco Giants Bobby Bonds. He is not apologetic and does not display humility nor grin to place White fans and sportswriters at ease. He is not gracious like others; in fact, with his lineage (growing up around a Major League clubhouse and being Willie Mays's godson) he is not only the best player of his era; he *is* baseball. He does not apologize for his position in life, nor thank Whites for his "opportunity." He is the ultimate BNS who eschews the racial contract and is unafraid to protest that race affected his life, despite his financial privilege. Bonds's posture and words serve as a rebuke of the inhumanities non-Whites have endured from Jim Crow and post-civil rights failed promises to the legacies of slavery, rape, murder, and oppression that have inflicted deep wounds on Black manhood and womanhood. His less-than-amiable behavior is considered proof that BNS are ungrateful, angry, mean, evil people, in the eyes of the sports media.

During Bonds's historic home-run chase of Mark McGwire's then record of seventy home runs in a single season, a sportswriter called his quest "anti-climatic" because McGwire had already broken Roger Maris's long-standing record of sixty-one home runs two seasons earlier. There was an unwillingness to acknowledge that the possibility of setting a new record was important! The real reason Bonds's feat was treated this way is that many sportswriters were angry that it was Bonds setting the record and not someone more affable like Sammy Sosa. Oddly, few seemed to care that McGwire was often surly and uncooperative with the media. (One can only assume that Whiteness got him a pass.)

There is no doubt that Bonds is hated because he lacks the proper humility fans and media expect of their Black heroes. During the 2004 season, Barry Bonds hit his 700th home run, and when he arrived at the plate, scant few were there to greet and congratulate him. During the 2004 World Series between the St. Louis Cardinals and the Boston Red Sox, Bonds, who had won the National League MVP for a record fourth consecutive time, was booed by the St. Louis fans. His appearance was brief and there was scant coverage of the event on ESPN or elsewhere. Of course, much of this is by Bonds's own design because he has kept his distance from the media. But much of it stems from a distaste for his confidence and style, which get him labeled as arrogant or a "bad" man.

He represents the first among a group of BNS from privileged backgrounds to produce at the highest level; he does not give a f**k if the world embraces him. Oddly enough, he turned down his first major league contract because they would not offer him what he wanted. He opted for college instead; an early sign that he would forever function on his own terms. Bonds, a product of the post-civil rights era and an example of BNS, refuses to make concessions. He rejects the lessons of the "Say Hey Kid," pushing American media to meet him on different terms.

These factors make him more prone to point out racism, make political statements from time to time, and march to his own beat. It is for this reason that I like Barry Bonds, former star outfielder for the San Francisco Giants, and current home run king. He is a member of the first post–civil rights generation; the initial generation that "benefited" from the struggles of the Civil Rights Movement. Indeed, hip-hop-generation athletes like Bonds understand the importance of being oneself. And, Mr. Bonds, love him or hate him, exudes Baller resistance.

He is indeed an example of what still happens to Black men who are too confident or unwilling to show humility. The punishment for Bonds was revenge in the way of a Bay Area steroid-use scandal. On 15 November 2007 he was indicted for perjury and obstruction of justice charges. Although he played well during his final season with the Giants, and he has yet to be convicted with evidence that he knowingly used steroids (as of 2009), or perjured himself for allegedly lying under oath during an investigation of steroid use in baseball, no team has offered him a contract. He reportedly is willing to play for the league minimum, but as of 2009 there have been no takers. The hate for Bonds is so deep that sportswriters illegally obtained court documents to write a book about Bonds and his alleged steroid use. This of course led to a public conviction of Bonds, labeling him a cheater.

But anyone who knows anything about baseball knows Bonds, who is nothing but pure talent, does not need to cheat. In fact, whether he cheated or not, what is true is that he competed in an era of steroids, just as Babe Ruth competed in a steroid-like era of overt racism and segregation. When I think of pioneer BNS, Bonds comes to mind. In the outfield he never merely made the routine play but his outsized talent allowed him to snatch pop flies out of the sky with a graceful swoosh—making the difficult look routine. He often posed after each of his home runs, as he watched them sail out of the park. The way he wore his uniform—with his very long pant legs and signature diamond-encrusted cross earring (not worn during the latter stages of his career) strategically placed in his right earlobe for all the world to see during each of his at bats—changed how baseball players began to present themselves in the 1990s. Bonds flaunted a diamond encrusted cross earring when it was not as popular to do so in the 1980s. He exuded a grace, cool, privileged background and level of performance unmatched by his peers.

Bonds is interesting because (steroids or not) he has aged like fine wine; at over forty he remained among the best in baseball, setting a new career home run record in 2007. Of course, one of his problems is the rumor that he knowingly took steroids to extend his career and achieve the all-time home-run record. He will go to court in 2009 to determine if he perjured himself. Meanwhile, there seems to be collusion among MLB franchises to keep Bonds, a player who was among the top ten in on base percentage during his last full season, out of the league. His production was better than 60 percent of the players currently in baseball, yet not a single team tried to sign him since his contract expired with the Giants in 2007.

Bonds is undeniably the standard by which baseball greatness must be measured. As the holder of a record seven MVP awards (voted by the very sportswriters who detest him), slugging percentage, and single-season and all-time home-run record, a batting title, and eight Gold Gloves, he is undoubtedly the most complete player in the history of baseball—right up there with his godfather Willie Mays. This pisses many people off—partly because Bonds, unlike his godfather, does not smile for the camera or go out of his way to make Whites feel comfortable. He also is not grateful or gracious toward the sportswriters who vote for him; and he is not as affable as, say, Sammy Sosa or the mythical Ruth, whose chummy relations with members of the media contributed greatly to his mythical greatness. No, Bonds has chosen the opposite path. He merely does his job and allows his achievements to do the talking. Media figures resent Bonds's aloofness, his unwillingness to please them, make concessions, or make them at ease in his presence with a joke, knowing wink, or grin. In this way, he is the antithesis of his godfather, Mays, who brought with him an aura of gratitude for being allowed the opportunity to play in the major leagues. Unlike Bonds, Mays followed acceptable athletic protocol yet was still unappreciated. But Bonds is different. He has been around professional baseball his entire life; he witnessed racism and inequity directed at Black players first-hand. As a child he witnessed the mistreatment of Black players (namely, his dad, Bobby Bonds) and will never forget. He seems to punish the media for it, making them uncomfortable every chance he can. Once when asked why he chose not to participate in the All-Star Game home-run contest, he replied: "I am a grown man and will choose what I want to do, which is not to participate in the contest." This is the swagger of a BNS.

In addition to breaking the home-run record, he has done something that may never again be duplicated: hitting 500 home runs and stealing 500 bases! Yet despite all his accolades, he disgusts most people because he is "arrogant" and controlling—the worst sins a Black man can commit. His mystery, and aloofness render him an enigma to sportswriters. He does not seek nor care for approval from media, so they make him out to be surly and villainous. In fact, he has been convicted in the media without proof (his trainer, unlike Roger Clemens's and Andy Pettitte's, has not testified against him). Perhaps his greatest crime, is not that he might have perjured himself, but that he repeatedly defies of the racial contract that demands and requires non-White humility and deference; he refuses to "monkey shine."

Perhaps Bonds rejects the "I am happy to be here" persona that made so many love Mays because he saw the media turn on Mays. Instead they chose to embrace Ted Williams and Lou Gehrig as the greatest living players. This is not a knock against Mays; he was, in my opinion, the best player of his era and perhaps, some might argue, of all time, but he emerged in baseball at a time when an affable "kid loving a kid's game" persona was the best route to celebrity for a Black athlete. When people critique Bonds, they tend to forget that he is the son of Bobby Bonds and spent much of his childhood in Major League clubhouses. As mentioned previously, it appears the price for his personality has been an unspoken collusion among major league teams to keep him out of MLB. This is the price of unreconstructed Black masculinity.

I suppose I like Bonds because he claims the privileges that the civil rights promised, and is unafraid to express his views regarding race in America—making clear he has few illusions. Although he lived next door to Whites as a kid, he soon learned that dating their daughters was considered taboo. Bonds senses that despite the fame or wealth he has achieved, race still poses barriers (and this enrages him). He has decided he will concede nothing, which frees him to shun the media and let his spectacular playing define his masculinity. He reminds me of the first Black heavyweight champion, Jack Johnson, who ushered forth a new kind of Black athlete. He too exuded confidence, fearlessness, and was flashy, bodacious, and creative. Bonds's emergence in Major League Baseball in 1985 came at a time when, according to Nelson George in *Elevating the Game* (1992), the acceptance of Black players led optimistic Blacks and well-intentioned Whites to concoct a grossly unrealistic and romantic notion of what the celebration of a few jocks meant about the perception of all Blacks. Through his father, Barry gained a more realistic view of life for Black athletes. He realized early that money did not curtail the rules of the racial contract. He saw this via the unrealistic expectations and unfair concessions heaped upon Black players like his father. My personal theory is that Bonds witnessed this, internalized it, and decided never to sign this racial contract. Now, with the steroids and perjury allegations surrounding him, his is paying the price for his behavior.

Bonds's privilege, wealth, and fame are what were expected by most from the post-civil rights generation. Bonds was never awed by professional baseball, nor did he feel the need to be "grateful" to baseball and its journalists. In fact, he seems to feel baseball should be grateful for having him, and that it owes a debt to his father and godfather. He saw players come and go as a child. He also got to see firsthand the pressures that Black professional ballplayers like his father and godfather faced. They had to conform to appease White society. Bonds has flipped the script, unwilling to conform or appease the world, making them accept him on his own terms, marching to the rhythm of his own drum. His silence speaks volumes, unnerving weaker reporters. This makes him America's greatest nightmare, perhaps the whipping boy for baseball steroids, and an example to other BNS who dare to forget their place.

*Floyd "Money" Mayweather Jr.*
Before retiring from boxing in 2008 with an unblemished record, Floyd Mayweather Jr. was considered the pound-for pound best boxer of this generation. (May of 2009 he unretired.) He won six titles in five weight classes. Mayweather, who dazzled America with dance moves that rivaled his moves in the ring, and mixed it up a bit in WrestleMania for a few extra bucks, epitomizes the confidence and bling of BNS. In 2007 alone he is reported to have earned as much as $50 million from boxing. He pals around with the likes of Mark Cuban, Chris Brown, and the rapper 50 Cent. He is no Mike Tyson; his fortune is in tact. His personality is outsized, so is his ego and his earning power.

He earned $25 million alone in 2007 for his victory over Oscar De La Hoya and is able to select opponents that net him the most money. Speaking of money and control, the baller in Mayweather compelled him to buy himself out from Top Rank in 2006. From that time until his first retirement he promoted his own bouts in order to earn the complete share of his ring earnings. No manager, promoters or backers direct him, he calls his shots. This is what being a BNS is about on one level. Or, as Mayweather put it best in an 8 June 2008 *NY Times Magazine* profile, "I can write my own ticket in boxing. Money Mayweather like to be outside the box." He is a noteworthy example of modern boxers because he managed to become famous, earn lots of money and control his own destiny in a weight class and sport where both rarely occur at the same time.

*Oscar De La Hoya: Golden BNS*

Oscar De La Hoya represents a transcendence of the New School Baller. He has charm, "crossover" appeal, and powerful friends; and other fighters like him because he has helped to make them quite wealthy and independent. De La Hoya is perhaps the best example of BNS come to fruition. He grew up poor in a rough Mexican community of Los Angeles and saw many fighters cheated out of their money by managers and promoters. His company, Golden Boy Promotions, advocates his belief that fighters should know what promoters and managers make, in addition to receiving a larger piece of the purse.

De La Hoya is a real Baller. He is the vision of what a New School Baller should aspire to be: taking, giving, and calling shots simultaneously. This is what he does in the sport of boxing. (He retired in 2009.) He is president of Golden Boy Promotions (founded in 2001) and was an active fighter. Using the clout from Golden Boy Promotions, he is slowly taking over boxing and heading toward new frontiers. For example, De La Hoya also owns *Ring* magazine ("The Bible of Boxing") as well as *KO, World Boxing*, and *Pro Wrestling Illustrated*. He acquired these publications through Sports and Entertainment Publications, a group he founded to explore publishing opportunities

With his good looks, easy manner, and charisma, De La Hoya has singlehandedly changed the game of boxing. Non-heavyweights now earn enormous salaries largely because of him. He has helped to shift the focus from the traditional heavyweight division, establishing himself as boxing's biggest star who appeals to English- and Spanish-speaking audiences.

In true Baller spirit, once he became the biggest attraction in Pay-Per-View history with several record-breaking promotions, specifically his 2007 fight against Floyd Mayweather Jr., which broke the Pay-Per-View record for buys of a non-heavyweight fight (over 1.4 million) and for ticket sales ($19 million), De La Hoya set out to challenges Bob Arum and Don King as boxing's top promoter. To date he has been quite successful.

So successful is De La Hoya that he has shaken terror into boxing's business model, which is filled with unscrupulous promoters who fix fights and take large percentages of money from fighters' earnings. He has brought the fighters closer to the money, negotiations, and power. De La Hoya offers an alternative that promises a truthful accounting of promoters', trainers', and managers' cuts from a boxer's earnings. What he is doing is honorable, making boxers such as Bernard Hopkins and Floyd Mayweather, Jr. more money and giving them more control than they had previously experienced. He is the Curt Flood of boxing.

But this New School Baller is not limited to boxing. Golden Boy Promotions has acquired a stake in leading Spanish-language newspapers in the United States, as well as a thirteen-story office building in downtown Los Angeles. In 2005 De La Hoya and James Long, a Los Angeles real estate developer, jointly invested $100 million to form Golden Boy Partners, which is investing in housing as well as retail projects in Latino neighborhoods in Southern California. All would be Ballers have to turn to De La Hoya as the blueprint for the future; he understands that his celebrity can garner him more than ads hawking shoes, drinks, batteries, or cell phones, but that real Ballers build institutions that have a lasting impact on communities and the world.

*Myron Rolle: Renaissance Baller*

Ballers are individuals who in lieu of calling shots do things on their own terms, embrace leadership, intellectualism, and their ethnic identity without apology. Most important, they all attempt to claim space beyond what the racial contract designates for them. One of my fondest contemporary examples of a Baller is 2009 Rhodes Scholar Myron Rolle. He was a defensive back for Florida State University. Rolle was the first prominent college football player in 25 years to receive the honor. He is a leader, outstanding student, superior athlete and humanitarian. Rolle graduated in less than three years with a 3.75 grade point average, is pursuing a master's degree in Public Administration, and attended Oxford in 2009 for a master's degree in medical anthropology! He makes the

Baller list because he is a member of Omicron Delta Kappa National Leadership Honor Society; was active on several campus committees; and will be both an NFL draft pick and a doctor! Indeed, he models what far more male athletes must strive for. (Many female athletes of color are achieving in this manner because of gender disparities in professional sport.)

All these BNS, past and present, male and female, remind us there is indeed a legacy of Baller spirit that has historically struggled against American racism with success. They also reveal that sport can be a powerful vehicle for change. While similar pitfalls face contemporary BNS in different ways, there are certainly signs of progress. Current issues at hand regarding White disapproval of modern athletes' aesthetics, is really a struggle over cultural sovereignty; it involves racial/cultural politics of power. Whoever can sway the worldview of the fans regarding acceptable style wins. The real fear is not about wearing throwback jerseys, hats, and jewelry but about ideological supremacy. Although BNS may not completely understand the stakes in this battle, they do understand the importance of being allowed to be free to be themselves.

Thus, when modern sports stars pierce their bodies, tattoo signs on themselves, wear their hair in braids, and wear sports apparel and we no longer discuss this in relation to "normal" and "acceptable" or morality, then progress will be upon us. When the transgressions of athletes of color receive the same latitude post-career as current NBA analyst Bill Walton (who used drugs while playing) or Marv Albert (who revealed an unusual sexual appetite), then we can say sport is leading the way.

Two things come to mind when pondering BNS past and present and how far we as a nation have progressed regarding race. First, I think former *Slam* magazine editor at large and author Scoop Jackson put it best when he posited that the current tension between modern athletes and the media is mired in White journalists' belief that their cultural values are the only relevant and good values. Again, Jordan was embraced primarily because he represented standards that meshed with the dominant culture's standards. People forget that the gritty, hip-hop, "do shit their own way" BNS are merely a variation of that early Jordan. Almost all BNS idolize the core elements of Jordan's style: his big diamond earring, success and acceptance, cockiness, baggy shorts, and entrepreneur spirit; some even admire his apolitical stance. As David Halberstam intimates in his book *Playing for Keeps: Michael Jordan and the World He Made*, Jordan was successful primarily because he avoided race, often ignoring it completely. This put people at ease with him. Indeed, he was acceptable as long as his Blackness was nowhere in view. Jordan's success saddens me, however, because it is a reminder of the limits of post–civil rights racial progress. It is a reminder that opportunity is attainable for non-Whites willing to embrace neo-Booker T. Washington politics of hard work, while ignoring racial, social, and political issues.

Looking at Ballers past and present, it is clear that while athletes in the modern era enjoy some basic privileges that those in the previous era could not, race still impacts their lives. The scrutiny remains quite high; there are still double standards. However, there is hope when one thinks of the Williams sisters, who have developed a global following; the success of the Jordan brand; and De La Hoya's Golden Boy Promotions, which garners boxers of different weight classes more money and gives them more control than they could have previously imagined.

Masculinity is deeply tied to American sport culture, often to a fault. In her book *Manliness and Civilization*, Gail Bederman explains the historical meaning of manhood in America. According to Bederman, manhood is a historical process whereby "individuals are positioned and position themselves as men or as women. . . . [M]anhood or masculinity is the cultural process whereby concrete individuals are constituted as members of a preexisting social category—as men" (7). And in America, bodily strength and social authority possess similar powers in defining manhood. For African American men, there is the constant threat, dating back to slavery, of being deemed as lacking manhood. Sport has been one way of legitimizing social and political disfranchisement. To watch the not-so-subtle signs in the images and language is to understand—even today—that manhood is always linked to Whiteness. Bederman does a fine job of explaining that manly power historically has been linked to "the racial supremacy of civilized white men" (22).

BNS such as Bonds, myself included—products of the post–civil rights, hip-hop generation—have a sense of the near and present danger of race upon their lives, the constant critiques, while struggling to live as a woman or man on one's own terms in America struggling against the rules of the racial contract. This is the legacy of the Original Ballers that modern BNS must uphold, hopefully with increasing political consciousness in the future. Like hip-hop—a cultural creation that is highly politicized and about controlling or carving out public space for the disenfranchised—BNS must force America to confront its race issues, such that there is appreciation for cultural difference and diversity rather than fear of the loss of White cultural supremacy.

Jack Johnson grinned, but it was menacing, and he was unforgiving in his selfhood, demanding to exist on his own terms unbound by race. Ali grinned, taunted, joked, and rhymed, without shying away from Islam or Black Nationalism. BNS have looked at such examples and forged similar but unique paths. In fact, BNS attitudes are a mixed bag of sorts. Some "don't give a f**k," while others are respectable, yet tied to masculinity and freedom in a way that reminds me of the late great poet Langston Hughes's famous remarks in his essay "The Negro Mountain and the Racial Artist." In this essay Hughes was responding to the pressures being placed on Black artists from both Blacks and Whites. He tells critics:

> If white people are pleased we are glad. If they are not, it doesn't matter. We know we are beautiful. And ugly too. The tom-tom cries and the tom-tom laughs. If colored people are pleased we are glad. If they are not, their displeasure doesn't matter either. We build our temples for tomorrow, strong as we know how, and we stand on top of the mountain, free within ourselves. (In *Within the Circle* 59)

This is the vantage point from which Bonds and some of the other BNS seem to take their swings. In doing it their way, we see great wealth amassed and burgeoning empires like those of LeBron James or Oscar De La Hoya. Gone is the era when pioneering athletes ate shit and grinned about it, complacently. While grinning does still take place and shit is still on the menu, it is not what it was. Ballers, past and present, make us painfully aware of American racism in sports, the racial contract, and beleaguered Black humanity. While discrimination functions in a much more sophisticated manner, opportunities are more prevalent than in previous generations. Is there still a price to pay? Certainly. Still, the majority of BNS are unreconstructed. Some of the more "successful" ones are more diplomatic or willing to "play the game." But what is interesting is that on some level they all strive to function, to some extent, on their own terms.

I cannot help but to look at figures like Tiger Woods when pondering the true measure of sport's racial progress. How far have we progressed when Kelly Tilghman comments that the only way for opposing PGA players to halt Woods's dominance is to "Lynch him in a back alley," and Woods chooses to ignore the comments as "a complete non-issue" out of fear of a "White lash" or media lynching? Woods has decided that he must deem a joke about lynching, used to murder 3,500 Black Americans between 1882 and 1968, as harmless. This is the state of progress, or the price of progress, in twenty-first-century America.

Just as Original Baller Jack Johnson's display of masculinity and disdain for White supremacy's racial contract earned him the moniker of "monster," modern BNS like Bonds enrage America and the sports-industry gatekeepers because they are not completely playing by the rules of the game; they are not smiling enough or thanking everyone for the opportunity. Still, change is within our grasps. All we have to do is harness the popularity of modern athletes across multiple socioeconomic and racial lines to change racial politics of old. The iconic status of Venus and Serena Williams, LeBron James, Allen Iverson, and Oscar De La Hoya makes them perfect instruments for changing the world if approached in an honest and humble manner. What if the most popular BNS carried the mantle of political activism as did Flood, Ali, Gibson, Brown, and others who took stands on significant issues like war and free agency? What if they formed an entity like the Negro Industrial and Economic Union (NIEU)? Since "keep it real" is the mantra of this generation, more pressure should be placed on teams, fans, leagues, and other affiliated entities to advocate for the next phase of inclusion or equality in the corporate sports world. Real Ballers call these kinds of shots.

# CHAPTER FOUR

## WHERE THE BROTHERS AND SISTERS AT?

America calling.
negroes.
can you dance?
play foot/baseball?
nanny?
cook?
needed now. Negroes
who can entertain
ONLY.
others not
 wanted.
(& are considered extremely dangerous.)

—Haki R. Madhubuti

> *One of the best kept secrets in sports is how you have all these African Americans playing sports, but so few African Americans covering sports. . . . That has got to have a huge impact on how the news is presented.*
>
> —Terence Moore

On 31 December 2007, NCAA president Myles Brand headed the NCAA convention, where he made a plea for equality on campuses for women and minorities in the field of head coach and athletic director. Brand cited the paucity of Black head football coaches as an "embarrassment" to college athletics and encouraged the leading members of NCAA institutions to take immediate action regarding the hiring of Blacks and other minorities into these positions because the historically slow rate of increase among minority head coaches or athletic directors. Furthermore, Brand, seizing the moment and aware of the racial inequities in collegiate sports leadership, reminded the gathering that if intercollegiate athletics is to play a key role of helping to promote social justice in higher education, as it should, then all of us, the NCAA national office and the universities it represents, must recognize the challenges and commit to meeting them.

This chapter extends a similar challenge, but not just to collegiate sports. Here the query is where is the diversity at the coaching and executive levels of American sport culture in the 21st century? For while there is little doubt that in the high-profile sports such as football, basketball, and baseball the presence of non-Whites speaks volumes regarding racial progress, positions of leadership beyond the playing fields are far from diverse. Contrary to popular notions, the world of sport, which has been lauded for its racial progress, is filled with discrimination, inequities, and lack of diversity. Racism, inequality, discrimination, and nepotism in sport are real. Instead of being frustrated by repeated declarations that race is a problem, what should be more frustrating is the variety of ways discrimination exhibits itself in American sport culture. In many ways, sport culture is a reflection of our society. Further, the disenfranchisement of people of color in sport culture reinforces false notions of intellectual inferiority, ensuring a regime of racial discrimination that systematically keeps people of color out of positions of leadership.[1]

During the 2009 college football bowl games bonanza in December and early January, I took stock of where in fact the brothers might be. Of the thirty-two games that were played, I noticed on the fields during games that Black players were in the vast majority of those involved in these contests. But when I looked to the sidelines for the men wearing the headsets and leading the teams, I found scant Black head coaches. Where were they? In fact, in 2009 less than seven of the 120 Division IA football head coaches in the NCAA top division were Black. And, of the top six BCS conferences there was only one Black coach! In 2007 there were less than ten head college football coaches and no more than twelve Black or Latino Athletic Directors (AD) in Division IA (according to the Race and Gender Report Card Whites held ninety-four percent of these positions in Division I, ninety-two percent in Division II, and ninety-six percent in Division III in 2006–07). In the twenty-first century, the number of Black head coaches allowed to lead big-time football programs is a shameful reminder that the racial contract is real.[2] Things are so bad that in 2009 Oregon House Bill 3118 was passed. The bill will require Oregon's state colleges and universities to interview at least one minority candidate before hiring a head football coach. Major League Baseball—while it has a fair mix of Asian, Latino, Black, and White players—also scores very low when it comes to non-White team managers, general managers, and team presidents, etc. And, American newspapers are even more segregated than MLB, touting deplorable statistics like an F for gender hiring practices and a C for racial hiring practices in sports journalism.[3] As outlined below, America still has a long way to go on the field of racial equality. My primary goal in this chapter is to encourage readers to face the continuing problems of discrimination and racism, but most importantly challenge American sport culture to actively seek true diversity for its leadership positions.

Indeed, there is a problem when, as the Institute for Diversity and Ethics in Sport reported in 2006 that nine out of ten sports editors are White males, as are at least eighty percent of sports columnists. Therefore, it is necessary to begin discussion of inequities, diversity, and racism in American sport culture with a critical examination of American sports journalism. I begin with the poor diversity of newspapers because, as the poet Haki Madhubuti once said, "ideas run the world." In fact, it is in the sports pages that many barriers, myths, and stereotypes plaguing our society continue to exist. The politics, ideas, and practices that deter or assist racial progress are covertly and explicitly expressed and reinforced in American sport journalism (the excessive criminalization of non-White athletes has been well documented). Although the sports pages are where people go to escape, it is also a space where their defenses are down long enough to move past myths and stereotypes. Unfortunately sport journalism offers subtle ideological agendas that support narratives of good, hardworking, and smart (White) and the bad, instinctive, physical, not smart (Black) on every level of sport culture. These subtle narratives criminalizing non-White athletes often go unchallenged. One reason for this is because, as statistics below reveal, there is too often one voice, or a lack of diverse perspectives driving sports reporting and narratives in America.

A study released in 2006 (at the request of Associated Press Sports Editors) revealed that Blacks held only 6.2 percent of sports writing jobs. Out of over three hundred newspapers that were surveyed in 2006, less than five had a Black sports editor. These numbers do not reflect the percentage of Blacks in the population, and certainly not the percentage that play high-profile professional and collegiate sports. If Black athletes have played a significant role in steering America to a more understanding view of race, if sport is a site of important gains, why is journalism so segregated? Why is the industry that casts very important judgments that shape the views of the average fan so lacking in diversity? Why does the press box remain the domain of White males? Sportswriters contribute to and shape the ideological infrastructure that perpetuates or ends misguided racial beliefs. Where the brothers (or sisters) at to balance these perspectives?

The 2008 Racial and Gender Report Card reveals interesting statistics that might help explain the biased reporting and racial tensions in sports media, and America. Quickly, here is what it revealed: There was a slight rise in the number of Black columnists, up from 7.4 percent to 10.7 percent, but White sports editors comprised ninety-four percent; Whites were nearly ninety percent of assistant sports editors; eighty-eight percent of sports columnists, eighty-seven percent of reporters and roughly ninety percent of copy editors. Looking at these figures how feasible is it that sports pages might reflect a diversity of opinion or voice? How fair is sports reporting/coverage of people of color in American sport given Whites comprise nearly ninety percent of most aspects of sports journalism? With such fragile diversity non-Whites cannot risk broaching too many racial issues without risk of losing their jobs or being censored by senior editors. The first step toward racial progress in sport culture is to diversify the newspaper industry.

The sentiment and diversity in American society in the twenty-first century sport culture suggests that there is a common belief that affirmative action, while initially useful to correct past injustices, is unwarranted in what many falsely believe to be "post-race" America. The common belief is that it no longer makes sense to assume that non-Whites suffer disadvantages in life or that there is a lack of diversity. In fact, many Whites complain of suffering from a diversity malaise. But in sport culture racial dishonesty is more transparent; there is nowhere to hide from the cameras. Take one look at positions of leadership in American sport culture from quarterbacks and pitchers to coaches, owners, and team executives, and what it reveals is that America still has demons of racism to contend with.

*Penalty for Unnecessary Roughness*

A better understanding of the paucity of non-White sportswriters, coaches, and administrators can be found in a study of football coaches in Division I NCAA institutions (Non-HBCUs) that reveals that less than ten percent of coaches are Black, while fifty percent of players are Black. Message: You can play for us, but we will not hire you to lead our teams.

Although the 2008 Racial and Gender Report Card gave college sport a B for its race hiring practices and a B for gender hiring practices, I suspect grade inflation when considering the dismal numbers. One reason racial tensions do not appear significant is because as Marcus Allen laments, the subject of race relations has gone "underground" and "racism is at its highest point since the civil rights movement in the 1960s and 1970s. . . . Yet the majority of today's athletes seem increasingly hesitant to stand up and speak out."[4] Race is clearly an issue when one considers the lack of male and female sports editors, head coaches, and executives in professional and collegiate high-profile sports that are overrepresented by persons of color on the playing field.

Certainly we cannot continue to turn a blind eye to race if a Hall of Fame athlete also concedes that racism and discrimination persist as problems. Racism does not transcend sports. Most sports journalists either avoid the question or in some cases contribute to tense racial dynamics. Few players speak up for fear of losing their jobs or future opportunities with colleges and professional teams. Key factors to this stalemate are attributable to the lack of sports journalists, executives, coaches, managers, and other sports executives of color in American sports. One reason for this is the lack of supportive networking, mentoring, and learning opportunities. Also, the majority of Black men in football, for example, are hired to coach wide receivers, tailbacks, and defensive linemen or act as recruiters. These jobs rarely lead to head coaching positions. An NCAA 2003–04 Student Athlete Ethnicity Report revealed that although Black men have been somewhat more successful in men's basketball and track, only thirty percent of assistant and associate athletics directors in 2003–04 were female. This NCAA report also indicated that most women and minorities don't have the opportunities to be the number one administrator or coaching assistant. What they often find they are up against is a process that is discriminatory and futile. One of the major reasons these racial and gendered glass ceilings persist is because many college presidents rely on services, with the cooperation of athletic directors, to personally recruit high-profile coaches from the same old pool of sharks.

What is clear about sport is that it puts a person's or a society's true character on display. Wayne Embry, the first African American general manager for a sports team, tells of the obstacles facing African American executives in his book *The Inside Game*. Embry recounts interviewing for the general manager position with the Cleveland Cavaliers and being asked: "If you get this job, will you feel compelled to hire a black coach?" (11). Unbelievable. No one asks White owners, general managers, or team presidents if they will hire White coaches. Embry received death threats during his tenure with the Milwaukee Bucks, and as he tells it, he "heard almost every racial slur and insinuation" (11).

Embry's situation is a good example of how racism is at the root of imbalance in positions of power. Many of the struggles and the scrutiny he endured were because of his race. Therefore the question "Where the brothers at?" is meant to suggest that the racial contract maintains a "racial order" that is responsible for the paucity of men and women of color in leadership/power positions in sport culture—a mirror of American culture. Further, the few athletes and executives like Embry who get an *opportunity* are burdened with using the platform to broach equity. Unfortunately, as Marcus Allen opines in his autobiography *Marcus*, the "black athlete of today has indeed gone silent."[5]

These athletes are silent because nobody wants to hear them say anything that is not scripted. Yet White players are not asked to serve as spokespersons for social and racial issues impacting White Americans. This is why it was amusing and frustrating when then–NBA rookies

Carmelo Anthony and LeBron James were interviewed about racial progress when the film *Glory Road* was released. No disrespect to them personally, but why ask eighteen- and nineteen-year-olds with all sorts of corporate handcuffs on them to affirm racial progress? Why not turn to experts like Black Coaches Association (BCA) executive director Floyd Keats or renowned sociologist Harry Edwards? What we might have heard is Keats explaining how basketball does better at hiring coaches because it benefits from a "different culture and thinking, but that much progress remains to be made." It does not fit the desired narrative.

Beyond and within the playing fields, the "qualified" question is like a nagging injury, especially when the subject is leadership positions for people of color. Racism, prejudice, and stereotypes are contributing factors. Indeed, the problem stems from management continuing to hold to some archaic, unspoken notion that Black coaches lack the intelligence and leadership qualities necessary for success. Also, sports journalism, with its biased reporting and abysmal diversity record, helps to keep these archaic ideas alive. Finally, with so many non-Whites dominating high-profile sports, one of the last alpha male positions remaining is the coach. Leadership positions in sports have remained central to White male identity. In sports, White male domination as the lead player or figure is central to masculine identity. Thus, the position of coach (quarterback too) is the final bastion that will be difficult for White men to relinquish.[6]

The threat to White male identity began on that fateful day of July 4, 1910, when the boxer James Jeffries (who at the time was considered the greatest heavyweight and originally tagged, "The Great White Hope") was literally lifted to his feet for a second time by a group of White male spectators after heavyweight champion Jack Johnson knocked him into the ropes. But coaching seems to be the space where White masculinity had to be reconstructed and reconceived (look at the treatment of Bobby Knight and Bill Parcells). As non-Whites take up more and more space on playing fields (primarily in high-profile sports), the status of coach, which signifies leader, has been raised to higher importance and celebrity; it is also the province of primarily White men.

According to Floyd Keats, a contributing factor to sports leadership inequities is unwillingness among team owners, university presidents, and athletic directors (96 percent of whom are White at Division I schools) to "be diverse in their thinking and diverse in their process."[7] Thus, organizations continue to recycle the same coaches and executives along with feeling comfortable only with hiring White coaches. In my conversation with Keats, he asked a brilliant and obvious question: "Why aren't college presidents, athletic directors, and coaches looking at historically Black colleges for coaches and athletic directors?" Keats is correct. These institutions are bursting at the seams with qualified, seasoned applicants in every phase of athletics. The blockade against Black coaches is far from invisible; there are severe social problems in college and professional sports, more so in the front offices than in locker rooms. Otherwise Eddie Robinson—former coach at Grambling and among the most successful coaches in the history of college football— might have been invited for at least one Division I job interview during his illustrious career. Very few women and members of minority groups are represented. In fact, it was so dismal that between 1995 and 1999 the number of athletic directors, assistant athletic directors, and associate athletic directors declined for minority groups, leaving ten "minority" athletic directors in Division I among 312 institutions. But college presidents, who hold much of the power for change, refuse to take the lead in diversifying athletic departments beyond the playing fields.[8]

*Black Coaches Anyone?*

Hall of Fame running back Marcus Allen also once observed that "even those who have managed to get a job on the staff of a pro team face long odds of one day ever becoming the man in charge" (209). When Art Shell became the first African American head coach in the NFL in 1989, although he was the man in charge, he was treated as a second-class citizen by owner Al Davis. Players are far more color-blind than management, whose discrimination is made clear by the lack of non-

Whites in sports beyond the playing fields and courts. Because the brothers are not in executive positions in sports organizations, it is at least clear where the brothers *are not.*

While sport culture may reflect some change, it also serves as a perfect vehicle for exposing the painful truth about racism in America. A brief look at the facts regarding NFL diversity is quite revealing. The NFL's history of racial discrimination and inequity past and present is not honorable. The NFL Black coaching ranks and executive positions tells the story. According to the 2008 Racial and Gender Report Card, while there were a record number of assistant coaches of color (172) in 2006, that number remained unchanged in 2007. Also, in 2008 there were twelve Black vice presidents, one less than in 2006. In 2008 only the Oakland Raiders had a female President/CEO, and there has yet to be a person of color to serve as president or CEO in the history of the NFL!

The 2008 season is a reminder of how much is possible, and how much still needs to change. The season began with six of the thirty-two teams being guided by a Black coach (three in the same division that only one can win!). By the end of the season the second Black coach led a team to a Super Bowl victory while the number fell to five before Tampa Bay hired Raheem Morris, returning the number to six.

This is less than 2006, when only seven of thirty-two NFL teams had Black coaches: Herman Edwards of the Chiefs, Tony Dungy of the Indianapolis Colts, Marvin Lewis of the Cincinnati Bengals, Romeo Crennel of the Cleveland Browns, Art Shell (fired in 2007, Lovie Smith of the Chicago Bears, and Dennis Green (fired in 2007) of the Arizona Cardinals. Again, what these men have in common besides the color of their skin is that they all were pretty successful (four led teams to the playoffs during that span) with teams that needed serious rebuilding. For example, Dungy turned the once miserable Buccaneers around and was fired the year before the team won the Super Bowl. He took over what had become a dismal situation in Indianapolis, returning them to playoff form, and in 2004 led them to the American Conference championship game, then in 2006 led them to the best record in the NFL, and in 2007 they became Super Bowl champions!

How did other coaches fare in resurrecting bad teams? Dennis Green's team rarely missed the playoffs during his nine-year tenure in Minnesota. Twice his team made it to the NFC championship game (both losses). His stint in Phoenix as the Cardinals head coach was less successful, but he made a visible impact on the attitude of the organization and quality of players drafted in less than three years (many of the players he drafted were part of the team that made it to the Super Bowl in 2009).

Marvin Lewis spent several years as the defensive coordinator and mastermind of the Baltimore Ravens defense, which in 2001 was touted as the best ever. Despite this achievement, it took Lewis several years to finally get a chance as a head coach in Cincinnati. In his first season, he led the Bengals to their first non-losing season in almost a decade, and in 2006 they won the division and made the playoffs. He experienced his first losing season in 2008.

Meanwhile, Herman Edwards took over a Jets team that had fallen on hard times and had instant success. He led them to the playoffs and back to being competitive before leaving for the Kansas City Chiefs head-coaching job, where success was difficult because of injuries to numerous key players in 2007 and 2008. He was fired at the end of the 2008 season.

Romeo Crennel earned five Super Bowl rings as an assistant coach or coordinator. Like most of the Black head coaches, he was handed a terrible team in the Cleveland Browns. His success in turning around the Cleveland Browns would have earned him Coach of the Year honors had his mentor in New England not led his team to an unbeaten regular season in 2007. Despite his success there was scant room for failure. In 2008, his inability to repeat the success of the previous season, despite injuries to both of his top quarterbacks, cost him his job.

Lovie Smith was the defensive coordinator for the Rams when they won the Super Bowl. In two seasons he managed to turn the lackluster Chicago Bears around, leading them to a division title, a playoff berth, and a historic appearance in the 2007 Super Bowl against his mentor Tony Dungy's team, all while also winning Coach of the Year. His teams have been up and down the past two years, which has placed his future in question.

Unlike his predecessors, head coach Mike Tomlin received a very solid Pittsburgh Steelers team that two years prior to his arrival had won the Super Bowl. While the season before his arrival was a disappointing one, the team he inherited had a very strong nucleus. Tomlin has responded well, guiding the Pittsburgh Steelers to two straight division titles since being hired in 2007. And in 2009, he became not only the second Black head coach to lead a team to a Super Bowl victory, but the youngest coach to ever achieve this feat! One would think that as the coaching carousel at the end of 2008 and early 2009 began everyone would be vying for the next Tomlin, but this was not the case.

Despite the success of the aforementioned Black coaches and diversity efforts like The Rooney Rule, why does the NFL continue to claim to have difficulty finding head-coaching candidates? There are organizations like The Black Coaches Association (BCA) eager and willing to serve professional and college teams looking for historically underrepresented coaches and administrators. As Floyd Keats, BCA director, contends, "There are no excuses." Indeed, what college and professional sports need to find out is how the NBA has managed to find at least thirteen Black head coaches for nearly half of its franchises." The NBA seems to have discovered "where the brothers at" (right in their face); the other leagues would do well to follow their lead in providing the same opportunity.

What is most interesting is that the successes of Black football coaches like Tony Dungy, Dennis Green, and Mike Tomlin disprove the myth of inferior Black leadership and intellect (as though it actually needs to be invalidated). It is common knowledge that Tony Dungy, the 2007 Super Bowl winner, successfully resurrected two different teams during his illustrious career. Not only did he turn the lowly Tampa Bay Buccaneers around, but also from 2003–2008 (when he retired), his Colts won at least 12 games during the regular season—an amazing feat. But because the racial contract makes it difficult for people to embrace the cognitive and leadership abilities of non-Whites Dungy's success as leader/coach of the Indianapolis Colts was often attributed to his White quarterback, Peyton Manning. Dungy's enormous success should have created more diversity in the coaching ranks. To be quite frank, Tony Dungy's tree of Black coaches such as Herman Edwards, Mike Tomlin, Lovie Smith, and Jim Caldwell (whom Dungy had a hand in selecting as his replacement), has done more to pave the way for Black head coaches than the "Rooney Rule."

Several years ago the NFL devised a wonderful public relations gesture when it invited the coaching staffs from small, predominately Black colleges to spend a weeklong all-expense-paid trip to their training camps to help them learn the pro game and acquaint themselves with the coaches. Despite this gesture, the head-coaching ranks remain the province of White males, who are recycled from team to team. Like our society, sports leagues, especially the NFL, fear relinquishing power and racial supremacy myths. Although the NFL alleges to place an emphasis on hiring more Black coaches and front-office personnel, consideration for these jobs are far less equitable than the struggle for roster spots on the team.

The best way to gauge progress is to recall that in a league where Black players represent at least sixty-five percent of the players, in 2004, four of the thirty-two head coaches in the NFL were Black (slightly over ten percent). As of 2009, on the heels of two Black coaches leading their teams to the Super Bowl in the same season (2007), and another winning in 2009, there are now six (which is one less than there was in 2006). That cannot be right. Where is the mad scramble to fill vacant head-coaching positions with Black coaches in the hopes of duplicating the success of the Colts, Bears, and Steelers? In 2008 the New York Giants shocked the world by defeating the then-undefeated New England Patriots in the Super Bowl. The architect of this overachieving group was the first-year general manager Jerry Reese, who also happens to be Black. As of 2009, Reese is one of five Black General Managers in the NFL. One would think that Reese's success as well as that of James Harris, vice president for player personnel for the NFL Jacksonville Jaguars, would open doors for other executives of color, but there has been little change.

The point is that sport does not escape the perils of racial discrimination. One would think that with the success of coaches like Tony Dungy and Lovie Smith, and executives like Reese would provide far greater opportunities for non-Whites in professional sports. But the racist "Old Boy" network of White privilege and exclusion is tough to crack—even in what is alleged to be a "post-race" America. In the end the question remains: where the diversity at?

This is also the question for Major League Baseball (MLB), which has never had a person of color as CEO or team president for any of its thirty teams. Two women have held this position, but no persons of color. However, there are two Black General Managers (Ken Williams for the Chicago White Sox, and Tony Reagins for the Los Angeles Angels), and one Latino (Omar Minaya with the New York Mets). MLB saw nearly a seven percent rise in 2008 for managers of color for teams. Meanwhile only ten percent of the team vice presidents were persons of color and sixteen percent were women. In 2007, according to the 2008 Racial and Gender Report Card, people of color comprised eighteen percent of senior administrators, and twenty-eight percent of the professional administrators. But on the field another dramatic shift has occurred over the last decade. Since 1997 the number of Black American players has dropped from seventeen percent to eight percent, while Latino and Asian player population continues to increase steadily.

However, not every league has failed as miserably as the NFL. The 2008 Racial and Gender Report Card gave the NBA the highest marks of all professional sport leagues. Perhaps the NBA has been more progressive in comparison to the other sports leagues (namely, baseball and football) because in the NBA over eighty percent of the players are African American. Some might argue that the NBA's extensive diversity initiative has resulted in it having the highest rates of diverse ethnic representation on the sidelines and front office. In 2008 the Racial and Gender Report Card on the NBA indicated high marks in the front office. The NBA had a two percent increase in people of color in administrative positions (currently twenty-eight percent), and twenty-two percent of the senior administrators for teams were people of color. Astonishingly, women held twenty-seven percent of these positions. From 2007 to 2008, people of color occupied fifteen percent of vice president positions, and the NBA touts the highest percentage of people of color in the history of men's professional sport in the category of CEO/President, vice president, and league office professionals! While Whites still have easier routes to leadership, and remain in the majority in these areas, this progress cannot be ignored.

Perhaps the NBA has done the best job of diversifying the coaching and executive ranks because it *desires* to. Still, the message in professional, and (as I detail below) collegiate sport, seems to be that it is okay for Blacks to be a field hand—to get dirty, sweat, jump, and run—but leadership positions are the province of White men and women.

*Illegal Procedure in College Sport*
As I pointed out previously, college programs often lag behind professional sports in the area of executive diversity. But how can institutions of higher education fail to lead the way in diversifying American sport culture when the presidents who run them are supposed to know better? The 18 November 2004 *Chronicle of Higher Education* article by Daniel Engber, "Lack of Diversity among Division I-A Leaders Is Reflected in Football Coaches They Hire" reveals the hiring practices of universities. His analysis is instructive for college and professional sports, as well as society in general. According to Engber, racial diversity among campus leaders and

conference commissioners in Division IA sports is closely correlated to the demographics of the head football coaches they hire. Based on the findings from the 1999 study by Richard E. Lapchick, director of the program in sports-business management at the University of Central Florida, only a small percentage of head coaches are African Americans or Latinos.[9]

As of 2009, the diversity among the college football ranks has gotten even worse. What this reflects is what Lapchick calls "an old-boys network that is very much alive and well." It is a network that "make[s] quick decisions [and] turn[s] to people among their colleagues and friends, and frequently end[s] up with people who look like them." To make matters worse, few if any of the African American presidents or athletics directors have hired an African American football coach, and only one Latino athletic director has hired a non-White coach. Why? Where is the open hiring process that promotes diversity? Where are the sisters and brothers at who do not sweat, run, and grunt? How come even the African American executives refuse or are fearful of promoting diversity on the sidelines the way it is promoted on the field? The most anguishing aspect of the racial contract is when the non-White signs the agreement when in positions to make a difference.

Actually, the struggle for diversity in sport mirrors the struggles of society at large. Diversity plagues professional sports in the same manner that it plagues higher education. The persistent problems are access and success, climate and intergroup relations, credentials and experience, and institutional vitality and viability. Just as the academy has been resistant in embracing diversity, American culture has resisted diversity with equal or greater passion. We think when we watch sporting events—especially baseball, basketball, and football—that we are witnessing diverse atmospheres that accept differences in personality, work style, religion, social economics, and education because we are watching teams working together toward victory. The myth is that American society practices pluralism, especially in sports. However, it is differences in work style, social economics, education, or race that keep coaching, front office, league commissioner, and other important positions in professional sports segregated and reserved for "Whites Only."

Race is indeed a dicey issue that impedes equal occupational opportunity in all facets of our society. Devah Pager, a young sociologist from Honolulu, studied the difficulties of former prisoners seeking work and found what most Blacks already know to be true. The study grouped three hundred-fifty equally well-spoken, well-groomed, college men with identical résumés to apply for entry-level jobs in Milwaukee. Pager had one man in each group (of Blacks and Whites) inform employers that he had recently served an eighteen-month prison sentence for cocaine possession. What she found was that even the White male with the criminal record had better success than the Black males without a record! The Whites with a criminal record had a callback rate of seventeen percent, while those without had a thirty-four percent callback rate. The Blacks from this group with a criminal record had a five percent callback rate, while only fourteen percent of those Blacks without a criminal record were called back. What the study reveals is that in America White privilege and racial inequities still rule. A White with a criminal record is more desirable than a non-White without one!  Similar inequities impact sport culture; the sweat free zones of leadership in sport culture face similar racial dynamics.

Oppositional "'vindicationist' scholarship is a necessary political response to fabrications of the Racial Contract" (Mills 119). Thus, the antics of coaches like Woody Hayes or Bobby Knight are repeatedly justified because they won. How can such men continue to receive coaching positions and acclaim while very qualified coaches of color linger on the fringes? A closer scrutiny of alleged great White coaches reveals that Woody Hayes was a disgrace (attacking his own and opposing players on national television); Paul "Bear" Bryant was racist and allowed cheating to get recruits; and Bobby Knight is a boorish man who is borderline racist and a poor role model. Yet in the case of Knight—despite his disrespectful, brutish, and embarrassing behavior—the media continues to lavish praise. He was featured on a TV reality show, and Madison Avenue hires him to endorse products. That these men are all held up as coaching gods is a clear example of the privilege that the racial contract accords Whites in our society.

Sports journalists speak favorably about Knight, Bill Parcells and other paternalistic, "throwback," or old school coaches who they believe can whip these BNS into shape. They send not-so-subtle messages that Black athletes are lazy and shiftless (a myth since slavery). Media selectively forget that modern athletes work hard, perhaps harder than athletes of previous eras, to stay in shape year-round and prepare themselves for what has become a market of highly skilled and conditioned players. What they also omit is that Parcells, Phil Jackson, and other successful White coaches are successful only when they *give* the respect they demand of BNS.

Perhaps the best example of the divisive racial tensions between BNS and the recycled aging group of White coaches who overpopulate professional sports is that of P. J. Carlesimo yelling at and denigrating the character and commitment of Latrell Sprewell (who infamously choked him for publicly demeaning him at practice), or Larry Brown, who regularly feuded with his star guards in Philadelphia and New York. But it is a new day that requires new blood in the coaching ranks. Allegedly the hiring progression has changed. Hiring coaches was the province of GM, but now owners are trusting fellow businessmen to help them select the right person. The focus during interviews now is not only coaching knowledge, but also organizational skills, thinking patterns, media savvy and business traits. Maybe the new criteria will result in a more diverse pool of candidates.

Unfortunately the men and women of color who aspire these positions still struggle extra hard to "earn" entry into this elite circle of privilege. The difficulty of racial inequality is that Black coaches and athletes are under extreme moral scrutiny, their margin of error always thin, whereas those like Bobby Knight can misbehave countless times (before retiring Knight had a history of outlandish behavior—from throwing chairs onto the court to brandishing a whip at Black a player, choking another, and assaulting a writer), yet remain revered by media and fans.

Meanwhile, John Thompson, the former Georgetown University men's basketball coach (affable, respectful yet stern), was castigated in the media throughout his career because his teams played hard, tough defense and he limited media access to his kids. They were labeled dirty players, even bullies, because the teams were all Black. They were consistently among the top five teams in the country, coached by a Black man who limited media contact with his players and made certain they graduated— all in direct contradiction to the racial contract.

Still, in NCAA Division I sports—despite the success stories of young Black coaches like Paul Hewitt (who led Georgia Tech's basketball team in the championship game), and the success enjoyed by John Thompson, John Thompson III, Tubby Smith, and John Chaney—the opportunities for African American head coaches, while better in basketball than football, has not grown as it should. It is important, however, to emphasize that BNS are going to have to step up to make change occur faster. BNS can make change happen if they use their star power effectively to demand diversity or by attending colleges willing to hire Black coaches.

What would happen if suddenly the players (primarily basketball because it is less costly to run) of the top two tiers of each high school recruiting class decided they would either go play for Black coaches or at Historically Black Colleges and Universities (HBCU)? Would the paradigm of coaching inequality shift? Two scenarios might take place. Once these programs beat the established programs, the networks would have to cut deals with Black conferences. The revenues earned could build the athletic department and universities. Perhaps more Black athletic directors and head coaches would finally get the notoriety they deserve. Some might be asked to coach (too late) a Florida State, Miami, North Carolina, or Duke, because of the courageous acts of young athletes using their talents to force change. People forget that a few ass-whippings from predominately Black teams forced the powerhouses like Kentucky and Alabama to integrate football and basketball programs, not social change or civil rights. We also forget the history of the Fab Five at Michigan, the five top high school players who all selected the University of Michigan in the early 1990s. That team appeared in two consecutive NCCA finals! Imagine what would happen if for five years the most talented Black football and basketball players committed to and transferred to traditionally Black colleges? It would draw on deep revenue streams, the publicity would increase enrollment, and it would effect change. Schools would change hiring practices to compete for top recruits. If the threat of lost revenue could desegregate buses during the Montgomery Bus Boycott, it certainly can diversify leadership in collegiate sport.

Again, much of this is contingent on the ability of young athletes and their families to think against the grain, work in the tradition of Black opposition, especially since they control the product everyone needs— their own talent. Philosopher Charles Mills calls this being able to "fight an internal battle before even advancing onto the ground of external combat" (118). This is a wild, desperate idea that could work. BNS must be encouraged and challenged to use this power.

### Where the Sisters At?

It is impossible to discuss inequality in sports, or ask where the brothers at, without also asking about the presence of women in the world of sports. One thing that the 2009 Racial and Gender Report Card revealed is that gender discrimination still plagues our society at an alarming rate. Only the WNBA rated an A-plus in the area of gender, and outside of the NBA no other organization from the NCAA to the NFL rated higher than a B-plus. Despite the strides of feminism and Title IX, women still lag behind, are omitted, disrespected, and ignored in the world of sports.

American sports culture remains a male province. Geno Auriemma  can coach the UConn women's team to multiple championships and emerge as the superior women's coach in America, despite the legacy of success and commitment the University of Tennessee's Pat Summit, *the* most successful coach in the history of women's college basketball. Summit has never been seriously considered for a men's coaching post, despite her enormous success. Auriemma can expect to entertain such offers. Moreover, since the advent of Title IX, more men have moved into the women's basketball coaching ranks. Also absent and equally problematic is the lack of Black female coaches, despite the large representation of African American players in women's college basketball. So it is only fair to ask, "Where the sistas *at*?"

Women are thinly present in professional sports management, coaching, and so on, albeit given ample opportunity to shake their behinds for male pleasure (the Lakers Girls and Dallas Cowboy cheerleaders are an institution unto themselves). The message sent in sport magnifies the one sent in our society: women are only necessary as objects of male desire, not to be taken seriously. What signals are being sent to young girls when females are largely absent from the American sport culture or when visible, they function in the capacity of cheerleader, or sexual object on the periphery of the games during time-outs? Years ago I recall attending a football game of a friend's nine-year-old son. The game was to decide the league champion. The park was packed, loud parents shouting for their sons, all eyes glued to the field, where the action intensified with each play. To my left, barely in view, I could faintly hear chanting that seemed to be coming from the mouths of young girls. Turning in the direction of the noise between plays, I caught a glimpse of the sound: it was the cheerleaders! Six little girls shouting their adorable hearts out, barely audible over the hum of the crowd. These little girls, working the sidelines, perhaps oblivious to the score, were virtually ignored as they cheered. Support for the boys, shouting for attention, and we were ignoring them. As the boys' huddle broke on the field for the next play, I panned back to the game so as not to miss any of the action, ignoring the girls again; but what about the girls? What does the scene say about gender, sport, masculinity, or our culture? These questions and recollections flood my mind as I stand on the sidelines rooting for my daughter's mixed-gender basketball team.

The impact of sexism has racial blinders. The messages sent to women in our culture are negative and disgusting at best. Girls are socialized early that it is best they are seen and heard off to the sidelines; that there is no place on the playing field for them. Even beyond sports, they see that our culture is dominated by and caters to men. I was at dinner with a writer who was lamenting about how perceptive his five-year-old daughter is regarding gender and society. He explained that as she acknowledged several presidents, she noticed that since they were all men, it was not something she could become. Livid, he raised his voice, explaining bewilderment that such a notion would enter her head when the conversation in his home is one of pride, self-confidence and encouragement unbound by gender limitations.

Sadly, this is not the message conveyed in American society outside of my friend's home. Society is not unlike its sport culture, which suggests that it is a "men's only" entity and that women need not apply except to shake their bottoms while scantily dressed during small breaks in the action. Unfortunately, it is sports that shape and confirm masculinity in American culture; it is the arena where boys become men, and men prove their masculinity. In the film *Girl Fight*, the protagonist Diana's initial presence in the boxing gym draws hecklers, laughter, and anger. Her physical presence threatens the ultimate expression of masculinity—boxing. The consensus is that she is a woman and thus an object, better suited for carrying around the card in between rounds while dressed in a bathing suit as sexual entertainment.

There is little wonder that my then five-year-old daughter told my wife that girls don't play sports, especially not football or basketball, only tennis (thank God for Lindsey, Monica, Serena, and Venus). When asked why she thought this, she retorted: "Whenever daddy watches football and basketball, only boys play; there are no girls." I could see that my wife was quite bothered by this, replying: "Well, Safina, it is simply not true. Girls can play any sport boys can play—look at Lisa Leslie, Cheryl Swoopes, and Tamika Holdsclaw, who play professional basketball. In fact, tomorrow I will show you that girls do play basketball." The next day She came home with a copy of the film *Love and Basketball*. She popped the DVD in and skipped to the relevant scenes to make her point. "Look at Monica [the protagonist]: she is playing basketball, along with many other girls." Safina was silent, watching with intensity. She had correctly noticed that women are indeed omitted from sports like football and baseball, but we figured basketball was a way to convince her otherwise. I realized that even in showing her *Love and Basketball*, I was also confirming her suspicions that sports culture is a male province because Monica is constantly frustrated by sexual double standards and inequities. After the film was over, I asked her, "So now do you still think that girls only play tennis?" She turned to me, still digesting what I suspect was her new discovery against what she had been seeing; somewhat convinced, she replied, "No, they play tennis *and* basketball." Not yet six years old, she had raised the important question: "Where the sistas at?" She also affirmed that they certainly are not well represented in sports.

So although we convinced her that women at least play basketball, she reminded us of how much parity is lacking for women's sports. Sure women are in the WNBA, which is where the film ends, but do people support the league? Are the women making a good or living wage equitable to men? What is clear is that problems of sexism and objectification of women in sports—even those involved in sports with star status—persist. Take, for example, Heather La Bella, the director of tactical marketing for the WNBA Los Angeles Sparks. La Bella posed topless for the August 2004 issue of *Playboy*. She was featured as the "Employee of the Month." (I cannot imagine a magazine asking the New York Yankees or Boston Red Sox young general managers to pose nude or in bathing suits for a magazine—whether or not people found them attractive). In the photo La Bella is featured holding a basketball inscribed with the WNBA logo. According to La Bella, whose job is to increase ticket revenues, she posed topless to increase ticket sales.

This speaks volumes about the devaluation of women in our culture as anything but sexual objects. The Don Imus "nappy headed hoes" comment about the Rutgers women's team reveals how bad things are for Black women. In addition to their bodies becoming fetish, their dignity is under attack as well. Of course, many female athletes choose this route because they have terrific bodies and are proud to display them to the world—which is fine. Indeed, they have this right, but the flip side is that the low salaries paid in women's sports play an equally influential role in such decisions. What does it mean that greater value is placed on women athletes posing nude than on playing? It means that more women like figure skater Katerina Witt, volleyball player Gabrielle Reece (both posed nude for *Playboy*), and WNBA MVP Lauren Jackson will be displaying their sculpted bodies in the buff. On a very real level, it represents a culture that refuses to view women other than as objects of sexual gaze.

For Black women the issue of the objectification of the body is especially problematic. Since slavery, the struggle to control their bodies and sexuality has been more complex than that faced by White women. As Beverly Guy-Sheftall cogently explains in her essay "The Body Politic," Black women's sexuality has been marginalized in the discourse on the female body (*Skin Deep, Spirit Strong* 14). One area where this issue is subverted is women's tennis, which has gained enormous popularity in the last decade, largely because of the sexual appeal of female tennis stars. Of course, these women are wonderful tennis players and exceptional athletes, but the scant dresses, short shorts, revealing shirts, and catsuits do not harm viewer ratings. Why else would Anna Kournikova, who never has nor ever will win anything, be among the most popular female tennis players? The difference between White female stars and non-Whites is, as

Guy-Sheftall reminds us, a case where "racial difference is marked in ways through the construction of gendered differences between Black and white womanhood" (14–15). The White female stars received labels that connote civilized womanhood, in contrast to the "others" whom are not associated with beauty or civilized womanhood but rather brute strength (the Williams sisters) and hypersexual and perhaps exotic or savage because of the differences in hair, body shape, and skin color. These ideas, dominant in seventeenth- and nineteenth-century European thought about the Black women in Africa (Sheftall 17), persist even today.

Despite great attempts to de-feminize Black women in American sports culture (Jackie Joyner-Kersee is a great example) Black women like Lisa Leslies, Cheryl Swoopes, and Venus and Serena Williams are changing perceptions. They bring a unique blend of unmistakable athleticism, beauty, and sexual freedom to the game that has not been seen since Florence Griffith-Joyner wowed the sports world with her grace, beauty, style, and power. In fact, Serena, with her catsuit or short shorts and boots during a match comes close to Griffith-Joyner in her assertion of the feminine, desirable Black female body as attractive on its own terms—in all her curves and hips. Yet Serena is aware of and embraces her sexuality, subverting the racial and sexual patriarchy that has so long controlled images of Black women's bodies and images of beauty. It is a tough struggle as the integrity of her body is interrogated during every match. Still, she asserts control over her sexuality (I cannot forget the numerous camera close-ups of Serena's bottom during her match in a black catsuit), seeking to represent the humanity of her sexuality and athletic superiority simultaneously.

A continuing problem for women in society, even in sports, is the skewed value placed on females as objects of sexual gaze, as objects of athletic or entertainment gaze. As writer John Updike reminds us in his essay "Venus and Others," the attitude toward women and their bodies has historically been one rife with contradictions: exalt and debase, serve and enslave, injure and comfort (495).

Indeed, it is a situation exacerbated in the case of non-White women, whose bodies are often denied aesthetic parity to White women. Despite Serena's occasional fetish to be blond, in other ways she has made a point of repositioning the aesthetics of beauty to include Black women who have historically been excluded as feminine or desirable. As Charles Mills reminds us, "Global white supremacy denies subpersons not merely moral and cognitive but aesthetic parity" (*The Racial Contract* 120). Still, in all capacities of sport, women are still not taken seriously enough; they continue to battle against being the objects of male desire. At the end of the day, men make the cover of *Sports Illustrated* because of the merits of their athletic performances, while non-athlete women and even women athletes make the cover because of their bodies. Serena and Venus are female BNS who reposition the double bondage of gender and race on their own terms, making clear that the world knows "where sistas at" and how to perceive them.[10]

*Fear of Black Quarterback*
While diversity has made strides on the field, the pace of progress continues to be slow for the most executive of positions in sport: Quarterback. The holder of this position is the general on the field, the leader, and the brain. It is no surprise that the top spot has traditionally been off-limits to non-Whites, whose role has historically been relegated to running and catching the ball. The cover of the 19 April 1999 issue of *ESPN: The Magazine* featured a story by Michael Wilbon entitled "Qballers: They're Bringing a Whole New Game to the NFL." The magazine cover featured four young quarterbacks of the class of 1999, who epitomized the revolutionary changes occurring at football's premiere position—the quarterback. Three of the four players were African American: Akili Smith, Daunte Culpepper, and Donovan McNabb, with Caucasian Cade McNown. Although not the first quarterbacks capable of running and throwing, they symbolized acceptance of the second coming (a quarterback who is smart, strong, and mobile). Both Culpepper and

McNabb flourished during their second seasons, while Smith and McNown struggled on subpar teams. But they were not the only revolutionary quarterbacks of the pre-millennium class, only the most visible signs of the modern quarterback.

I conducted a search in 2002 to determine how many Black quarterbacks exist in the NFL and was shocked to discover that of the one hundred quarterbacks only roughly twenty percent were Black. Improvement? Depends on how you examine it. From my perspective, it says that teams will only take the very best Black quarterbacks; it says teams are unwilling to have too many Black quarterbacks around unless they have extraordinary ability, unlike the sixty-odd White backups. Yes, I said it. To be Black, you have to be twice as good, or at least very good. The NFL has plenty of space for brothers on playing rosters, except at quarterback. While the figures improved a bit more in 2008, there are less non-White starting quarterbacks in 2008 than there were three or four years ago. This number is astonishing considering the growing number of non-White quarterbacks leading top college teams to high rankings and championships.

In a 10 August 2004 *USA Today* article, writer Larry Weisman indicated there were five sets of brothers playing quarterback in the NFL! That was an incredible number. Koy and Ty Detmer, Matt and Tim Hasselbeck, Brock and Damon Huard, Peyton and Eli Manning, and Josh and Luke McCown represent the five sets of brothers playing quarterback in the NFL. No one can accuse the NFL of discriminating against brothers. It just is not enthusiastic about too many Black brothers so to speak, unless they have mega talent. Of the five sets of brothers, three are starters, and the combined passer rating of the group hovers below 75 percent. Basically, paternal brothers have a greater chance of making it to the NFL than *brothers* who excel as college quarterbacks for top schools.

Among the four teams competing for the chance to go to the Super Bowl in 2002, two of them (Tennessee and Philadelphia) had quite spectacular Black starting quarterbacks, and one (Tampa Bay) had a former starter as a backup. Although none of them advanced, it says that Black quarterbacks, who comprised less than one-third of the quarterbacks in the league, represented one-half of the quarterbacks leading their teams into league championship games. (Donovan McNabb led his team to four consecutive NFC championship games and to the Super Bowl, yet remains maligned.) And while the numbers have increased, the success ratio of those leading NFL huddles suggests that there should be far more starting Black quarterbacks in 2010 than there were in 2002.

The truth is that although most teams want to win, sadly they may not want to win at the cost of having a Black leader. How else do you explain the success of so many Black quarterbacks in major college programs, yet their overwhelming absence in the NFL? Of course, the 2005 NFC championship game marked the first time that two Black quarterbacks played each other for the right to lead his team to the Super Bowl (Michael Vick and McNabb). When I was doing my roll call, checking the list of Black quarterbacks, I noticed that most of the White quarterbacks came from schools that were relatively unknown and would get creamed playing the big-time schools, yet these players are nearly 80 percent of the quarterbacks playing (the racial contract strikes again). How could so many of the quarterbacks playing for the top twenty-five college programs be so ill-suited to perform at the next level? And if these White quarterbacks from lesser programs were not highly regarded enough to lead the top schools, then what suddenly made them qualified to play quarterback as professionals?

Whenever Black quarterbacks have been given an opportunity to play, the scrutiny has been intense, if not unbearable. It is as true now as it was in 1958 when Willie Thrower relieved George Blanda during a game as a quarterback for the Chicago Bears, marking the first time an African American was behind center to call signals. It would be ten years before Marlin Briscoe of the Denver Broncos became the very first African American to start at quarterback in the NFL. He did not fail miserably, but he did not shine and thus did not last long. But he broke ground, paving the way for Joe Gilliam of the famed Pittsburgh Steelers dynasty team of the 1970s and early 1980s. Few recall that in 1974 Gilliam beat out Terry Bradshaw for the starting job when Bradshaw and other players joined a strike. Gilliam went 4–1–1, but he was booed by his home fans during a 17–0 loss to the Oakland Raiders (his only loss). The Pittsburgh fans desperately wanted Bradshaw back. Gilliam gave in to the pressures and began using drugs, which soon led to his departure from the league.

Gilliam told of receiving hate mail and death threats and being hurt that so many fans revealed a racial tone in their anger toward him. The franchise even received bomb threats on Three Rivers Stadium if he were not removed from quarterback. Of course, Steelers coach Chuck Noll explained that his decision to give the job back to Bradshaw was influenced by Gilliam's drug problems and had nothing to do with the racial pressures that contributed to it.

The Gilliam story is sadder still because he died in late December 2000 of a heart attack, just prior to his fiftieth birthday. He had been drug-free for almost three years, but at different points in his life he had lived on the streets in Nashville, sold his Super Bowl rings for cash, even lived under a bridge in a cardboard box for two years, partly because he could not handle the pressures of intense racism directed toward him, despite playing well. Gilliam is proof of the long history of the fear of Black quarterbacks that persists even today because of the racial contract.

The same contract was also responsible for the intense scrutiny Doug Williams endured when he emerged as the starting quarterback in his rookie season with the Tampa Bay Buccaneers in 1978. He became the first Black rookie to start at the position. He led the team to a playoff berth and a playoff victory over the Philadelphia Eagles. This was unheard of for a first-year player. After leaving the NFL in 1983 for a brief stint in the newly formed USFL until it folded in 1986, he was acquired by the Redskins as a backup to Jay Schroeder, whom he eventually beat for the starting job and led the Redskins to a record-setting Super Bowl victory, where he became the first Black quarterback to win and be named MVP (throwing for four touchdowns and 340 yards). Despite all these accolades, the following season Williams lost the starting job to Schroeder and at the end of the season retired.

What few want to accept or engage is that America's national ethos is inseparable from the legacy of racism and racialism that bars non-Whites from positions of leadership on and off the playing field. Cultural and social forces have a severe impact on human behavior and instigate backward arguments about inborn racial differences in mental and athletic ability. It explains why star college quarterbacks whose football teams contended for championships like Charlie Ward, Turner Gill, Tony Rice, and Andre Ware (all quarterbacks of championship Division I college teams) never made it in professional football. Further, it offers an explanation for the initial lack of opportunities and success for talented players like Warren Moon (who in 2006 became the first African American quarterback inducted into the NFL Hall of Fame). He opted for the Canadian Football League, despite leading his college team to Rose Bowl victory in his senior season! Moon is an interesting case because despite his stellar senior season, the NFL did not initially draft him unless he would agree to switch to wide receiver or the defensive back position. Moon had to prove himself by winning five consecutive Grey Cup Championships before the NFL Houston Oilers sought his services!

Other notable star college quarterbacks who endured NFL resistance were Rodney Peete (drafted in the second round), Joe Gilliam, Doug Williams, Vince Evans, Andre Ware, Jeff Blake, Randall Cunningham, James Harris (now personnel executive director for the Baltimore Ravens), Kordell Stewart, Shaun King, Charlie Batch, Quincy Quarter, and Akili Smith, the list goes on. Whatever their shortcomings on the field, the color of their skin gave them little room for error, essentially sealing their fate as professional quarterbacks. Why else would the Philadelphia Eagles' quarterback Donovan McNabb be booed on draft day and continue to endure such harsh scrutiny despite leading his team to four straight division titles and appearances in the NFC championship game, along with a Super Bowl appearance? The racial contract maintains that positions of leadership, prestige and power are reserved for Whites—even in sports. The lack of non-White quarterbacks and coaches support this accusation.

*Myths Die Hard*

When Rush Limbaugh made the racially charged comments about Donovan McNabb, all hell broke loose, confirming long-held feelings about the ineptitude of Black quarterbacks and the racial stereotype that Black players are not smart enough to effectively lead a team successfully. Doug Williams, the first and only African American quarterback to win a Super Bowl, concedes: "As a black quarterback, sometimes they're a little tougher." Indeed, Limbaugh, who at the time was an analyst for ESPN, charged McNabb with getting "a lot of credit for the performance of [his] team," credit that he did not deserve because "the defense carried the team."

Commentators argue that a quarterback's statistics are unimportant as long as his team wins. For example, Bob Griese (Miami Dolphins), Trent Dilfer (Baltimore Ravens), and Brad Johnson (Tampa Bay Bucanneers) all have in common that they were average to above-average quarterbacks whose teams managed to achieve the bottom line: Super Bowl victory. But for the brothers (Black quarterbacks) the criteria is different. Black quarterbacks catch hell both ways. On one side, when players like McNabb lead teams to the playoffs with solid leadership and above average statistics they are crucified by the media and fans for lacking stellar statistics. Then on the other side, when Doug Williams, Warren Moon, Daunte Culpepper, Randall Cunningham, and Steve McNair have posted great numbers they are told statistics are less important than victories. This embodies the history for Blacks in America: the rules are always different us—fluxing as we scale barriers. Even Hall of Fame quarterback Warren Moon acknowledges there are still stereotypes out there, that there remains prejudice and bigotry in sport. We would all like to think that if a person can play well, the color of his skin should not matter, but the truth is that it does. The scrutiny these field generals endure is similar to that endured by Marlin Briscoe when he first broke the quarterback barrier with the Denver Broncos in 1968, or what many non-White professionals endure on his or her job.

*Changing the Game? Rules the Same*
In college and professional football, it is well known that racism exists in the form of stacking Black players into offensive positions such as running back and receiver. For example, several NFL players and even future Hall of Fame inductees were once quarterbacks in either high school or college: Marcus Allen, Jerry Rice, Woody Dantzler, Tony Dungy, and Antwaan Randle El to name a few.

The unique mental skills required for the multitasking modern quarterback is turned into something negative. NFL coaches do not regard highly this ability to avoid tacklers, get outside the pocket, and apply pressure (on defenses) by creating something that couldn't possibly have been diagrammed on the sidelines or predetermined in the huddle. In the past it was acceptable for a Roger Staubaugh, Steve Young, John Elway, Brett Favre, or Fran Tarkenton to scramble out of the pocket for time and first downs, but whenever Black quarterbacks do the same, they are criticized for being unable to read the defense or being impatient in the pocket (Vick and McNabb are nagged by this sort of criticism).

Few want to admit that the new crop of quarterbacks entering the game on their own terms are changing football a bit from the traditional pocket passer. Both Steve McNair and Donovan McNabb came close to winning a Super Bowl, a sign that, these new school quarterbacks have changed the game with their quick wits, fleet feet, and rocket arms. The fear is that there is really no way to effectively defend against them, or control them. McNabb, Vick, McNair, Blake, Stewart, Culpepper, Young, and others are the modern era of quarterbacks who have received more opportunity than the Black quarterbacks of yesteryear, but just as much scrutiny regarding their intellectual capacity to play the position. Disagree? After Vince Young, the star quarterback for the University of Texas beat superpower USC with both his legs and his arm for the National Championship in 2006, there were still questions about his ability to play quarterback. The way he led Texas to a come-from-behind victory with great passing and running was truly amazing, yet the experts had him ranked as the third or fourth best quarterback coming out of the draft! Many thought it a mistake that he was picked as high as third in the 2006 draft. Of course, he went on to lead the Tennessee Titans to a respectable record and win Offensive Rookie of the Year. But despite his long list of accomplishments, there remains a long list of doubters regarding his ability to play quarterback in the NFL. And, in 2008 he was demoted to back up because of alleged emotional/psychological instability.

It appears that the superlative performance of Black collegiate and professional quarterbacks past and present is having minimal impact on the pace of progress for Black quarterbacks. Many successful Black college quarterbacks have historically gotten the cold shoulder from the NFL. One famous example is Turner Gill, the brilliant field general of the top-ranked University of Nebraska scoring machine, never even considered declaring himself for the NFL draft once his college career ended. He saw the bleak future and opted to stay at Nebraska as an assistant coach. He has gone on to have a successful career as head coach at University of Buffalo, leading the school to a football bowl game and conference title.

Although the Super Bowl victory and MVP honor of Doug Williams was historic, Randall Cunningham was an early New Jack Black quarterback. Cunningham, after fifteen seasons, decided to retire (then briefly returned for a few brilliant seasons with the Minnesota Vikings). Cunningham, the little brother of Sam "Bam" Cunningham (star running back for the New England Patriots in the 1980s), completed his career 21 passing yards shy of 30,000 for his career, 207 touchdowns, and 134 interceptions, with 4,928 rushing yards and 35 rushing touchdowns. As an

Eagle, he holds four team records: most 300-yard passing games (13), most yards passing in a single game (447), and longest punt (91 yards). After six years of missing the playoffs, he led the Eagles to three consecutive playoff appearances. During his three seasons with the Vikings, his team set an NFL record of 556 points in a single season (the 2007 New England Patriots broke the record) and advanced to the NFC championship game. Cunningham could run and throw and had his own style and flair. He could dominate and take over a game. Cunningham is a modern pioneer for Black quarterbacks, yet unlike Warren Moon, who was elected into the Hall of Fame in 2007 he may never make it in.

*A New Day?*

The latest Black QB sensation is Michael Vick (arrested in 2007 for financing a dog-fighting ring, suspended from the NFL and reinstated in 2009), the slick moving left-handed gunslinger out of Virginia Tech University. The Atlanta Falcons gave up the farm for the opportunity to draft Vick, and he produced. But despite his off-field troubles, Vick is even more revolutionary than McNabb, McNair, or Culpepper. He is one of the fastest players in the NFL and has the strongest arm in the league too. People hail him for these natural gifts, but few mention his intellectual acumen. Like his Black predecessors, Vick is a continuation of the evolution of the position, moving it further away from the old school drop-back mentality. Before his legal trouble, Vick was the face of the NFL.

Despite resistance, these quarterbacks are placing a different stamp on the position. Unfortunately, some views die hard. For example, former New York Giants general manager Ernie Accorsi felt McNabb, McNair (deceased), Culpepper (retired), and Vick are exceptions to the drop-back rule and with his lottery pick chose Eli Manning. And while Manning's team won the Super Bowl in 2008, it was often despite him, and because of an outstanding defense. Manning's job is to play within the game and to avoid mistakes. As a pocket passer his play is average. Although he was awarded MVP of the Super Bowl many agree that the

Giants defensive front line was the true MVP. People like Accorsi maintain that the greatness of a quarterback is judged by being in the pocket, making plays. But the truth is that the new wave BNS are mobile and multitalented threats using both their arms and legs to create big plays. Watching Vince Young of the Tennessee Titans in 2006 and 2007 lead his team from being dismal and then back to the playoffs during his first full season as a starter is proof that this is true. And a few mobile quarterbacks (except Roger Staubach, Steve Young, and John Elway) have won a Super Bowl, but none have been non-White.

Perhaps the unspoken reason that Black quarterbacks are given little room for error, or scarce opportunity in the NFL stems from a combination of the racial contract and the pervasive fear of moving beyond the institutional comfort zone. The Black quarterback stigma minimizes intellect and places a premium on speed and strength; it is directly tied to the racial contract and remains difficult to kill. In the NFL, opportunities for those selected as quarterback still pale in comparison to opportunities to play running back, receiver, defensive back, defensive end, linebacker, and other roles that Black players are stacked into. Despite the past success of Cunningham, Williams, McNair, Moon (the first Black Hall of Fame Quarterback) and the recent success of McNabb and Vick, the position of quarterback or leader is still somewhat "Jim Crow": reserved for Whites only.

*Few Brothers Representing*
With all the talk about contracts and racism, I would be remiss if I failed to discuss the large number of Black athletes who choose not to hire Black sports agents to assist them in their sports career. David Falk did and still does hold the reins for a large number of Black NBA players (much of his power was culled from representing Jordan and everyone wanting to be like Mike). I truly do not understand this phenomenon, except to suggest that players have accepted a colonial attitude that believes White is better. I cannot help but hold athletes accountable for failing to give more non-

White agents an opportunity. The workings of the racial contract delve deep into the psyche of the non-White. Too many players believe they will get a better deal if they have White representation. The irony in all of this is that the Falks, Steinbergs, and countless other sports agents who represent Black sports stars might not deal with them on any other terms. These men are "sharks in suits" whose loyalty rests wherever the money is. It is about money, pure and simple. Athletes who claim that there simply are not enough Black agents, are incorrect. Unfortunately too many still believe the racial myth that the White agent will get them the best deal and endorsements. The key to the deal is the product or brand—the athlete!

One White agent (whom shall remain nameless) told me that he did not feel it was fair to penalize him because he was not Black. He feels it is discriminatory for Black athletes to primarily hire sports agents of color. When I asked this agent if most of his clients were people he would hang out with, he said no. However, the unwritten rule in business is that people do business with people they like, yet my agent friend felt it was not detrimental that his clients are not the type of people he cares to "kick it with." As an academic, I know that a primary criterion used to hire academic candidates, besides effective teaching or research, is likability, being able to connect with the candidate as a person.

Certainly the first place to turn when exploring the questions of sports agents of color is to athletes who decide whom to hire. Where the brothers at? It is important to know that in the modern world most top prospects as soon as they show potential get swarmed by a bevy of individuals who are not from their community. People who would never venture into or care about the Black community fearlessly appear out of nowhere. Still the pressing question is where are the brothers or sisters? To gain a better perspective, I turned to sports agent Glenn Toby. When I asked him about being a sports agent in the twenty-first century, here is what he had to say:

The colonialization is correct, but the social subsets that have been created are the key in creating further separation of athletes of color and agents of color. It is those sets that further pull them back from what we need. I was fortunate to get with Alonzo Shavers as unlicensed partner and handle management, marketing, and infrastructure for NFL agency. I took my street swag, hustle, creativity and put it with structure of the NFL rules, and we won and we are winning with our clients. The world of sport is getting more and more sophisticated, so we have to find ways to generate more revenue.

Let me give you an example of the pitfalls and risks of this business. Michael Vick had a deal with AirTran, and the day he got in trouble, they pulled the ad and the deal. It's a tough game. [Vick was in jail for financing dog fighting. He lost his endorsement deals, and the Falcons even want the salary they already paid him!]

Here is where the game is now. If you take a look at the fact that it cost $1,500 to take the test [to be a sport agent]. It is gonna cost at least $50,000 to operate in the first year. And if you don't get a client a big contract, even if their performance is not up to snuff to move up the scale, the player will get a low offer, which puts you out of business. That client is going to grow tired of waiting for you to make something happen. This is a tough business.

Toby explains that the financial risk is huge.

With any given athlete you represent, you may have to deal with the following: past debts, baby momma, financing relatives who want to come out to the draft or combine, educating the client as you go along, vitamins, special twitch muscle speed training, and all the while you are praying they don't get hurt, get cut, or get caught up in off-field nonsense. Then they have to perform so you can negotiate for the next contract that you only get three percent of annually, of a non-guaranteed contract. Now, the big money is off the field, where you get fifteen to twenty-five percent off marketing, but players must be big enough and willing.

The reason more ex-athletes are not agents is because the marginalization of agent's business is difficult. It is becoming a world where agents are facilitators of athletes' core needs, from getting a house, marketing, life decisions, getting through life on daily basis.

What I see happening is that players hire an attorney to negotiate contracts, and they will hire managers to handle off-field activity. I personally believe we will soon see the end of agents as we know [the business] today. It will not be an affordable effective situation.

Big agencies will give rebates to keep the athletes, even if they get down to one percent. They will just shift the business anyway to stay in business; this leaves small guys out of the game, and they must convert themselves to managers. More agencies will practice in big outsourcing of the money to find guys like us who can transition and manager players.

People have to be creative; a lot of these guys' friends will be managers and may not have the license. Once athletes really understand their value, I think they will be able to financially capitalize on every aspect of their existence, from a cookout to speaking engagement.

If players are not second-round selections, they lack confidence to push for more money, so they can move their money position or seek endorsements. Many are afraid to work the backwoods and take advantage of it; just looking to profit as a number one player. But this doesn't mean everyone cannot be a player.

What players see with me is that "Glenn realizes this potential and [this] makes him special." These guys are treated as a commodity, a product, and I treat them as human beings and change the course of their lives; they also earn lots of money.

Look at LeBron James; he fired his agent and hired a group of nineteen-year-olds. In fact, they started their own company!

They seemed to do a good job, look at his endorsements. These modern Ballers are about to become the shot callers. There are many big-name players who are negotiating their own contracts (NFL and NBA).

Let's look at boxing for a minute. More than sixty percent of boxers who are sanctioned will have neuro issues five years after boxing. Boxing is unregulated and so open that many boxers have been taken advantage of. Managers often get one-third; promoters get ten percent, sanctioning fees, licenses, taxes. All of this comes out of a boxer's purse while he is taking all the risks in the ring. King is one brother who has made a name for himself in the boxing game, but how different is he from White promoters? As you pointed out earlier, De La Hoya is really making a difference in the boxing game.

What makes Glenn Toby different is my concern for boxers' health. I also take a lower percentage, flat rate; my concern is for boxers' physical and financial health. They are charging boxers back for expenses—even paying them less than marquee fees and forcing them into mandatory bouts. There are not many wealthy boxers. I want to change boxing by helping fighters like Oneil Bell (former Cruiser Weight undisputed champion of the world) break bad contracts and liberate them from exploitative situations.

The way upstart agents, especially young brothers, compete with big boys is with service. We understand baby's momma; we understand why young brothers want bling. We understand the frustration and the pain of people from other communities speaking to them without respect, or why brothers may not want to wear a belt. As Black agents, our relationship is a healing process and a revealing process. The guys my company represents will go out of the game with lots of dignity and a platform that allows him to dictate his policy by performance on the field and in the community.

If we are measuring the coldness of ice, our guy is in the top one percent. Our ice is just as cold, but it ain't dirty. One of our top clients, Asante Samuels, was a fourth-round pick—no off-field issues, has learned the system, he did everything they asked of him. Yet the Patriots were unwilling to pay him a long-term deal. Why? It's about market value and business. He was franchised in 2007 and signed a $10 million per year deal with the Philadelphia Eagles. The data shows he has outperformed everything in the league, but they were not willing to take the franchise tag off him. They did not want to pay him because it is business, so we had to take his services elsewhere. But where do we divide racism from colonialism and economics?

In the end the ball is in the athlete's court to choose an agent. They actually pave the way for others, if they believe a non-White can represent them appropriately. What most fear is that the non-White may not have the rapport to get the best deal for them; their very fear of unequal dealings between management and a non-White representative speaks volumes regarding their true feelings regarding racism or the racial contract's impact on non-Whites. So when we ask "where are the brothers and sisters?" we have to initially direct these questions to athletes of color. They must understand the leverage they have to diversify the agent pool. One thing that can be said of LeBron James (who fired his original agent, hired his homies, and they started their own management company) is that he is a BNS in the truest sense—he has kept it real and seeks to call his own shots. His team management landed him some outstanding endorsement deals. It is important to emphasize that one is not advocating discrimination but equal access. James is an example of effectively using leverage to open doors that racism has historically closed.

*How to Reverse Trends?*
The actions of LeBron James and select others are one of the most effective ways to reverse past trends of discrimination. Although the Black Coaches Association (BCA), Jesse Jackson's Operation Push, as well as the late Johnnie Cochran and others have worked hard to force American sports

teams to hire more people of color as coaches and executives, to have comprehensive diversity programs, the institutions implementing them must sincerely be interested in change. They have to want to do it. It is that simple. The key dimensions of any successful diversity program rely on three things: (1) access and success; (2) climate and intergroup relations; (3) institutional vitality and viability. Without all three elements, along with feelings of openness and trust, success is doubtful at best.

Is real change occurring? Yes but it is limited and slow. I once read a story about how former San Francisco 49ers head coach Bill Walsh was committed to mentoring his Black coaches. Walsh understood that unlike most institutions, professional sports executive positions go to those in small circles. Thus, he made a point of bringing his Black coaches into these circles (the "Old Boys Network") so that they got an opportunity to socialize with owners and other upper-echelon individuals in his organization and other organizations. The result: his coaches received head-coaching and offensive or defensive coordinator positions over the years. Perhaps the sports world and society could use men like Walsh who was willing to force real change to occur.

It is also healthy to note that the NBA expansion team the Charlotte Bobcats became the first minority-owned franchise in 2004. In major league baseball, the Anaheim Angels were sold to a minority owner. So while slow and spotty, there are some signs of progress. But I am reluctant to jump for too much joy when I see our culture's structures, symbols, and sentiments (especially in sports) still laden with a racial contract that leaves in its wake racial road signs and racial carnage that indicate not much has changed. This is especially true of college football, which has not opened the process of hiring from a diverse pool of head coaches.

For every collegiate program that fails to diversify, prospective athletes, their parents, and coaching candidates should indeed guide their children to programs that are willing to engage coaching and administrator inclusiveness. Floyd Keith, the director of the Black Coaches Association

(BCA), called on prospective coaches and athletes to shun the University of South Carolina at Columbia for ignoring the association's recommendations for an inclusive hiring process. Protesting programs like South Carolina might be an answer to such behavior. Another option is to issue Title VII lawsuits against schools like University of South Carolina that fail to employ open hiring practices. Even former NCAA president Myles Brand admitted that more opportunities are necessary for people of color and women in coaching and administration.

Ironically the real Ballers, the power brokers, at least in college sport, are the athletes. Players hold enormous power. I cannot emphasize enough how important it is for modern athletes to become much more politicized and to participate more fully in forging change. They have to assume a much more active role in using their power and influence in a culture that worships sport heroes to help *make* real change occur. BNS cannot stand on the sidelines and allow inequities to continue; universities begging them to play for them will respond to diversity demands. There is no singular act or person that can change the world but we all must do our part in our own space and time. Collegiate athletes' space and time happens to be very influential. Just as the previous generation sacrificed to integrate all-White athletics to prove they belong, this generation must hold institutions to a higher diversity standard, or consider a reverse exodus back to Historically Black Colleges and Universities until positions of leadership in athletics are more proportional to the starting lineups of top Division I football and basketball teams. Athletes can change these racial inequities. BNS have to make choices that truly "keep it real." Boycotting discriminatory programs and toppling the myth, much like Western Texas did when it defeated Kentucky in 1966 to win the NCAA basketball championship, are the most effective contributions BNS can make to the struggle that the BCA and others are fighting.

In fact, the truth is that after five decades of African American success in American collegiate and professional sports (high profile, high revenue producing ones), not enough progress has taken place in the areas of adminstration, ownership,management, team presidents, or coaches. The world of team sports leadership remains guarded; race may matter far less on fields of play, but when it comes to leadership positions, opportunity is stifled.[11]

The best way to grow diversity is to attack institutional traditions that made diversity work necessary in the first place. This means coalitions, clear goals, systemic change in hearts, minds, and institutional cultures, and learning the systems that erect barriers in the first place. The prescription outlined here is not one that recommends "reverse discrimination," but requests that the most qualified people get an opportunity. To achieve this, everyone must be assembled into the room for an interview so that the committees can pick the best person. As long as an increasingly diverse committee regularly selects from a diverse pool of candidates, the diversity will become manifest.

However for this to occur, institutions have to change ideologically. We have to cultivate an institutional vision and atmosphere that wants to challenge an intellectual and social climate that supports the racial contract. Historically, such change has always become manifest via unconventional methods considered outrageous at the time. As the most recent College Report Card reveals (2009), there is still much to be achieved in the way of equity. Collegiate and professional sports culture must make greater attempts to address issues of diversity and American pluralism. Although change remains slow, the racial contract can be broken with clear focus on institutions and the people who run them. Only "real" BNS will play an active role in shredding it to pieces—White and Black. How many are willing to keep it real?

SECOND HALF

# CHAPTER FIVE

## BIG PIMPIN' IN AMATEUR SPORT

*Look at the money we make off predominately poor black kids. We're the whoremasters.*

—Dale Brown (former coach at LSU)

*Maybe the NCAA can keep a straight face as it gorges on its new $6 billion TV deal, then belches out the same old claims that college players don't deserve to get the money they generate.*

—Peter Keating, *ESPN: The Magazine*

In December 2002, a group of Harvard economists named the NCAA "the best monopoly in America" (Keating 56). The only remedy is for someone to launch an antitrust challenge against the NCAA, because it is a contradiction to sell television rights to the highest bidder, yet forbid amateur athletes from earning one penny of what the market will pay them. The spoils of war go to coaches and administrators, who get raises, perks, commercials, and endorsement contracts totaling in the millions, while athletes are pimped and punished if caught accepting payment beyond tuition, room and board, and small stipends.[1]  "Education" and "protection from exploitation" are a smoke screen for exploitation.  In American culture, college athletics has become wholly commercialized. It shamelessly exploits amateur athletes, especially youth of color in high-revenue-producing sports like football and basketball where their graduation rates lag. While the graduation rates for all college athletics are not alarming, a fire alarm needs to be sounded regarding football and basketball athletes, where the numbers tend to slip, particularly among Black athletes.

Currently roughly 42 percent African American football players in Division IA graduate compared to 55 percent of White football players. In basketball, among the African American players on the sixty-four teams in the 2001 NCAA men's basketball tournament, close to half the teams graduated less than 35 percent of these players! Few are willing to broach how Black bodies fuel the growth of institutions of higher learning then are discarded. These bodies just happen to be concentrated in the highest revenue-producing collegiate sports. Perhaps few care because the money at stake in these sports is too great. Football and basketball are the cash cows for many colleges and athletic departments. These sports draw huge alumni revenue streams, publicity, and hundreds of millions of dollars from BCS bowl games, NCAA basketball tournament appearances, and television contracts. And the majority of the cows producing the most milk in the highest profile programs are often black and brown. While it is old news that college athletics has veered down the wrong path, what is not discussed enough is the exploitation of the young Black men that heavily populate the highest revenue producing sports (football and basketball), yet consistently have the lowest graduation rates.

Beginning in the 1960s, predominately White colleges actively began to recruit Black players and enjoyed great success. Schools like Kentucky and Alabama reluctantly joined the fray because they were forced to change to stay competitive. Moreover, before the 1970s most colleges in the South did not have integrated football teams—or any teams for that matter. A famous turning point was when USC beat the University of Alabama, 42–21. The star performer of that game was a Black running back named Sam Cunningham. He dominated so thoroughly that at the end of the game, the Alabama fans were chanting, "Get us one." Hall of Fame coach Paul "Bear" Bryant acquiesced in order to win, not to make social strides. To remain competitive Bryant got himself a Black running back the following year, and soon many other colleges followed.[2] Today, if you look at the top schools in football and basketball you will notice that they are usually represented by a starting lineup that is 70 percent players of color. Sadly, the graduation rates for these same athletes are often among the lowest on the team and athletic department (there are schools that are exceptions but are in the minority). Given this horrible truth, it is only right to call for collegiate sport to be drastically altered. Either it adheres to its stated intent or is treated as the for-profit business that it has become.

With the help of their Black studs, top ranked universities and coaches reap the economic benefits of the harvest (a winning season). Their spoils span from endorsement deals with sports apparel companies, commercials, million-dollar contracts and video game revenues to Bowl Game money and publicity that ramp up admissions along with school profiles. Coaches enjoy bonuses, endorsement deals and television shows, while athletes get room, board, books, tuition, and perhaps illegal payments on the side. What gets glossed over is the enormous revenue surrounding high-profile college athletic programs. The entities profiting most from college athletics escape scrutiny for exploitation, while athletes asking to be compensated for their lucrative labor are criticized. The universities and NCAA (like a pimp) enjoys the bulk of the profit from the labor and product the players bring to these spectacles. If pimping is about control, universities and the NCAA have mastery over players, rules, and a system that allows them to generate enormous capital, manage all the money and makes all decisions, while declaring a tax-exempt status. Even their mission is similar to that of a pimp. The NCAA and universities claim to provide athletes with: protection and management. Like a pimp their rap is also similar: if left to their own devices athletes (prostitutes) would make the wrong decisions and be exploited by those unconcerned with what is best for them.

Indeed, they are vulnerable to exploitation because high-profile collegiate amateur sports are big business, which explains why universities, coaches, and the NCAA are "big pimpin'." So why should athletes participate for the honor of the game, or accept as their only reward an "education" when everyone around them gets rich from their efforts? This is the same "education" some claimed New School Baller LeBron James was missing out on by declaring himself for the NBA draft right out of high school. The same people who criticized him for taking his enormous talent directly to the NBA ignored the specious morality of his high school, which profited from selling the rights to televise several of his games on ESPN. The bottom line in American culture is cold, hard cash—dead presidents. And, those who produce must be paid.

Academics and education is a myth, a lie. In fact, academics is often competing for the time of athletes involved in revenue-producing athletics like football and basketball. Unfortunately school often comes second because the stakes are high. Football teams receiving a BCS bid in 2009 earned their conference $18 million—win, lose or draw. If a second team from a conference qualifies, the conference shares an additional $4.5 million. In 2006–07, the thirty-four of schools entered into the NCAA basketball tournament from major conferences on average earned revenues of $9.4 million and an average profit of $4.4 million—an amazing 47 percent profit margin! (But basketball players did not receive a salary) However, the NCAA Presidents' Commission is hesitant to make any sustained or comprehensive reform of intercollegiate athletics. Why? Too much money is on the line. So with that in mind, it is evident that "big pimpin'" will be hard to stop. It is now time for athletes to either get paid or remove the nonprofit status of the collegiate sport. It cannot continue to exist both ways. If University of Connecticut head basketball coach Jim Calhoun feels he is justified in earning several million annually because his program produced a multi-million dollar profit, then why is it wrong for his players, who *earned* this money, to get paid as well?

*Personal Fouls in the College Game*

Unfortunately colleges, universities, and even the NCAA are a sort of mafia that shakes down student-athletes for all their talent and sweat equity in exchange for "illegal" booster payments, "free tuition," and an "education" (that there is scant time to achieve between preseason, summer and spring workouts and practices, film sessions, weight training, and travel). The pimps are the NCAA, coaches, and colleges that receive outrageous performance bonuses and revenues because of players' performances. For the most part, a college "education" is a joke at most Division I universities. California state senator Kevin Murray, D-Culver City, compared athletes to sharecroppers, where the post-slavery, post-Reconstruction vocation left many forever in the debt of the White landowners whose fields they worked. Like sharecroppers who rarely left with a profit because of their debt to landowners, modern collegiate athletes are in a similar state. They have everything to lose. If they receive money, they are expelled; there is no health insurance for athletes participating in "voluntary" summer workouts—which are "strongly urged" if one is interested in renewing his scholarship. These sports-croppers are annually in debt to a coach who has the power to renew (or rescind) scholarships.

Sports have changed drastically, particularly on the collegiate level, where everyone "legally" profits from players' sweat and toil, except players! Even AAU and high school coaches receive money, sneaker and sports apparel deals from the sweat of their players' performances and to guide them toward certain schools. The college game is even worse. Coaches' careers hinge on the signing of top-notch recruits. So much money is at stake that middle-aged White men will walk into the toughest housing project or neighborhood to get the recruit who will bring him conference titles, bowl bids, appearances in the Sweet Sixteen or Final Four, and, oh yeah, more money. Modern slaves (who receive food, shelter, and basic "education") fill stadiums, draw television contracts, and bring exposure to programs along with pay raises, perks, and bonuses for coaches. BNS are angered that they do not see one "legal" cent from revenues generated, and that if caught with "extras" they stand to lose everything. This is unacceptable. How can every entity involved in sports from junior high school to college sports profit except the field hands? Such inequities must be challenged. It is time for exploitation to end and for revenues to be shared with players.

In addition to the racial dynamics, let us consider how so much has gone wrong in "amateur" sports so fast and why the entire system must change. When I was a kid, we played on vacant lots, back alleys, up against abandoned buildings with milk crates for baskets, and between parked cars on small side streets for fun. We played ball for whatever school district we lived in. No one systematically tracked us coming out of junior high school or cheated the system to get us to play for their team. There were no bidding wars among junior high and high school coaches. If enough people who played certain sports well attended a school at the right time, the team prospered.

During my junior year at Sumner High School in St. Louis, Anthony Stafford was one the most sought-after running backs; he was recruited by nearly every major football program in the country. We all figured he was lucky because he was getting free trips to Notre Dame, Oklahoma, and other top schools, along with the free gear they gave him. We had no idea that the stakes could be as high as they are today. Never in our wildest dreams could we conjure the $21 million surplus the NCAA cartel would collect in 2000–2001, or the 11 year $6 billion deal (roughly $545 million annually) the NCAA would sign with CBS to broadcast "March Madness" basketball games. Who would have imagined that in 2008 the University of Kansas basketball program could generate revenue of $13.2 million and a profit of $7 million, or that the North Carolina basketball program of 2006-07 could generate revenue of $17.2 million and a profit of $11.6 million? All we could envision was a full scholarship, free meals, an education, and a chance at a professional career in sports. Of course, modern athletes are far more sophisticated. They understand the money on the table for the NCAA, coaches, colleges, and universities. As the late rapper Biggie Smalls proclaimed, "Things done changed." The pressure of money over time has created a situation where education is less a priority. (However, a degree can be achieved, but requires extraordinary commitment to summer school and perhaps a sixth year in college.)

Indeed, things have changed since the original intercollegiate contest took place in a Harvard and Yale boat race in New Hampshire in 1852 (Shulman and Bowen 5). The participants of that race regarded it as merely a "jolly lark" and not the 20th century enterprise amateur athletics has become. In the early half of the twentieth century there were no big-time programs as they exist today. There was not as much focus on money, resources, administration, and admission slots. Sports were definitely lower key, part of student life, something students did because they enjoyed playing. The experience was similar to what I experienced as a college student at the Division III University of Rochester and what I experienced as a professor at Willamette University, a liberal arts college where roughly 40 percent of the students participate in some sport, without *most* of the pressure and demands of a Division I program (except football and basketball).

Perhaps the way things used to be in college sports were not so bad. Scholarships were once given as four-year awards. Players were paid a salary to attend a university and represent its team. But lawsuits shaped the rules into what they are today. Now coaches are almighty with the power to renew or rescind scholarships on a year-by-year basis. Thus, to really understand how and why college sports have spiraled out of bounds, one must briefly look at the history of regulating college sports.

Before 1956 there were no athletic scholarships. They were legalized to deter the widespread practice among schools of paying athletes based on athletic ability instead of academic need. However, many contend that the legalization of scholarships actually encouraged their proliferation and in effect raised the bar of athletic competition (Shulman and Bowen 12). After World War II, the NCAA and college sports (football and basketball) embarked on a path of avarice and never looked back. Before 1984, the NCAA held control over television football rights for all of college football. However, since the Supreme Court ruling that freed individual schools and conferences to negotiate their own contracts, big television contracts bring big money, which altered the focus, wealth, and power of the NCAA and participating schools.

However, at least some colleges were willing to continue to uphold their academic integrity. The Ivy League (which popularized college football and was the first college sport monopoly) became an official conference in 1956—ironically because of the legalization of athletic scholarships (which they opposed). In the latter portion of the twentieth century, Ivy League presidents decided to harness the distressing academic profiles of students by imposing "formal admissions regulations—to protect themselves from themselves" (Shulman and Bowen 13). What they arrived at was a complex admissions requirement that considered the athlete in relation to the overall academic profile of students in the school (13). Prior to that, the Ivy League schools consistently balked at officially forming a conference (17). Hence, maintaining the educational mission for these schools superseded sports despite the overwhelming growth of the entertainment industry and societal forces shaping the institutionalization of college sports. As James L. Shulman and William G. Bowen articulate in *The Game of Life: College Sports and Educational Values*, athletes from the 1950s and modern athletes emanate from vastly different ecosystems (27).

In the present system, the NCAA seems to function as a fox watching the henhouse of college sports, forming its own rules, fattening its pockets from the slaughter and sale of the chickens it is supposed to protect. The very opportunity for a "free education" that athletic scholarships offer is impugned by "sports-related" obligations. Players spend summers preparing for the seasons in "voluntary" workouts, while during the year there are mandatory film sessions, weight training, practice, and away games during midterms and final exams. Football players spend the spring, after football season is over, participating in practices and intra-squad games for several weeks. Baseball players participate in winter workouts. These obligations devour a major portion of the very "college experience" that many self-righteous purists argue is important for young men's and women's development.

Clearly, as this brief history details, college athletics did not set out to embark on this path. The original intent of college athletics and the achievements of student-athletes were far different from what it has become. The societal forces such as the growth of the entertainment industry and the commercialization of college athletics, along with the increased specialization of athletic talent, are largely responsible for the drastic changes that chart the new course for college and university athletics. Moreover, as Shulman and Bowen elucidate, "there is no direct connection between organized athletics and the pursuit of learning for its own sake" (3).

As I compose this chapter, the NCAA Final Four Tournament, affectionately known as "The Road to the Final Four" (it should be renamed "The Road to NCAA and University Riches") is just getting under way. For several weeks schools have been battling in conference tournaments (making more money) for the right to spend three weeks chasing a National Championship. Conference and NCAA tournaments are set up right behind each other, so players spend an entire month traveling the country playing games. I began to think about how teams that wrapped up conference tournament play on Sunday were on the road again Thursday to the city where they would play regional games and perhaps not return to campus until Sunday for another brief stay. How can all this occur right around midterms? Where are the pundits that claim these kids are students first to argue it is wrong to require such hectic practice and travel schedules during the most important point of the semester? It is a great three weeks for the school and fans, but bad for the athlete-students, who, during mid-term exams are consumed with travel, practice, and playing. If the NCAA were really serious about academics, the schedules of sporting events like this tournament would accommodate the "education" and academic schedules of athletes instead of catering to money. Many are culpable for the state of college athletics, from the NCAA and the media, to universities and the American public that consumes it. The next time you are watching March Madness, think about how many students are missing school or exams for your entertainment.

Embarrassed by the woeful graduation rates of basketball and football players (the two big-money sports), the NCAA launched a new set of academic rules in 2003 to turn things around. It had to respond to the ream of ethical, financial, and academic violations that have been mounting in recent years. A brief examination of the academic evidence will reveal why the NCAA had to act fast. Studies have revealed that only 41 percent of male Division IA college basketball players graduate, and the rates for Black athletes are appreciably lower. Furthermore, a 1989 cohort of athletes who played in high-profile sports had grade-point averages as a group that put them "at the 25th percentile of their class" (Shulman and Bowen 62). In fact, over 80 percent of the high-profile athletes (in football and basketball) in Division IA private universities are landing in the bottom third of their class (64). In the 1950s athletes compared much more favorably to students at large—they were nearly even.

Today fewer athletes in the two biggest sports earn degrees, especially non-Whites. In all fairness to the programs, the statistics look worse because many players turn professional early, which works against graduation rates. However, even if those turning professional early or transferring did not count against the final tabulation of graduation rates, the numbers would still look bad for colleges. The only thing the NCAA has not admitted is that a college education is an afterthought; and it is not why athletes are given scholarships. On the surface these rates appear to compare favorably to student graduation rates at large, but closer scrutiny reveals that Black players in the high-revenue-producing sports have the lowest graduation levels.

Students' academic health must compete with the reward system for coaches, whose jobs and salary correlate with the competitive success of their teams. Given the current economic realities, it is unlikely that most coaches can be committed advocates of academic achievement, for it shifts focus from sports and winning—their lifeline. The billion-dollar collegiate sports economy is responsible for the numerous cases of academic fraud and illegal wagering, which have gotten worse in the last few years. Real advocacy on the part of coaches would place academics on par with athletics. Real advocacy on the part of institutions would place a value on graduation rates that rival team victories. True student advocacy would make student athletes' academic performance THE most important job performance item for coaches.

Check some of the evidence that things have gone totally wrong and need a major overhaul. In 2003 St. Bonaventure in Olean, New York, allowed a player with a welding certificate from a junior college rather than the associate degree to transfer to its school. At Fresno State, the team statistician completed the course work for some players. A University of Georgia assistant basketball coach who was teaching a class on basketball coaching gave very good passing grades to a top player who did not attend class. In 2001 the University of Michigan basketball team was suspended from postseason play for a scandal involving booster payoffs to players. It was reported to be the largest financial scandal in NCAA history to date.

If there was no financial pressure to recruit these players, these individuals would never have been in college and this would not be a problem. Certainly, the issue here is not to strip opportunity from minority athletes who lack an adequate academic preparation from an opportunity to attend college, but to make certain that such students actually make education the priority once admitted.

All the while, colleges, universities, and the NCAA contend that they are giving these wide-eyed young recruits an opportunity to develop themselves. BNS are about getting paid and many take money "under the table," but what they receive is peanuts and what they risk is enormous. And just like a pimp, colleges, universities, and the NCAA get the glory and money, while the cash cow is milked for every last drop until his eligibility is gone or he is injured. While these are not the only two outcomes, as some players use college to launch a professional career or use sport to earn a free education, too many fall by the wayside. Many BNS understand that college sports are a profitable business for universities, colleges, and the NCAA, who hide under the guise of nonprofit organizations and education. For example, in 2008 the NCAA men's Final Four alone generated $47 million! (This is not including ticket sales or spending by local residents and other boosts to the economy.) Athletes know this type of revenue is flowing from their toil and sweat.[3] They understand that their talents create this profit and they want to be compensated for their work, which is why many leave college early for the pros or take money "illegally."

BNS know that billions of dollars are being generated from college ball and believe they should be paid. So for many years, top college basketball and football prospects have opted out of college, using the "hardship" card to declare themselves early for professional drafts. For example, in basketball the list of famous players who turned pro early include Michael Jordan, Isiah Thomas, Earvin "Magic" Johnson, Julius Erving (Dr. J), and Connie Hawkins. In fact Spencer Haywood, Moses Malone, and Darryl Dawkins pioneered skipping college ball, and jumping directly to the professional ranks. The 2005 NBA draft was the last one to allow players to skip college before turning professional. In football the deal has been no different except players are ineligible unless they are three years removed from high school. College football players celebrated a brief moment of triumph in 2002, when Maurice Clarett (a tragic individual) won a lower court ruling allowing him to join the NFL without waiting the mandatory three post–high school years. But it was a short-lived victory, as the NFL and college pimps got a higher court to overturn the ruling.

On the one hand, America embraces the notion that people are free to sell their services to those who desire to pay for them at the highest price he or she can negotiate. Athletes excelling in tennis, hockey, golf, baseball, and (until the last couple of decades) basketball are free to turn professional as teenagers, if there is a demand for them in the marketplace. But as Spencer Haywood, the man who broke the age barrier for professional basketball players, poignantly states, "Only football and basketball—the big revenue-producing sports for colleges—instituted rules about when you could turn pro. . . . [I]sn't that a strange coincidence?" (Milan Simonich, *Pittsburgh Post-Gazette*, 11/28/03). Indeed, Mr. Haywood, indeed. It also reeks of the stench of the racial contract that denies equal economic freedoms to the primarily non-White amateur athletes who represent the bulk of those that slave at these sports.

When Haywood broke the NCAA/NBA slavery barrier in 1970, after averaging 30 points and nearly 20 rebounds the previous year with the ABA Denver Rockets, it took a federal court injunction to allow him to join the Seattle Supersonics. It was not a pretty sight, as lawyers for the NBA struck back, challenging Haywood's right to work in most of the league's seventeen cities. Often, just before tip-off, Haywood would be served with court papers prohibiting him from playing in that evening's game. Thus Haywood played in less than half of his team's games that season. The Supreme Court would not rule in Haywood's favor until 1971. But the decision affirmed the lower court's ruling, establishing him as a "Pioneer Baller" who cleared the way for all qualified players into the NBA. Modern athletes are indebted to Spencer Haywood for refusing to slave on the college courts for nothing, while his mother slaved for two dollars a day in cotton fields. BNS had better recognize "Hollywood"

Haywood for making a way for young qualified players who don't play baseball, hockey, tennis, golf, or other White-dominated sports to get paid. BNS should get paid in college and still be allowed to choose to skip college or to leave early just as tennis, hockey, and golf professionals do.

There is no coincidence that the primary money-producing college sports have such restrictions. In fact, NBA commissioner David Stern would like to increase the minimum age to twenty or to two years out of high school. He does not care about young athletes, but that the two or three years in college increase his marketing edge and anticipation for athletes' move to the NBA. Jermaine O'Neal, former power forward for the Indiana Pacers, concurs that racism might have something to do with the NBA's desire to put an age limit in the next collective bargaining agreement. "In the last two or three years, the rookie of the year has been a high school player (LeBron James in 2002 and Amar'e Stoudemire in 2004). There were seven high school players in the All-Star Game (2005), so why we even talking an age limit?" O'Neal said. O'Neal is among a large group of players who disagree with Stern's agenda, saying: "As a black guy, you kind of think [race is] the reason why it's coming up. You don't hear about it in baseball or hockey. To say you have to be 20, 21 to get in the league, it's unconstitutional. If I can go to the U.S. Army and fight the war at 18 why can't you play basketball for 48 minutes?"

In the modern era, before Kevin Garnett, Kobe Bryant, Kwame Brown, Jermaine O'Neal, Tracy McGrady, and LeBron James (the first crop of players in twenty years to jump directly from high school to the pros), there was high school phenomenon Stephon Marbury, who attended Georgia Tech for a single year and is a model of sorts. Marbury is a good example of a BNS, strictly about getting paid and calling shots. According to Luke Cyphers and Chris Palmert, "Marbury watched a new cultural industry—commercial street ball—grow up around him, embrace him, make money off him" (Cyphers and Palmert 66), and he was not going to be pimped. Marbury understands the Benjamin factor of college ball. He spit out business stats from his single season at Georgia Tech like KRS-

One or Jay-Z spits rhymes: "Every game was sold out. We went to the Tournament. We were on national TV 20 times" (70). What Marbury is articulating is that all of these facts translate into more money for Georgia Tech because of his presence. Impact recruits like Marbury deserve to get paid.

He also kept it real about going to college and making a career from playing ball. Marbury eschews the bull about learning life skills or getting an education. He explains, "I let it be known when I was a freshman that if I was going in the top five in the draft, I'm coming out early. I caught a lotta [flak] for that. But I wasn't going to lie" (66). And when he was chosen fourth in the draft, school was history. Marbury felt that one year in the NBA exceeded what four years of college could have provided him developmentally and financially. While Marbury's assessment of college is debatable, his anger about exploitation is not. College is the perfect place for young people to grow and make mistakes without paying the penalties the real world extracts for flawed decisions.

However, I am bothered by those critical of amateur athletes taking cash under the table or leaving the college farm systems early, when they know the system focuses more on profit than student education. I assume this position because athletes are being exploited by a cartel or monopoly. Football is perhaps the most exploitative system because, unlike Major League Baseball and the NBA, which have farm systems (although the NBA now restricts anyone under nineteen), it relies on colleges to maintain a free and efficient farm system. Major League Baseball spends, on average, at least $9 million to maintain its minor league system, while the NBA finances its developmental league. In the free college farm systems, players assume all the risks while the professional leagues assume none. College sports (particularly football and basketball) generate hundreds of millions of dollars without paying salaries to players. Ironically, sports dominated by White athletes such as tennis, baseball, hockey, and golf are void of age restrictions or scrutiny. In fact, youth is celebrated. I think these contradictions are matters of race and class and because these are not big-money college sports.

As Stephon Marbury astutely points out "Nobody says anything about tennis, or baseball, or hockey, and they're all coming out of high school" (70). Indeed, there does seem to be a contradiction that the only sports enduring antitrust labor violations are those predominated by athletes of color. Now, this could just be a coincidence, or it could be that Black athletes happen to dominate the highest revenue-producing sports and it is merely a case of "Benjamins" over race. But I have a hard time discerning the difference between a fourteen-year-old pro golfer and an eighteen-year-old pro football or basketball player (the latter are much older). Perhaps what distinguishes them is that colleges lose the revenues from football and basketball if players skip straight to professional status. The truth is that colleges need those basketball and football "prostitutes" to turn the tricks that put millions of butts in stadium seats and garner multibillion-dollar television contracts and related ventures.

Colleges and universities cannot deny the money train that pulls into the station after ticket sales. There are booster donations, apparel and sneaker endorsement deals to be had, along with additional marketing exposure for institutions (Shulman and Bowen 4). All of this extra money fuels the university engine, covering a wide range of expenses. Far too often kids leave war-torn neighborhoods to play sports that generate enormous wealth for colleges, then they return to the hood with little to show for their efforts—definitely not a degree or a coaching job. A quick glance at the grades and graduation rates of Black football and basketball athletes makes this an easy argument to make.

*Pimpin' Ain't Easy*

The Colorado, Missouri, and Ohio State infractions magnify the problem with amateur sports in the United States. Yet no one wants to progressively discuss how to deal with college athletes in the modern world of college sports. College athletics are about one thing: the Benjamins, baby! For any effective recovery to take place this fact has to be admitted. How can any ethical person argue that it is fair to run a nonprofit business (college sports) yet generate billions of dollars without paying the primary workers? The NCAA, colleges, and universities want to hold firm to its cash cows—even if it means violating antitrust labor laws. To change the systems the pimps have to be willing to release athletes from servitude.

Let us look at how the pimps (Division I schools) play the game, and the money at stake if their cash cows were put out to pasture. Without age limits in professional football and basketball many athletes would leave college early and work for themselves. The college product might also be less entertaining and lucrative. There are millions at stake. In 2004, $17 million was paid to each conference whose team won a Bowl Championship Series (BCS) game, and by 2009 the amount has reached $18 million. The teams that play get a larger share of this money but it is a nice windfall. Compared to these earnings, the $3,000 stipend that the NCAA president proposed for players in 2004 is punk money. The stakes for sports revenues are so high that a group of college presidents of the forty-four colleges excluded from the football BCS formed the Coalition for College Athletics Reform to push for inclusion in the big-money games in postseason football. You would think that college presidents would have more important things to do, like run their institutions and focus on academic excellence.

The NCAA alleges that it gives 94 percent of every dollar it receives to the universities, which supposedly trickles back to student-athletes. Even if this were true, receiving roughly 6 percent of nearly $400 million for the basketball contract, not to mention college football regular season and bowl games, and the growing popularity of the College Baseball World Series is a huge income. And while the financial situation of athlete/students has improved with more NCAA funds being made available for emergencies and other needs, a quick look at compensation for the "bigwig" executives and administrators at the NCAA will reveal that athletes are not receiving fair market value for their services. Those charged with protecting athletes from the villains are being well compensated for their services.

The NCAA officers' and directors' salaries and benefits are quite astonishing. Prior to 2009, the two senior vice presidents averaged $267,000 annually with benefits of about $93,000, while the chief financial officer pulled down $206,354 each year with benefits totaling $158,088. Even the lower-level officials are getting paid quite well in the business of college sports: General counsel commands over $200,000; vice president of marketing earns $168,700; vice president of enforcement, $158,200; vice president of education services, $157,200; and the vice president of championships only asks for a meager $156,460 (these figures are higher for 2009). The NCAA, which alleges to protect the welfare of the student-athlete, fills the pockets of everyone except the players they "protect." The NCAA's egregious administrative salaries and profit seem to have clouded their vision of what it means to "serve" the student-athlete.[4] Are these salaries really justifiable? The original goal of the organization was to protect amateur athletes from exploitation and to promote education, but neither of these objectives are effectively being met.

What is even more telling of how players are being exploited is revealed in the NCAA president's salary (which has doubled over the last six years) and the seven figure salaries of big-time college coaches (which have risen at a similar rate). As of 2008, the late NCAA president Myles Brand earned a salary of roughly $935,000, which included over $150,000 in benefits. Now Brand, who inherited this great fortune, cannot be blamed for the scale of his salary, but its heft certainly could not be ignored. Ironically, the public feels paying players is unreasonable but is not bothered that NCAA officials, college coaches, and administrators charter private jets for travel and receive outlandish salaries at the expense of athlete generated streams of revenue. Meanwhile, players receive tuition, room and board, and book expenses as payment (certainly we all know that many players get paid illegally, but if caught they risk losing everything). Scholarship athletes in the high profile sports that produce millions are just not being fairly compensated.

If collegiate sports are not about money, why do NCAA officials, coaches, and athletic directors earn such enormous salaries? Equally ignored is the fringe cash derived from tickets, food, stadium advertisements, and the sale of T-shirts, hats, and the scores of other products that produce billions. Contrary to what programs claim, money is very important in sports. Who gets paid when *Sports Illustrated* sells that yearly issue that includes a "free" book chronicling the national champion in football or basketball? One thing is certain: not the players! In 2004 I found an interesting article in the *New York Times* questioning the ethical concerns of colleges' jersey sales. Today names and logos are licensed and protected by the NCAA, which prohibits a university from using athletes' names or images to promote a commercial venture. However, the rules do not prohibit colleges from featuring the numbers of star players on jerseys and hats to increase sales. Thus, during the basketball and football postseason play, jerseys, T-shirts, and hats with numbers of star players on them sell for up to $50 a pop! Athletes want a share of these profits and have complained, to no avail, about this shameless exploitation, citing the contradiction. And although late NCAA president Brand admitted being uncomfortable with the ethics of such practices, he did not act to forbid colleges from selling merchandise bearing star players' numbers. However, he stood firm that players should not make money from uniform sales or their celebrity while under scholarship. Furthermore, Brand was of the opinion that giving players free jerseys would place athletes in the position of a professional endorsing a product. News flash: college athletes already endorse a product called college sports! Such obtuse thinking suggests there is slim hope for real change. The refusal to pay their slaves (athletes) means plantation owners (the NCAA and colleges) will continue to get a large slice of the revenues.

Of course, many will continue to argue that a scholarship is payment enough, but one cannot take this position without considering the business of college athletics. No self-respecting capitalist would agree that players and teams that produce are fairly compensated. Another common argument is that college athletics enliven college life, providing the poor with educational opportunities that they would otherwise not have. However, as Michael Mandelbaum makes clear in his book *The Meaning of Sports*, the relationship between major team sports and institutions of higher education is a uniquely American "unholy alliance that, because the ethos and the commercial orientation of major sports are at odds with the purposes of the university, has a corrupting effect on institutions of higher education" (xvii).

*More Bad Ethics and the Money Train*
In addition to college football and basketball being big business that pimps a large African American contingency, it also draws bad behavior in the name of money. To get a shot at all the money on the table, many universities were willing to risk a seemingly endless number of infractions. In 2003 alone, numerous infractions occurred. For example, the University of Rhode Island settled a sexual harassment lawsuit with a former secretary in its athletics department who charged the then men's basketball coach Jim Harrick Sr. with improperly touching her and using abusive language toward her. At the University of Georgia, Harrick Sr., was suspended and then quit after academic fraud and improper benefits to players were discovered.

Other infractions in college sports include the San Diego State University football team being punished for holding improper summer workouts. The NCAA took scholarships away from the University of Arkansas at Fayetteville's football team because a booster improperly paid players. Nine University of Georgia football players sold their championship rings on eBay. The University of Washington head football coach Rick Neuheisel was fired after he admitted that he bet over $6,000 on the NCAA Division I men's basketball tournament. Rutgers University athletes were discovered to have competed while ineligible but received minor punishment. A University of Alabama fan, Logan Young, was indicted for paying a high school coach in Memphis $150,000 to steer a star player to Alabama. In September 2003 the American Football Coaches

Association released a survey revealing that most football players spend more time in practice than is allowed under NCAA rules—surprise, surprise.

In 2004 the infractions just kept coming as seven women alleged sexual misconduct by Colorado football players or recruits in various incidents dating back to 1997. Also, sex was used as a recruiting tool with player-hosted visits to strip clubs and the hiring of escorts. In light of these allegations, head coach Gary Barnett was placed on paid—yes, paid—administrative leave and then reinstated after the school's investigation revealed he was absolved of any violations (he was eventually fired at the conclusion of the 2005 season). But players found guilty of transgressions will always serve as examples of discipline, as some were suspended and a few lost scholarships. What does this say about privilege and power?

Maurice Clarett and Ricky Clemons are prime examples of the racial contract in collegiate sports, its hypocrisy, and the vulnerability of amateur athletes in the culture of big revenue college sports. Although Clarett is currently serving a prison sentence for stupid crimes and proved to be a nightmare to himself and those advocating for his rights, his case should be examined. Clarett led Ohio State back to prominence and to an NCAA national championship as a star running back during his freshman year. Later that spring Clarett was charged with falsifying a police report about the value of items stolen from a vehicle loaned to him by a college booster. Suddenly, stories surfaced soon after the stolen-car incident to suggest that Clarett alone was unethical. There were rumors about his grades and possible special treatment in a Black studies course. The only person punished was Clarett, who was suspended for the entire season. Even when Clarett spoke out against the university, telling of how he received money and cars that his coach knew about, nothing happened to Ohio State. Incensed, Clarett left school and briefly won the right to declare himself eligible for the NFL draft when U.S. District Judge Shira Scheindlin ruled in his favor. (Prior to Clarett's victory, the rules prohibited college athletes less than three years removed from high school from entering the draft.)

Although the ruling was later overturned when the NFL launched a successful appeal to block the ruling before the April NFL draft, Clarett's victory, albeit a short one, was analogous to a runaway slave being returned to his master (the NCAA). For a fleeting moment, Clarett made it possible for teenage football players to enter the draft straight out of high school, much like in baseball, tennis, and hockey. Predictably, Art Modell, longtime team president of the Baltimore Ravens, deemed the initial Clarett ruling disgraceful, advocating that players "finish schooling academically and athletically and then come to our [NFL] sport." Modell and others felt the Clarett ruling was bad for the NFL and the young athletes because it raped the colleges. However, turnabout is fair play, for the colleges have been raping athletes for decades.

The NFL ruling is age discrimination; it violates antitrust law, an infringement of Clarett's freedom to enter the marketplace to earn millions of dollars. (Clarett eventually got his chance. He was drafted in the third round by the Denver Broncos and cut during training camp.) Sadly, if Clarett had decided to join the armed forces directly from high school, nobody would have objected to him being unfit for combat. Judge Scheindlin cited the NFL's rule as "precisely the sort of conduct that the antitrust laws were designed to prevent" (Chaka Ferguson, Associated Press). While not all eighteen- or nineteen-year-olds are ready for the professional draft, some may be. However, it is important to allow individuals the freedom to choose in a meritocracy. Collegiate sports tread very dangerous water, threatening to drown in a cultural embarrassment.

Ricky Clemons's story is equally depressing. The former star guard for the University of Missouri basketball team personified the cultural embarrassment that college sports have waded into. Clemons's basketball brilliance seemed to matter more than a high school diploma (which he did not have upon enrolling). His play was so dazzling that Missouri miraculously found a way for him to complete twenty-four credit hours in a single summer at three different colleges to qualify to enroll at the University of Missouri in time for basketball season. While at Missouri,

Clemons went to jail for second-degree assault for choking his girlfriend. Clemons alleges he was told to plead guilty so that he could continue to play ball. (By doing so, he only had to serve sixty days in a halfway house, and be allowed to keep his scholarship, and resumed playing after a year.) But when Clemons was dropped from the team, things got interesting. Left without a scholarship, as damaged goods, sitting in jail, Clemons began to talk. In taped jailhouse conversations, he tells of being paid, along with other star players, at least $500 at a time for playing for Missouri. Despite Clemons's accusations, Quin Snyder (then the head coach of Missouri)—a media darling—emerged from the fire a phoenix rising, for the NCAA was unable to support allegations of player payoffs and academic fraud. However, Snyder (who was fired a few years later) apologized for his assistants' poor decisions, accepting "full responsibility." His assistant coaches who allegedly doled out the money paid a price. Tony Harvey resigned, and Lane Odom was placed on paid suspension. The University of Missouri's personal investigation of the basketball program revealed that Snyder did not "specifically" intend to violate rules; his violations were "unintentional, and violated secondary rules, not major ones."

Since he "unintentionally" violated rules and those rules broken were merely "secondary rules," the university meted out punishment for Snyder. First, Snyder's base salary was frozen for two years (although he was still eligible for his supplementary income from the university and endorsements), and he lost one entire scholarship for the 2005 recruiting campaign. Additionally, Snyder was restricted from off-campus recruiting for seven days in the month of July 2004, and prospective recruits were limited to a single visit during the probationary period. The university gave Snyder a pass, but instead fired members of his staff: two international associates, one marketing coordinator, and two student manager positions were eliminated. Meanwhile Clemons was the real loser—he lost his *renewable* scholarship (often mistaken as a four-year guaranteed scholarship). Clemons returned home to North Carolina without a scholarship or team to play for, his credibility and morality tarnished.

These are two of thousands of similar hardships in a bad system where this has been going on for decades.

Two decades ago, Digger Phelps and Bobby Knight complained that blue chip players cost lots of money. Knight went so far as to say that "some . . . players are being paid more money to attend college than the professors who teach at the schools they attend" (Keating 57). Notice that Knight did not include coaches in his comparison. The truth is that if the NCAA were honest with itself and players were paid a salary, the Ricky Clemons and Maurice Claretts of collegiate athletics might have turned out differently, for they have not sinned alone. At least if they were thrown out of school, they would have been paid for their services and could have avoided returning home broke and bitter.

*Show Them the Money*
In an August 2003 opinion article in the *New York Times,* Jeremy Bloom, who at the time was a sophomore receiver with the University of Colorado, argued that college athletics should pay amateur athletes or allow them to earn money while on scholarship. Bloom deems the NCAA as more of a detriment, a hinderer of the opportunities of student-athletes, than a body that truly serves them. Its tactics are outdated for the very commercial, highly lucrative modern world of college athletics. Indeed, the NCAA holds a monopoly on college athletics. And like any good monopoly, there is no competition—it keeps much of the television royalties and other revenue of college athletics, while distributing the earnings at its discretion to the 1,200 member institutions.

Bloom's bitterness stemmed from being forced to abandon endorsement opportunities he secured as an Olympic moguls skier to play football for the University of Colorado in 2002. His opportunities ranged from endorsing ski equipment to modeling for Tommy Hilfiger. Bloom's request for a waiver of NCAA rules that bar endorsement earnings was denied in 2004. The lower court found that the NCAA was not inconsistent in applying its rules barring players from receiving customary income for a sport because players are not allowed to engage in any endorsement contracts or other income to remain eligible in amateur competition. Bloom was unsuccessful in his attempt, and, to date, there is not progress on this issue.

Unfortunately, while the financial scope of college athletics has changed drastically, the status of student-athletes has remained stagnant. Bloom and others are critical of the inequities in profit sharing. To quote Bloom, "It [the NCAA] prohibits us from having sponsors or appearing in advertisements, even if the products have no relation to the intercollegiate sports we play." Many other athletes concur with Bloom. Former UCLA linebacker Ramogi Huma is also an advocate for college athletes. He lobbies for workplace safety protections and benefits for college players via his Collegiate Athletes Coalition. The ultimate contradiction is that personal player endorsement earnings are illegal, but the NCAA advertisements using the names and images of star players to promote college sports are perfectly legal. Sounds, smells, and looks like bondage—at best indentured servitude. Bloom gave up trying to convince the NCAA and returned to his skiing career and his endorsements—he had no choice.

The rules that were instituted in 1992 forbid athletes from promoting commercial ventures and prohibit universities from using athletes' names or images, yet the images of star players are used to market college games and sports apparel. In fact, the University of Oregon once featured a huge advertisement for its football team on a billboard in downtown Manhattan, using the image of a star player. When all is said and done, it is estimated that the top-producing Division I schools usually sell roughly $7 million in T-shirts and other apparel each year! Of that amount, at least 6 percent is generated directly from replica jersey sales. Despite these revenues, the mantra of college sports is that only twenty-five schools' athletics departments break even or make a profit while the rest lose money each year. Still, those programs that earn profits like the 17-47 percent mentioned earlier in the essay need to share the money with players.

Of course, the issue of paying players remains contentious. There is a litany of reasons why players should not be paid. One argument is that Title IX makes it difficult to give all players equal pay; there must be equitable opportunity. Other concerns are that there would be recruiting wars for the best players and facilities—an arms race would ensue, and big income schools would always dominate (which is the case now). But the primary argument against paying players has been that the value of an education and the other benefits given to scholarship students are ample payment: tuition, room and board, books and fees, free tutoring, life skills, and, in some programs, illegal payments from coaches and boosters.

But who can blame players like Bloom and others for feeling undercompensated when the NCAA collects billions of dollars off of the blood, sweat, and tears of players, yet denies these same players compensation for their services beyond tuition, room and board, and books? It is understandable that others like Bloom would be angry when the *Kansas City Star* revealed on 22 May 2001 that the salaries of Big 12 Conference coaches have placed many in the "Millionaires Club." Oklahoma and Texas paid their head football coaches roughly $1.4 million annually in 2004. Few flinched at Oklahoma's Bob Stoops's $100,000 bonus for landing Oklahoma in the 2004 BCS title game or the additional $150,000 on the table had the Sooners won the title. Nobody judged or questioned Ohio State head coach Jim Tressel for signing a deal after claiming the national title in 2003 that guaranteed him $200,000 for each return trip to the title game until 2009 (they returned to the title game in 2007 and 2008). Surely the "studs" that make such salaries possible deserve a little piece of that bonus.

Even fewer people acknowledged or seemed to care that University of Oregon's head football coach Mike Bellotti (and former athletic director) had a lucrative deal for reserved ticket sales written into his contract that paid him between 4 percent of gross receipts for sales between 17,500 and 20,000 and up to 8 percent for sales of 35,001 to 40,000 tickets. Bobby Bowden (Florida State), Bob Stoops (Oklahoma),

Frank Beamer (Virginia Tech), Bill Snyder (Kansas State), Phillip Fulmer (Tennessee), and Mark Richt (Georgia) all earned between $1.5 and over $2 million annually in 2005 (those still coaching earn even more now).[5]

It's sad how the rules of the racial contract deride LeBron James and Carmelo Anthony as being greedy for skipping college and signing multimillion-dollar endorsement deals as teenagers, while Stoops, Tressel, Bowden, and Bellotti are deemed shrewd businessmen deserving of whatever the market bears, although it is on the backs of teens like James and Anthony. In 2007, the University of Alabama awarded Nick Saban $32 million over eight years to become head coach of their football team. No critiques are launched against these men for being greedy and this is wrong; there can be no double standards.

Why is it acceptable for a student on a music scholarship to play night performances for money without jeopardizing their scholarship but scholarship athletes cannot earn money from their celebrity? College athletes' performances net huge profits for the NCAA and universities but they receive little of this revenue. States like California introduced bills advocating student-athletes' rights. In Nebraska a bill passed in the legislature that would require Nebraska football players to be paid (only if three other states with Big 12 schools pass the same measure). Although many claim the "free ride" is adequate compensation, many feel that it is un-American or institutional exploitation that deters players from capitalizing on their celebrity. In 2004–2005 the University of Texas football team generated roughly $50 million, yet scholarships (room and board, tuition, books) only cost the program $2 million. It looks like there might be a profit somewhere for player compensation.

A quick glance at what is required to maintain the "free ride" that football players receive confirms they work hard and should be paid. Take for example, the University of Colorado where players get up at dawn, do an hour of wind sprints, go to classes, spend two hours in the weight room, devote a couple hours to seven-on-seven drills, study for school, and try to have something of a social life. And this is their off-season! But the hours increase once the season starts. There is the addition of film study, special meetings, and travel. According to Bloom, even if one were to consider the scholarships that athletes receive to be "payment," they are compensated at less than the minimum wage. Who can argue with these truths? To retain scholarships, players must focus on sports to the detriment of the "free education" they are receiving. An injury, placing class before practice, or refusal to participate in the "optional" off-season training could easily result in the termination of a scholarship. In response to this exploitative situation, Bloom drafted the Student Athletes' Bill of Rights, which he hoped would allow student-athletes to "secure bonafide employment not associated with his/her amateur sport" and collect money generated by the sale of apparel that bears their names and jersey numbers. The goal was to use revenues from the Bill of Rights to help student-athletes cover school-related costs beyond what their scholarships pay for.

We have to reexamine a system where athletes in football and basketball generate hundreds of millions of dollars, which fund facilities and other sports, but does not compensate them adequately beyond tuition, a small stipend, room and board. It makes sense that so many opt to move to the professional ranks as soon as they can. It is preferable to being victimized by an industry that uses their talents and gives peanuts in return under the guise of an education. If someone would please "show the players the money" it would stop the ruse that college sports are harmless fun and games. In its present state, college sports are nothing more than a profitable business that monopolizes cheap labor. The commerce of college athletics must undergo dramatic reform to eliminate infractions, immorality, and other problems.

*Can Colleges Reform?*
Modern college sport (primarily basketball, football, and perhaps baseball) is a troubled entity. It is a "Baller" in its own right, calling shots and making big bank while posing as a nonprofit entity. As I alluded to earlier, the

NCAA is aware that things have gone awry. However, the question is whether the NCAA has retooled its enforcement division and rewritten its rules effectively enough. In 2004 Myles Brand, the president of the NCAA, announced that he was increasing the number of field investigators from twelve to eighteen. All this is in response to the scandals of the previous years ranging from academic fraud and sex parties to murder. Brand explained the move as an effort to "make sure we do an effective and efficient job on major infractions" (*The Chronicle* A37). Because so much money is involved, unethical behavior and scandals abound in college sports; it appears that success on the field is inversely related to success in classrooms. In the end, those who suffer most are the athletes. When caught, they suffer the consequences of expulsion from the team, school, or both. Professional teams use these suspensions to drop players into lower rounds of drafts and to get them at bargain-basement prices during negotiations. Meanwhile, when scandals occur in a program, coaches (as was the case for Pete Carroll, Jim Harrick, Bob Knight, Quin Snyder, and Rick Neuhiesel) get second, third, and sometimes fourth chances. They receive paid leaves—or they just get paid to leave. These coaches (mostly White men) are offered limitless opportunities for redemption, largely because of the White privilege associated with the racial contract in America, which thrives in the world of sports.

For over two decades now, the NCAA claims it has struggled to convince coaches to recruit academically eligible athletes. Now, in an effort to stem the corruption, teams are penalized if their players fail to meet academic standards. Schools whose players fail to complete twenty percent of their degree each year risk losing eligibility for players, scholarships, postseason bids, recruiting privileges, as well as NCAA membership rights. The NCAA has also instituted reforms that require players coming out of high school with low SAT scores to have much higher grade-point averages. The impetus is to make a kid with a 400 SAT eligible as long as his high school grade-point average is a 3.55 or higher. The faint hope is that the new reforms will somehow change the big-money dynamics of college sports (particularly football and basketball).

Schools that fall below the standards receive warning letters the following year. Consistently poor performing teams could begin losing scholarships in the third year. But these measures are ineffective, especially the rule stating that postseason privileges and money from NCAA tournaments take effect the fourth year from the start of the infraction. And a linchpin term for punishment such as "consistent" is a specious loophole for colleges at best. Colleges will only become more accountable when the steps to punishment are instituted. In contrast, athletes caught taking illegal gifts are immediately suspended from teams, so why give so much rope to college programs on the issue of academic accountability? I always hear the NCAA, sportswriters, and play-by-play personalities discussing the respect of the game and how college is a place for education first. If they were really honest about college sports, they would acknowledge college sports as nothing more than a business, then work tirelessly to end its disdain for education. I adamantly advocate the sharing of profits with the athletes because when capitalist commercial entities are forced to share profits equally, they usually cease to exist.

The NCAA's new requirements are weak rules that have not improved graduation rates nor ensure athletes were better prepared when entering college. It did not alter the amount of academic fraud. In fact, fraud increased as colleges and coaches learned creative ways to forge the necessary grade-point averages and course credits. But more than anything, the statistics released in October 2007 give a clearer picture of the situation. The NCAA annual report on graduation rates for college athletics revealed that most of the teams that are doing well on the field are not doing very well in the classroom. The 2007–2008 national championship game combatants, Ohio State and LSU, graduated within six years 53 percent and 51 percent, respectively, of their players who entered college on scholarships from 1997 through 2000. To better understand my argument about high-revenue athletic pitfalls, notice that 77 percent of athletes participating in all sports in the nation's biggest colleges graduated. However, this number drops off greatly in football and among African American players. At Georgia the study noted that 67 percent of White players graduated, while only 29 percent of African American players graduated.

Unfortunately, the late Myles Brand's new reforms get failing grades simply because they take three years to go into effect, will only result in a few warnings or minor punishments, and fail to hit institutions where they really hurt—their pockets! The threat of potentially losing millions of dollars if banished from the big tournaments might force some surface changes in college sports, but they will be minimal since many infractions occur before any penalty flags are thrown.

In 2007 Brand proclaimed that despite the dismal graduation rates for college athletes in football and basketball "the idea of academic performance is taking hold." How could he make such a claim knowing that education is secondary in the minds of most coaches, players, and institutions? For example, the football powerhouses like University of Oklahoma, LSU (2004 and 2007 national champion), University of Texas (2006 champion), Ohio State (2003 national champion), had a long-term graduation rate of below 45 percent between 2002 and 2007. In 2004 and 2005, National football champion USC had an equally low graduation rate in the 40 percent range. Some NCAA statistician might try to argue that among scholarship athletes that entered college since 1996, 62 percent graduated within six years, while only 59 percent of the general student population graduated in six years. Although defection to professional leagues does skew these statistics a bit, there is still no denying how deplorable the football and basketball graduation rates are. But we are led to believe the enormous profits are not encouraging big-time college athletics' disdain for educational missions.

These rates are even worse among Black athletes. In the same six-year time frame, only 38 percent of Black basketball players graduated (shockingly these numbers represent a 10 percent increase over the previous year!). The numbers are a bit more respectable in football, where 42 percent graduated. So, not only are these statistics a cultural embarrassment, but a racial statement as well. The graduation rates for athletes at Texas and Oklahoma are lower than the non-athletes.

However, there are schools that manage to perform well on and off the field, such as Michigan and Penn State. Both revealed graduation rates in 2007 of more than 70 percent of their players, and Boston College touted a 93 percent graduation rate (90 percent for African American players) among football players. While in the minority, these programs prove it can be done—if you are willing to sacrifice winning a national championship or being ranked in the top five at the end of the season. The NCAA knows that it still has a long way to go, acknowledging that football rates fall short of where they want them to be.

There are three situations that, for me, exemplify the anti-intellectualism of America and the woeful state of college athletics. The first example is former Notre Dame football coach Bob Davie, who had the wonderful distinction, the year he was fired (2001), of a 100 percent graduation rate of his senior class! His flaw? The team had a mere .500 winning percentage and missed out on millions in bigger bowl game money. (I won't even touch Notre Dame's firing of Davie's successor, Tyrone Willingham for performance and retaining Charlie Weiss.) The second and most troubling example is former Georgetown University basketball coach John Thompson, who routinely received hell from the media for refusing to allow them access to his players. Thompson was notoriously protective of his players and boasted a very high graduation rate among Division I college coaches; he ran a clean, tight ship, yet he was maligned as surly, rigid, and unfriendly in the media. Perhaps Thompson's flaw was being a confident, successful, unreconstructed Black coach of a program that dominated the Big East in the 1980s. The final example is the best example of the mythical student-athlete. Robert Smith, the former star running back for the Minnesota Vikings, ran into severe academic/athletic conflicts while playing football for Ohio State. In college Smith decided that he wanted to be a premed major but was thwarted in his efforts by coaches because the premed labs and other courses conflicted with his football obligations (and they are numerous). The compromise? None. He had to choose one or the other. Smith chose to take a year off from football to pursue the education his scholarship allegedly promised.

Where are the college presidents at Division I schools who value the mission of education they were hired to commandeer? It is hopeful that the NCAA is trying to produce real student-athletes (whom we can honestly call students) and better athletic departments and coaches, while also curtailing academic failure in Division I schools. However, the shortcomings stem from an inability to admit to and address the main problem: College sports are a big-time, very lucrative business that cares more about cash flow than the education of its athletes who produce enormous wealth. Of course, there are some coaches that place players' education above or on par with the fiscal goals of their programs, but they do not last very long (take Bob Davie, who was fired despite the high graduation rates of his players at Notre Dame).

The way things stand now, college players should be correctly addressed as athlete-students because athletics demand so much of their time and focus. Athletics is the reason institutions want them to attend and what they are asked to dedicate the bulk of their energy toward. Their athletic acumen is what they are expected to bring to the student body— nothing more, nothing less than team victories.

Unfortunately, Brand's reform has done little to change academic performance in high-revenue sports in major conferences. The new rule requires athletes to have a 3.55 or higher grade-point average and an SAT as low as 400 or a 2.0 grade-point average and 1010 SAT or higher to be eligible for college. As Ohio State's athletic director, who has little faith in the reforms, contends, "You'd have to be beyond dumb to get yourself in trouble with that thing" (*USA Today*, 11/19/04).

*A New Brand of Leadership?*
In 1905, shocked by the level of violence in college football, President Theodore Roosevelt called the Harvard, Yale, and Princeton presidents and football coaches together to meet about restoring the nobility of

college football (note that this was the only game in town—it was *the* college sport). This meeting led to "a gathering of college presidents who formed the group that would eventually become the NCAA" (Shulman and Bowen 7–8). The late Myles Brand, former NCAA president, is the college president famous for standing up to legendary bully Bob Knight at Indiana. He claimed he was trying to refocus intercollegiate sports much like the gathering of presidents who formed the NCAA did over a century ago. Brand wants sports to focus on teaching life skills such as striving for excellence and having a strong mind and healthy body. But he never really understood that many of the existing problems could be alleviated if players were either paid or the big money was completely eliminated from intercollegiate sports. Since the latter is impossible, paying players is the most viable solution. Only the University of Chicago was brave and committed enough to its educational mission to drop its football program in 1939.

But there are few contemporary college presidents as tough as Robert Maynard Hutchins, who dropped the University of Chicago's football program. Brand himself admitted that collegiate sports are big money—big media events that generate wealth, publicity, and exposure—making it hard for colleges and universities to walk away from its spoils. It will be difficult for the NCAA to walk away from deals like its contract with CBS Sports for $6 billion over eleven years for basketball alone. The difficult task Brand faced was to somehow find a middle ground for college sports, which are no longer governed by student-run clubs and now are institutionally managed ventures. As Shulman and Bowen presciently explain, this transformation "has led to a tacit or explicit sanctioning of the goals, values, and norms associated with college sports in a way that has allowed the athletic enterprise to have access to the inner chambers where the educational mission of the school is defined and pursued" (9).

Still Brand, the first non-coach or non–athletic director to preside over the NCAA, was optimistic that he could achieve his mission to "move toward a much more balanced approach to college athletics" (*Rochester Review* 2005, 29). In 2005 Brand ordered a task force to examine recruiting rules and define "inappropriate" activities. He insisted that his reforms were not merely temporary solutions. The conundrum or contradiction Brand faced was that the NCAA organizes, orchestrates championships for, and markets a sports product, while also claiming to protect students that produce this product. Achieving the latter has historically been woefully unsuccessful in the top two money-earning sports (football and basketball). The problem in Brand's mission was that he served two masters as he sought to balance athletics with the academic mission of the institution. There are no easy solutions, but certainly a school like Ohio State, whose football program earned nearly $29 million in the 2005–2006 school year will have difficulty placing academics first.

*The South Africa and Vermont Model*
One possible solution to all the infractions and immorality plaguing college athletics lies in South Africa or the University of Vermont. Perhaps North American universities need to take a cue from academic institutions that have taken a practical approach to college sports. One such example is the University of the Witwatersrand (known as Wits) and other South Africa universities, which have flipped the script and eliminated many of the ethical issues that plague American sports. They avoid going through the motions of acting as though student-athletics and commercialism are separate entities. The Wits University team, which also goes by the name "Clever Boys," plays in the Professional Soccer League, which is the highest level of soccer in South Africa. Indeed, South African universities, in keeping it real, have managed to flip the script on college athletics and academic integrity!

In South Africa, institutions seem to accept the division between athletes and students. Therefore, institutions like the University of Witwatersrand pay athletes very handsome salaries to play soccer.[6] However, players are more than welcome to attend classes at Wits or elsewhere, without the burden, the threat, or the sham that leads to suspensions or bogus majors and courses that plagues North American universities. As Henk Rossouw points out: "North America is the only place in the world where institutions of higher education sponsor amateur sports teams that develop elite athletes and draws hordes of fans and television viewers" (*Chronicle* A32). Rossouw is correct. The players recruited by American universities are recruited for the same reason players are recruited to play at Wits in South Africa: athletic talent and money. The academic reforms of American universities and its failure are proof that the athletes' academic résumés are weak in comparison to most of their classmates'. In South Africa, rather than offering tuition, room and board, and books in exchange for players' services, they are paid decent salaries, and institutions like Wits get "monthly payments of about $50,000 from television revenues" (A33) along with some publicity. The script is definitely flipped in both parties' favor. Furthermore, because the team's status is nonprofit, if it wins a tournament, that money also goes to the team.

Following the South Africa model or adopting some aspect of paying players could help rid North American universities of problems with violations. Many NCAA rules would vanish along with athlete exploitation and public sparring over money from lucrative bowl games and network-television rights. In the same way that we are able to admit that professional sports are a business with a bottom line of winning, providing entertainment, and making money, so is big-time revenue-producing collegiate sports. South African universities definitely have one pragmatic and effective strategy that American amateur athletics would do well to heed: profits go back into the club for salaries and scholarships. Thus, if a player desires, she/he can attend Wits without paying the tuition fee (currently only two Wits players are full-time). But like American universities, only a handful of athletes (in big revenue-producing sports) are taking academics seriously.

Another option is to follow the lead of the University of Vermont, which eliminated varsity football after the 1974 season. They continued to use the football stadium, but for soccer. But all that began to change when Doug DeLuca enrolled at the University of Vermont in 2006. DeLuca played football in high school and felt there was no reason to quit playing in college. So, within one year, DeLuca got the permission of the university to use the school colors, raised enough money for equipment, and garnered interest among students to field a tackle football team. In September 2007 using Facebook, he had assembled a coach, certified athletic trainers, a place to play, a million-dollar insurance policy, and fifty players to round out the team. Roughly two thousand fans showed up to watch Vermont's assemblage of former high school players with no college football experience defeat a local semiprofessional team!

There are many other universities and colleges like Vermont that have turned to club football teams. And while many of these institutions may never have or revisit fielding an "official" football team, the formula seems to work. It works for several reasons. Students like DeLuca can now use tools like Facebook, a Web site, and e-mail to recruit students to play. It certainly offers the option of a football team to root for without corrupting pursuit of an education.

In the fall of 2008, Vermont's club team played junior varsity teams from New England colleges and two semipro teams. And while they lost many games in 2008, the enthusiasm and passion among the Vermont players was wonderful. They are true student-athletes who play sport as an outlet and because they love the game, while focusing on being students first. There are no threats of losing scholarships if they cannot practice. Games and practice schedules do not conflict or supersede classes or exam schedules. Perhaps an alternative to big-time athletics is club teams like Vermont's.

One problem with the Vermont model is that sports teams serve several purposes for universities and colleges. They generate revenue, increase school spirit, and function as a great form of advertising. Small unknown schools lacking national presence have long reported sharp increases in admission applications once their schools appear in the NCAA Elite Eight, Final Four, or bowl games (Davidson and Gonzaga University are good examples). A sharp rise in applications normally increases revenues, SAT scores, and overall school profiles. As sports teams do well, wealthy alumni give money to either athletic or academic missions. Sports are important. The solution to all this madness could exist in the models that they have in South Africa and Vermont, or perhaps in the Lewis model that I outline below.

*The Lewis Model*

The premise behind my proposal underlies my acceptance of collegiate sports for what they are: a revenue-producing business in need of repair. The bare truth is that when people think of Notre Dame University, University of Nebraska, University of Oklahoma, Ohio State University, USC, UCLA, and other universities with successful sports programs, they think of sports before they think about academics. It is also true that winning and generating profit are more important than education for their athletes. Collegiate athlete-students pursue big-time athletics while they are unable to develop fully academically, intellectually, socially, and personally. Athletic excellence is demanded while educational mediocrity is accepted. America would do well to heed John Gerdy's eloquent advice in *Sports: The All-American Addiction* (2002) that "our society is the problem and we need to change. To bring forth change" here is my challenge: First, eliminate the commercialization of Division I football and basketball, perhaps form clubs (Gerdy also proposes this in *Sports*), and then a real discussion can ensue regarding *education* and *student-athletes*. Then, and only then, will there be more players like former Ohio State running back Robert Smith who are committed to athletics and education.

Next, force college presidents to summon the courage to use their power to make changes that will embrace education first and only. The major conflict is the one between being a student and an athlete because coaches' careers depend heavily on the performance, talent, and focus of the players they recruit. Moreover, the myth of a free education is just that, a myth, since the primary, if not only, focus is sports. Athletes involved in revenue-producing sports are missing out on the full benefit of the great set of life skills that a college education offers because of the demands of their highly commercialized scholarship opportunity (playing football or basketball). My model accepts this as fact and attempts to remedy the situation. Finally, strip the NCAA of its tax-exempt status—see it for what it is *not* in its current state: games played by kids who must return to class.

Basically, college sports need to adopt three changes. First, raise the annual stipend for athletes to at least $7,000 annually for players ($1000 per month of practice). Second, in a true spirit of meritocracy, consider paying players for their services based on individual performances and team performance. Third, the salaries of the coaches, athletic directors, NCAA officers, and other athletic administrators should be reduced significantly. Let's see how committed they really are to team, morality, and developing educational and cultural leadership when they are making less money. Divide what they used to earn among the players, and place it into an account that grows. Upon *graduation* this money is then given to players so that they have some financial security. (You cannot send these young men back into their neighborhoods empty-handed after all they have sacrificed and produced for the universities.) Here is how it will work. The money can be given to those who fail to make a pro team but graduate within six years. If the university is really a nonprofit entity, as it claims, it should be willing to share this revenue with players from profit bearing programs.

Like the South Africa model, the American sports programs that regularly declare a profit on paper (forty to fifty institutions) should think hard about eliminating the educational mission ruse, separate from the NCAA, and function as businesses or clubs that universities sponsor. Under this approach, players get compensated and schools can pursue legitimate educational missions, without compromising academic integrity. However, because of how greedy the NCAA and universities are, an alternative plan of action similar to the one listed below might also remedy the situation:

> 1. Make all scholarships guaranteed for three to four years as long as players maintain and are given an opportunity to maintain academic eligibility. (Coaches have far too much autonomy in deciding the fate of athletes, whom they can cut or suspend from the team at their discretion.)
>
> 2. Reduce the salaries of coaches, athletic administrators, and NCAA officials, and pass the cash over to players in a trust (received upon graduation or one semester from graduation) and a reasonable annual stipend.
>
> 3. Divide the net revenues equally among coaches, universities, and players annually based on performance. (There is much to divide from bowl games, television contracts, conference tournaments, merchandising, advertisement, etc.)
>
> 4. If a player is a starter and performs, he should be paid according to how much he plays or produces, like in the professional leagues (perhaps too drastic, but it should be mentioned).
>
> 5. In addition to the annual stipend, a portion from the remainder, based on how well the team does each season and on bowl game revenues (which should result in extra pay just like professional playoff bonuses), should be placed in an retirement or some interest-bearing account annually that players can collect only upon graduation or if they come within one semester of graduating within six years.

6. Players failing to graduate after six years forfeit half of their escrow to the general pool for other players on the team.

7. Players that complete at least three years with a major and have at least a 2.5 grade-point average can receive one-half of their money accumulated in escrow, while those coming within a single semester of graduating can receive all of their money.

8. Encourage more African American athletes to attend historically Black colleges or colleges like Boston College that graduate at least 90 percent of players. Although several Historically Black Colleges and Universities (HBCU) have come under fire for low graduation rates, this is an issue of finances. There is still evidence that Black students' academic performance is better at these institutions because they endure less isolation or negative feelings about college, and easier cultural adjustments.

9. Draft and institute an Athletes' Bill of Rights for all fifty states that advocate income for college athletes to be paid in income-producing sports.

Let us "check game," so to speak. While I am most adamant about items 1, 2, and 9, the remaining six can be useful guides for revising aspects of the current system. Since college sport is a multibillion-dollar industry the proposed reorganization must be treated like a business deal. But if the NCAA fears revealing itself as the professional for-profit entity it really is, then the measures outlined above are necessary. I am not optimistic that under the current structure of college athletics can change direction. Too much revenue is at stake to fairly compensate athletes. John Gerdy reminds us: "America is the only country in the world where athletics is so intimately intertwined with the education system" (233). This tangle will forever endanger the education of athletes.

*A New Playbook*

Superstar high school basketball athletes could simply go overseas for one or two years and earn millions. Also college athletes might consider trying to unionize, or defect to Historically Black Colleges and Universities (HBCU) to change the leverage a bit. Just as the bus boycott got equal seating in Montgomery, Alabama, and Western Texas's victory changed the racial landscape of southern college athletics when it defeated Kentucky, shifting the star power to the HBCU playing fields could perform a similar leverage for change. Those in power only respond to money and power, and the shift of top prospects to HBCU athletics, would make a strong statement. I am certain such a shift will bring forth new and more stringent rules (because non-White institutions will be benefiting from the talent) that will alter college athletics for the better. African American athletes no longer have to attend predominately White universities to prove that they can compete. Western Texas's victory over favored Kentucky, and similar incidents settled this matter long ago. But the defection of top stars in the top two revenue-producing sports will also force changes in hiring practices and bring much needed additional revenue and exposure to these institutions.

The fear of losing the "Negro cash crops" or "Black Gold" from the football field and basketball courts at large majority White instituions will force real discussions about ending the exploitation of athletes as well as the coaching and administrative discrimination in college athletics (certainly there is no guarantee that a HBCU will not exploit athletes, but my faith in racism makes me optimistic that the NCAA will be watching a HBCU more closely than they did their White counterparts). Since many African American male athletes at predominately White universities report feeling "that they are unfairly treated, experience demoralization in academics, and think less of their academic ability" (Harrision and Valdez

2004), defecting to a HBCU could be a welcome change. More important, HBCUs will find new visibility and revenue streams that will improve facilities, faculty salaries, recruiting, marketing, and financial aid.

Union or no union, athletes could create real change if they withheld their services from the major colleges or boycotted national championship games in football and basketball until their demands for a fair division of the revenue and more diversity in coaching were met. If athletes really claimed the power that their talent gives them to force change, we would live in a drastically different world. In essence, athletes have to function as paid members of clubs affiliated with colleges or unionize their independent voices to gain momentum for organizations like the Collegiate Athletes' Coalition.

*Illegal Procedure*

Everyone protests when the economic rights of college athletes is the issue, or when players opt out of college athletics for lucrative contracts to endorse the apparel of Nike along with soft drinks, candy, and Radio Shack. But the unspoken truth is that the those who suffer from their absence are college coaches and universities that would have made billions from their presence. There is no mistaking the revenues that collegiate athletics produces. If the focus of big-time college sports will continue to be avarice over academics, amateurs will have to be paid salaries that take into consideration their "star status," the school's ranking, and similar criteria used to determine coaches' salaries. It would be refreshing to hear more members of the media discuss the egregious salaries of college coaches (many of whom make more than college presidents) and athletic administrators in comparison to the salaries of university faculty and administrators—the engines of the *education* they seem to value so much.

The biggest infraction I find in college athletics is the literal pimping of college athletes, particularly those of color in high-revenue-producing sports (football and basketball) in the guise of scholarships.

Although Black students comprise less than 5 percent of the student body on major predominately White campuses, on football and basketball teams they comprise 50 and 80 percent respectively.

My proposals, while perhaps somewhat extreme, are a cry against avarice and exploitation in collegiate athletics. I am tired of watching and reading sad stories of athletes, especially Black athletes (mostly male), returning home to a dilapidated community after their playing eligibility expires—often with little to show for their efforts. Since the one hundred-ton sports train cannot be derailed, then some reform is necessary to slow it down. The free college education is a partial truth. While these kids do enjoy the perks of being a star athlete in a big-time program, if they do not make it professionally, they become just a piece of Sports Century highlights. And, in football and basketball, they often generate far more revenue than their scholarship is worth.

The NCAA has to work harder to make academics the primary focus for high-revenue-producing athletics. Since it is unrealistic to hope that the NCAA will turn down millions, the only option is that athletes be paid for their services in the income-producing sports. The solution is quite obvious: either follow these proposed reforms, or state legislators and boards trustees of private academic institutions throughout the country must sit the NCAA down for antitrust discussions, reminding them that slavery was outlawed over 140 years ago, and that while pimping still occurs—it too is illegal.

# CHAPTER SIX

## ALL ABOUT THE BENJAMINS!

*Nobody is complaining about the owners'
salaries. So don't complain about us.*
—Barry Bonds

*You can't knock the hustle.*
—Jay-Z

People complain that modern athletes earn too much money, are greedy, and do not care about the team, but rarely is there outrage that team owners, presidents, and league executives earn too much money. Why? Could it be because the latter are primarily White and male? What we too often hear are recitations of how athletes, especially those of color, are not worth the money they earn, or unappreciative of their opportunity. How dare Rasheed Wallace (then of the Trailblazers), tell Portland reporters that all he was concerned with was for them to "just cut the check" (JCC), or Latrell Sprewell complain that several millions is not enough to feed his family. In fact, the Portland area was outraged when Wallace appeared more concerned about his money than what fans thought about him.[1] But sport has always been about money. There is no secret that it is a billion-dollar industry. Fans clamor for players' autographs because they are worth money. Romantic is the notion that team, fans, or racial goodwill and equity are guiding forces in American sport culture.

Historian Davarian L. Baldwin perhaps best expresses this point in his book *Chicago's New Negroes* when he explains:

> While great, benevolent "white fathers" are credited with the eventual opening of the gates of heaven to "promising" young athletes like Jackie Robinson, it was actually the other way around. "Good ol' boys" networks were pushed, kicking and screaming into the twentieth century. The New Negro sporting life continually agitated for inclusion and excelled in "racial" exile until both the pleasures and profits of black play could no longer be repressed or denied in the radical, yet uneven and incomplete, transformation of the American cultural landscape. (232)

Clearly, as Baldwin details above, money always has been and will continue to be the bottom line. Sound economics is the basis of what many mistaken as benevolent social goodwill in American sport culture. It has always been about making money more than about making change. Earning dollars has historically made the most sense in America. Most civil rights progress was pressured by impending economic perils. Humane acts, especially in sport, have been less about social progress and more about economics progress. It is, as some might say, "All About the Benjamins." From Fritz Pollard and Joe Louis to Kenny Washington and Jackie Robinson, change that involved profit has always made sense.

Sport culture has become corporate, and modern athletes now function as small corporations. As American sports culture has generated more money, BNS have demanded to be shown more of it (thanks largely to Curt Flood). But many fans and members of the media become angry with BNS for getting their "hustle on." The racial contract tells them that BNS are unworthy of wealth and should show gratitude, short of groveling, for the money they are allowed to earn as professional athletes. Floundering insurance giant AIG gives executives bonuses despite receiving billions in federal subsidy and in six months America gets over it, but people are still pissed that A-Rod earns upwards of $22 million annually playing baseball for the New York Yankees.

In fact, discussions about racial progress in sport are expressions of a mythical, racial feel-good mentality that is void of the historical truth of strife, struggle, and the "good ol' boy" resistance to change, with its inherent double standards. The real source of the flak that BNS receive stems from their refusal to abide completely by the rules of the racial contract.

So when BNS and NBA All-Star Rasheed Wallace said "JCC," no one should have been offended.[2] It is indeed, to paraphrase rappers P Diddy and Mase, "All about the Benjamins"! Yes, it was money ($35,000 to be exact), not a belief in equity and justice that got Tommy Burns to risk his belt and racial supremacy on 26 December 1908 against Jack Johnson. After Burns was beaten Jim Jeffries the "Great White Hope" left retirement to fight Jack Johnson (for the amazing amount of $100,000); it was as much about making lots of money as it was about putting Johnson in his place. Although Johnson pummeled them both to become the undisputed heavyweight champion, throwing notions of White racial supremacy in peril, they took the risk for one reason: money.

While sport culture has rightly been acknowledged for its symbolic importance to the struggle for freedom, justice, and equality, one must remember that money was usually a greater factor than social consciousness. No, making money and winning to make money have always been the determining factors. BNS intrinsically seem to understand this and thus vie for all they can get in the open markets. But any discussion of progress and sport must begin and end with a discussion of the economics that have compelled acts of integration and progress. For example, after the Harlem Globetrotters beat and embarrassed the mighty Minneapolis Lakers, the NBA had to consider opening its doors or risk losing its status and fan base.

Perhaps the best way to begin a discussion around money, sport, and racial progress is to begin with an investigation of the greatest of all social progress myths: Jackie Robinson's entry into Major League Baseball (MLB). Branch Rickey offered many, sometimes conflicting, reasons for his desire to integrate baseball. Rickey maintained that he hired Robinson because of his desire to put the best possible team on the field. Before multimillion-dollar broadcasting contracts were the norm, teams relied almost exclusively on ticket sales to pay their expenses—spring training, travel, player salaries, and stadium upkeep—and to make a profit. Attendance was always higher for winning teams, and Rickey was not alone in believing that African American players could improve his team, and his attendance. He saw the popularity of Negro League stars and their All-Star games and Rickey began to raid the Negro Leagues' talent. The Dodgers succeeded well with such black stars as Jackie Robinson, Roy Campanella, and Don Newcombe.

In a 1955 interview, Rickey later declared that in addition to making money, his belief in equal rights was also a strong motive for signing African Americans to the Dodgers. The Dodgers signed Jackie in 1945, expecting him to debut in 1947. They also believed that Jackie could draw a Black crowd as well as new Whites who were curious or hoping for Jackie's failure. Not coincidently, the year they signed Robinson, 1945, attendance soared to one million despite the team ending the season eleven games out of first place. Robinson's presence certainly had a huge impact on attendance for the Dodgers during the early years of his career. Indeed, the Dodgers drew a large spike in attendance in Robinson's first two years from curious observers and die-hard fans. Judging from the attendance statistics from 1945 to 1949, it is clear that Branch Rickey hedged a good economic bet. He knew that the Negro Leagues had outstanding stars and a strong fan base. Between 1946 and 1949, the Dodgers had an average annual attendance of over 1.5 million, enjoying an incredible attendance mark of 1.8 million in 1947, which was Robinson's rookie season.[3] Playing the angles he figured he would shore up his fan base and profit, drawing the committed and curious interested in watching Robinson play.

So, money was the primary force driving "the experiment." Another glance at the Dodgers' attendance statistics also reveals that in 1943 and 1944 the annual attendance for the season was roughly 600,000. The combined attendance for those two years is less than the 1946 season attendance! In fact, the 1947 season attendance tripled that of the 1943 and 1944 seasons. There is no coincidence between attendance and Robinson. His presence made money.[4]

Also, the year Robinson joined the Dodgers, they won the pennant, making the first of six trips to the World Series during his ten-year career—and by all accounts, Robinson was not the best Negro League player! The Dodgers' winning streak and soaring attendance compelled other teams signing Black players, but racism prevented too many on any single team, or an invitation for a Negro League team to join the White league.

Rickey was not the only White owner that saw the profit and popularity of the Negro League star players. They knew that the National Negro League East-West All-Star games of the 1930s were huge events whose crowds at times *exceeded* the attendance at the Major League version. The crowds at these events, which tended to last the entire weekend, drew crowds as large as or more than 50,000. As Davarian Baldwin also notes, the Negro League East-West All-Star weekends were so popular and profitable, that many argue it was a significant catalyst for the integration of Major League Baseball. While White owners may have despised the signature styles of these players, they saw the profitability of Black players who branded themselves in ways that set them apart in the marketplace. The owners wanted to make money; social progress was an afterthought, if a thought at all.

In professional basketball the Black star laden American Basketball Association (ABA) had a similar impact on the NBA. The ABA made "street style" basketball popular as players came from the streets of inner-city America. The most famous "street" tournament was the Rucker in New York. Many pro players played in that tournament and brought their styles to professional basketball in the ABA. The renegade, upstart league contending for a place in professional basketball, instituted a strategy of drafting and playing more Black players, then acquiescing to their styles of play. This primary component set it apart from the NBA. As a result, ABA games were entertaining, wide-open scoring affairs played high above the rim. Julius Erving (Dr. J) became the most famous player of the era, but he played in the ABA. The desire of fans who wanted to see star players like Dr. J play against NBA stars, gave the ABA owners the leverage they needed to join the NBA. While this certainly contributed to the huge influx of Black players in the NBA during the 1970s and early 1980s, it was simply the best way for ABA owners to force their teams into the NBA.

So while it appeared that the ABA, with its Black players and adoption of their signature styles, was interested in integration, innovation, and breaking racial barriers, it was always about making money, getting a piece of the NBA pie. In 1976 when the ABA finally merged with the NBA, it was clear that although more Black players had gained entry into the NBA, the ABA used Black players to rival the NBA and force a merger.

*Show Them the Money*

In the film *Jerry Maguire*, Rod Tidwell (BNS) tells his agent: "Show me the money." People chuckled and the phrase was used for all occupations and situations, yet it remained negatively attached to BNS in American sport culture. In America, everyone wants to be shown the money. America embraces free enterprise, capitalism, and self-preservation, yet modern Black athletes have become the poster children for greed and avarice. Team owners never endure such scrutiny or criticism. How can this be when so many American businesses generate enormous wealth from sports on every level?

Peter Keating called it right when he said: "Real amateurism still exists where competition is its only reward, from small-town field hockey to varsity crew. . . . But once fans pay to see a sport and networks bid to show it, dollars enter the mix and the game changes."[5] Perhaps the Wu-

Tang Clan's signature hit and ghetto anthem "C.R.E.A.M." ("Cash Rules Everything Around Me") best explains the reality of professional and amateur sports in America. Indeed, sports, like all American businesses is about profit. The only fidelity seems to be to cash. Always when athletes are paid well, the central focus is the salary of players, rarely the owners cutting the checks. One cannot help but wonder why it is okay for the New York Yankee's owner George Steinbrenner to earn enough profit to afford a payroll of over $200 million, while the $25 million that Alex Rodriquez earns annually is deemed excessive?

What I find excessive and outrageous is that since 2000 $13 billion of public money has been spent to build stadiums across America, while public schools, hospitals, and many communities need jobs and languish in poverty. I am outraged that many American banks and financial institutions received billions in federal dollars in 2008 and 2009 because they lost money then had the nerve to dole out millions in bonuses to employees. Where is the outrage that the New York Yankees, the richest franchise in professional baseball, asked the New York state government for $250 million in tax-exempt bonds to build the new Yankee Stadium? Where is the outrage that the Mets received millions in tax-exempt dollars to help build a new stadium as well? There can be no double standard. America is indeed broken if there is more scrutiny of athletes' salaries than there is of fraudulent activities of financial institutions, professional teams, and local officials.

In May 2008, former NFL Players Association president (deceased) Gene Upshaw complained that NFL owners had voted to opt out of their collective-bargaining agreement with players in 2011 (two years early) because players were demanding transparency. Upshaw's estimates projected total NFL revenue at $7.6 billion, and operating income for 2008 at roughly $18 million per team! Upshaw contended that this is only an estimate because team owners do not allow the union to peruse their books. Because the owners' books are closed to the union, the profit margins are difficult to verify to ensure players get the proper share of the pot.

The owners dislike the collective-bargaining agreement but have yet to be called greedy or unethical. To make matters worse, although team owners refuse to allow the union to see their financial records (and the players union should be suspicious of any new labor deal without viewing financial records), it is players, not owners (who refuse a more transparent financial disclosure), that will be seen as greedy. How can that be?

Jerry Richardson, owner of the Carolina Panthers, rationalized the owners' decision against opening the books to the union as simply running "counter to his most basic principles." Those principles being to generate as much cash as they can with a salary cap (projected at $137 million in 2011), and a rookie wage scale (similar to the one the NBA has) that caps rookie salaries to keep market forces in check for veteran deals. So it seems that the owners are "all about the Benjamins" and being "shown the money," and not the other way around. Responses to player salaries and owner revenues represent double standards that may go deeper than the racial contract in action in American sports culture. However, I am troubled that the media seems intrinsically to attack players for avarice, while accepting the economic self-preservation narratives of team owners, most of whom are White.

## Racial Contract and Money

Since sports are a major cog of the modern American empire, it is only natural that there would be outrage over salaries of non-White players. Players from the big three (football, basketball, and baseball) are often derided as overpaid. But one cannot help but wonder if these sports receive extra criticism because the racial dynamics have changed more than in equally "overpaid" sports like golf, hockey, race car drivers (I hesitate calling them athletes), tennis, or soccer. I rarely hear criticisms about the salary of a tennis player, golfer, or race car driver. Why? Could the racial contract have any bearing on such obvious double standards?

While professional sport emphasizes a team concept that requires sacrifice, ironically it rewards players based on individual performance. Many middle to upper-level executives are compensated for performance, but in sport the undertone is that the high salaries of many athletes challenge the values that represent Whiteness in the American empire; it violates the rules of the racial contract. While there was outrage that in 2007 and 2008 executives of major companies and bankers received multi-million dollar bonuses during one of the worst economic crises in over 60 years, athletes who have performed remain grouped with these underperforming financiers.

I must confess that I am bothered that entertainment is valued more than intellectual endeavors, but I am equally bothered that primary targets of the "overpaid" critiques happen to be athletes involved in sports dominated by non-Whites. The films *Jerry Maguire* and *Any Given Sunday*, although only fictional, are excellent examples of the racial dynamics in American culture. In *Jerry Maguire*, Rod Tidwell is a loud-mouthed, arrogant, egotistical, money-hungry, typical modern athlete whose only loyalty, his only concern, is being "shown the money." This mantra, which dominates the film, is supposed to epitomize modern professional athletes of color. What is often glossed over is Tidwell's motivations to take care of his family, and his deep-seated love of family, which forms the basis of his desire for more money. He has many responsibilities; lots of people depending on him. One positive aspect of the film was its depiction of the very corporate business of professional sports, where loyalty is a meaningless word. It is a world where "show me the money" is a natural response to owners whose negotiating tactic is "What have you done for me lately?"

The enduring depiction of Black athletes as immoral and avaricious is an equally dominant theme in the film *Any Given Sunday*. Oddly enough, it is through the lowest-paid quarterback on the team who also happens to be Black. One scene reveals the double standard dynamics of race in American sport culture. Willie leaves his very modest apartment and travels in his loud yellow truck to meet his coach at his ostentatious home, where they engage in a discussion about racism or "placism" and money. Willie explains to his coach during their heated exchange that the racism is "the same in the pros as it is in college, except that in the pros the field hands get paid."

But what was odd about the film is that all while Willie and those like him are being labeled greedy, those making the most money, those being shown the real money, happen to be White; their wealth is never questioned.

Although "the field hands get paid" in the pros, the system itself is akin to an open slave market. Like human chattel they are poked, prodded, measured, timed, and their strength tested. Then they are selected or purchased by the highest bidder—with the highest draft status. Of course, athletes are not slaves. They are paid well for their services, but the process still involves mostly White men who do the gazing, bidding, prodding, buying, and selling of mostly Black and Brown men. (More persons of color are scouts, general managers, and owners who judge the players, but the system is offensive.)

The racial contract slips coaches, executives, and team owners through the privileged cracks. In the empire, it is acceptable for them to earn huge salaries. They are thought deserving, and in line with the metaphysical obligation of Whites to rule less advanced people (Said 10). Most sports team owners, if not all of them, are on the Forbes list of the richest Americans. Team owners (who are roughly 95 percent White and male) have influence that stretches far beyond the NFL, MLB, NBA, or NHL. Revenues from sports teams is side money, but they earn enough from owning a sports team to dole out annual payrolls of $100 to over $200 million (the 2005 New York Yankees had a payroll of $207.2 million) and still make tremendous profits!

Why do the earnings of team owners—shrewd billionaire businessmen who keep their books closed—receive so little criticism? Moreover, the enormous salaries league officials like Roger Goodell and

David Stern earn, and White players like Tom Brady or Peyton Manning also receive less scrutiny than Black athletes like Terrell Owens, Randy Moss, Manny Ramierz, or Albert Haynesworth (who recently signed for a record $41 million in guarantees). Personally, I think they are all overpaid. Certainly there are other occupations more deserving of high salaries (like teachers, scientists, and counselors), however, if the market is willing to pay millions to athletes, I wish them well. But the racial contract privileges White owners, league officials and athletes to be overpaid with far less scrutiny than their non-White counter parts.

Rarely is the lead news story the mega-television, cable, or radio deal an owner has struck, or the huge profits from selling stadium marketing space, or taxes the public pays to have stadiums built, or the owners' closed-book policy, or the millions in profit a team earned after paying expenses. The focus is always on how much players earn, especially non-White players. The message, according to the racial contract, is that the services of non-Whites are devalued; they are only entitled to so much.

Forgotten in all this is that only until recently did players begin earning more money and freedom to avoid spending their entire career with a single team (thank you Curt Flood). People often try to deny that race and racism are a real source of tension in modern American society— and sport culture is no different. So, when Rasheed Wallace told the *Oregonian* newspaper in 2003 "JCC," evoking ire, shock, and disgust, the racial undercurrent was that he failed to show enough gratitude for being allowed to earn so much money.[6] The true tension was that he had forgotten his "place."

Wallace's interview with *The Oregonian* was enlightening because it revealed a BNS wary of the NBA's exploitation of young Black athletes via rookie salary caps. (While it was thought ridiculous to many, he did have a point, because rookies are no longer privy to open market bidding for their services.) There was total outrage after Wallace proclaimed the league to be full of "false screens." Wallace, at the time a member of the

Portland Trailblazers, did not mince his words. To punctuate his insights, he pointed out that "the commissioner of [the NBA] makes more than three-quarters of the players." To this, David Stern, who indeed earns over $10 million annually, not counting bonuses and perks, responded that Wallace's comments were a "hateful diatribe...ignorant and offensive to all NBA players." But no one followed up to investigate or discuss Stern's salary or whether Wallace's claim was really "ignorant" or inaccurate. Racial dynamics being what they are, in the sports pages the next day Stern emerged as the good guy...and Wallace? Well, I think you can guess.

What was most telling in this exchange was the information that was emphasized about Wallace. The article saw fit to remind readers that Wallace rarely spoke to the media, was suspended for seven games for threatening an official, and that he set an NBA record with forty-one technical fouls during the 2000–2001 season. Also, Wallace's annual salary of $17 million was mentioned several times, along with opinions assessing his morality (a common racial contract tactic). But his accusation about Stern's salary was never confirmed or disputed—it was ignored. Even Stern's rebuttal was limited to calling Wallace "ignorant" and "offensive," but he never declared Wallace incorrect, because rookie salaries are capped. First-round players can only earn so much during their first two or three years. Furthermore, Wallace, in all his "ignorance," was citing the contradiction of Stern's support of league owners, during the lockout in 1999, for a new bargaining agreement that saved owners hundreds of millions of dollars, but allowed Stern to continue to make over $10 million as commissioner. The young Black athletes to whom Wallace was referring were then rookies like Carmelo Anthony, Dwayne Wade, and LeBron James, upon whose shoulders the NBA was wagering its future. Now megastars, they sell out arenas wherever they play. But their salaries were capped for their first two or three years in the league to keep future earnings in check. In fact, to be fair, Wallace was wrong, Stern only makes more money than 60 percent of the players in the NBA.

Meanwhile, no caps were placed on the salary of Richard Grasso, the former New York Stock Exchange chairman and chief executive who in 2003 received a $187.5 million compensation package. Nothing stopped CEO Dennis Kozlowski from receiving an $18 million crash pad, the four GE executives from receiving apartments in New York, or former Global Crossing CEO Robert Annunziata from getting a Mercedes-Benz SL-500, corporate jet for commuting, and first-class airfare for his family to see him once a week. Oddly, there was minimal hostile reaction from the media or the public over these perks and expenditures. Nor was there much outrage or charges of greed when NHL players demanded the majority of the league revenues. Ironically most of the NHL players are White.

*Racism and Money*

The double standards outlined above are driven by race and racial privilege. As Hernán Vera and Andrew M. Gordon explain in *Screen Saviors: Hollywood Fictions of Whiteness* (2003), "In the United States... those who are not considered white are often automatically assumed to be smelly, 'greasy,' less intelligent, lazy, dirty, not in control of their emotions, unreliable, and so on" (12–13). Such racist descriptions of athletes of color are conveyed, stated, or implied in the world of sports journalism. Why else would sports journalists make certain to report large annual salaries of professional athletes but rarely the earnings of coaches, league officials, and owners?

The real problem with professional athletes like Rasheed Wallace, Curt Flood, Barry Bonds, and other BNS is that they are what poet Quincy Troupe calls "unreconstructed Black men."[7] Such men, despite newfound privilege or wealth, continue being themselves (they keep it real) and are unwilling to turn a blind eye to their roots, social inequities, impropriety, exploitation, or racism. They are not afraid to lose their newfound, yet delicate "advantages." Not all of them are muted nor blinded by their own good fortune; many see their good fortune for the aberration it is in a climate of heightened racial hostility and regressive legal policies. They know, for example, that in the real world beyond sports, when it comes down to equity, a White male with a criminal record has a better chance of being employed than does a Black man without a criminal record and a college degree. Sociological studies have proven that such discriminating practices exist. And although few are doing enough to make real change, BNS know all too well that the neighborhoods from which they hail are bankrupt of opportunities for a reason.

In the final analysis, American sport is primarily about the "Benjamins." Everything else is secondary. BNS know that when you can no longer produce, you are sent packing, so they try to earn as much money as they can, when they can. NBA Hall of Fame member and former NBA league MVP Charles Barkley echoes this point when he recounts his college coach asking him: "Charles, you want to play basketball or you want your degree?" It is about money from the college ranks to the pros. Business is definitely first and all else is a distant second and third. BNS know this much to be true. Sebastian Telfair, among the last high school stars to jump straight to the NBA, conveyed the essence of this when asked what he needed to do to be successful in the sports world. He was savvy enough to respond that it required playing two games: "basketball and business."[8]

BNS, like Jack Johnson and Curt Flood before them, understand the importance of earning all that the market will bear for their services because the window is so small. Instead of constantly questioning the morality and value of professional athletes, the media should scrutinize revenues of owners—and of course, the universities that exploit amateur athletics under the ruse of education. The media might do well to listen to the critiques of those like Wallace who charge usury and the racial double standards. What we cannot deny is that while sport is "all about the Benjamins," race still effects who is deemed worthy of earning them and who is not. Thus, given these dynamics all BNS like Rasheed Wallace concern themselves with is making teams "Just cut the check."

# CHAPTER SEVEN

## THE MAKING OF MEN IN AMERICAN SPORTS FILMS

*Hollywood movies continue to glorify white heroes and
to turn minority characters into symbols.*
—Hernán Vera and Andrew M. Gordon in *Screen Saviours*

Film representations are part of a larger subset of systems of social representations that determine how people live (Vera and Gordon 185). The images of non-Whites in contemporary sports films are quite unsettling. Since slavery, Black masculinity has been framed in notions of Brute Negro, Stud, noble savage, Uncle Tom, and Bad Nigger, while post-Reconstruction/neo-slavery images (1865–1954) have portrayed the Irresponsible Negro, Terrible Freedman, Uncle Tom, Stud, Buffon, and reprised Bad Nigger. In the modern world, sports films frame Black masculinity as the Hustler, Militant/Bad Nigger, Super Jock, or Womanizer—lazy, flashy, and consistently anti-intellectual or dumb. To counter these negative images, Black films in the early 1970s—beginning with Melvin Van Peebles's successful, yet at times problematic, *Sweet Sweetback's Baadasssss Song* (1971) and subsequent films like *Shaft* (1971) and *Superfly* (1972)—hit the screen with financially lucrative results (Bogle 240). But the films primarily featured heroes who were apolitical flashy individualists and also sexually audacious. To some extent such images were necessary to counter earlier images. But one consistent element with all of these Black heroes or anti-heroes is that they were renegades who were never intimidated by Whites. They were all the antithesis of the asexual, accommodating Uncle Tom.

Film has been a dominant purveyor of the discourse of White supremacy, a notion effectively situated in sports—particularly the arena of prizefighting. Modern sports films have emerged as a common launchpad for reprising many of the aforementioned stereotypes. As feminist critic Gail Bederman has noted in her insightful *Manliness and Civilization: A Cultural History of Gender and Race in the United States, 1880–1917* (1995), prizefighting played a central role in the construction of twentieth-century American masculinity, especially for White males. Jack Johnson's dominance placed the masculine White self in peril. Thus, the twentieth-century obsession of White males focused on putting Black masculinity back into its place. While impossible in the real world, sports film has been an effective vehicle for achieving this goal. In the litany of modern sports films, Black men usually emerge as bad men who are inherently aggressive, violent, and whose intellect is highly questionable, but who can be saved by great White fatherly figures.

Pioneering Black film critic Donald Bogle posits in *Toms, Coons, Mulattoes, Mammies, and Bucks: An Interpretive History of Blacks in American Films* (rev. ed. 1989) that sports heroes have been strategically placed in film, especially during the 1970s boom years when many African Americans became movie stars. The film industry was able to take the most powerful or superhuman Black athletes and manipulate, even counter, "the myth of the athlete and to alter his legend to fit the mood and tone of the times" (243). Bogle goes on to outline how the athlete as movie hero was seldom depicted as "a thinker, questioning his role in society. And almost always . . . the politics of the black athletes are far more populist than revolutionary" (243). This is a trend that persists in films like *White Men Can't Jump, Wildcats, Rocky II, Rocky III*, and *O*, among others.

Cultural critics, film critics, sociologist, and race theorist such as

West, Bogle, Snead, Cripps, and others remind us how films fuel a social order that is institutionally racist and a hierarchy that is racially coded to glorify White heroes. In modern America, where many of the heroes in high-profile sports (such as football, basketball, baseball, and boxing) are Black athletes, sports films rescue White masculinity; they provide him a space to be a hero again.

Images and spectacles shape the structuring of the modern visual world; they embody society's basic values and dramatize realities and conflicts. Therefore one cannot regard lightly the many spectacles of the Black male sports film characters. They are selfish, hypermasculine, criminal gangstas, or boys who become men with the guidance of a great White father. There may be some exceptions to this rule, such as in films like Coach *Carter* or *Cross Over*, but this is usually the norm.

As these films bludgeon the world with images of Black men as purveyors of hypermasculinity, society ignores the prevalence of these characteristics in mainstream American institutions. Derek Iwamoto describes this in his essay "Tupac Shakur: Understanding the Identity Formation of Hyper-Masculinity of a Popular Hip-Hop Artist." According to Iwamoto, America socializes men in general through movies (for example, *Terminator 2*, *Casino*, *Die Hard*) to prove their manliness, as well as through sports and television shows (45). Meanwhile, in the same films, in direct contrast to the negative images, are images of heroic, kind, and brave White Americans. There are also fatherly figures in films like *Finding Forrester*, *Glory Road*, and *Any Given Sunday*. In many American sports films, White men are natural leaders, deserving of the admiration and loyalty. Like American culture, sports films exaggerate and limit images of non-Whites males. The common trope is undisciplined, greedy, and unethical bad men whose sole purpose seems to be bolstering White masculinity. In fact, since the 1980s American culture has intensified its focus on the male body, emphasizing bigger, stronger, more muscular representations of American masculinity. In general, manhood and respect seem ever more entrenched in physical strength, violence, or the threat of violence. Because athletes usually are the males who fit this description in American culture and the majority of those in the public eye participate in sports dominated by non-Whites, modern sports films work hard to recalibrate the status of White masculinity.

But, of course, contemporary American sports films hardly exist in a vacuum. Indeed, they pick up where D. W. Griffith's silent film *The Birth of a Nation* (1915), based on Thomas Dixon's 1905 novel *The Clansman*, left off. *The Birth of a Nation* was a seminal film that set the tone and terms of racial cinematic depictions in American film. Again I turn to film critic Donald Bogle, who explains that Griffith's film presented all the stereotypes with "such force and power that . . . [it] touched off a wave of controversy and was denounced as the most slanderous anti-Negro movie ever released" (10). It is a film that seemed to suggest that order could be restored if Blacks were kept in their place.

The story is an idyllic tale of the old South where White men are benevolent and gentle and slaves are content with their lot, singing and dancing for their master, until the Civil War and the Reconstruction period disrupt this order. During the war and subsequent Reconstruction, slaves no longer dance or work; they abuse Whites on streets, take over the political polls, and disenfranchise Whites (12). The Blacks in Griffith's film gain freedom and lust after White women; they are arrogant, stupid, and lacking in social or political decorum. The rise of the Ku Klux Klan is all that can halt these Black rebels, whom they defeat to retain the honor of White women, White people, and American order.

Clear parallels exist between *The Birth of the Nation* and many modern sports films. First, in modern sports films there is commonly an archetypal big, bad, Black Buck who is either oversexed, violent, or a bestial psychopath; a Black villain lusting after a White woman (the ultimate symbol of White power, beauty, and pride). Second, in addition to these tired stereotypes is a tireless quest to restore White male supremacy. The modern twist is that characters are usually in need of the counsel of an intellectually superior or paternal White male to lead him in the right direction toward a better life.

Historical representations of non-Whites have supported what sports film critic Aaron Baker and sports historian Randy Roberts describe as a belief among Whites (still held today) that non-Whites, particularly the Black male, are incapable of performing in organized team sports that rely on "mental acuity, careful planning, and coordinated execution" (Roberts quoted in Baker 15). Indeed, it was believed that "nature had designed them to laugh, sing, dance, and play but not to sacrifice, train, work, compete, and win" (Baker 15). The common notion for several decades in the film industry has been a pronounced feeling that non-Whites are ill-suited for hard work, self-reliance, and deferred gratification (15). This type of racist imaging is prevalent today, reinforcing White racist images around the world (Vera and Gordon x).

Like Jack Johnson (a sports "bad man" pioneer), BNS are comforted by their own knowledge of their competence. But the brand of self-reliance and deferred gratification that BNS display has resulted in a continuation or backlash of images and critiques of inferior mental acuity or an unwillingness to sacrifice and compete. Such stereotypes persist; in fact, they bulge at the reels of modern sports film—primarily in response to athletes half a century removed from Jackie Robinson and unconsciously emulating Jack Johnson. Much of this acrimony stems from BNS's skepticism of the merits of deterred gratification. They hedge at embracing the American value system or its racial contract. Modern sports films often confirm but sometimes respond to racial segregation and stereotypes regarding masculinity and White supremacy.

Once the post-civil rights era demolished arguments of biological supremacy, Whiteness was placed in peril. It is a crisis that film seems to be working overtime to restore. As Vera and Gordon make clear in *Screen Saviors* (2003), "The new images apparently recognize the humanity of minority groups but actually misrecognize the true relations between minorities and whites" (187). In essence, not only do modern Hollywood sports films perpetuate mythologies such as Uncle Toms, coons, violent, hypersexual, hypermasculine non-White males, but they have aided the concept of "Whiteness," (invented during European colonization of Africa and the Americas), giving it space to reconstruct itself "in response to changing political and economic needs and conditions" (Vera and Gordon 11–12). Ironically, when Jack Johnson marred the myth of superior White masculine male by making handiwork of the Great White Hopes like Tommy Burns and Jim Jeffries, film footage from Johnson's victory was banned. Since it is no longer cool or easy to ban film footage, it has become necessary to "construct a public fiction" of White male athletic dominance and superiority using American sport films.

As Vera and Gordon indicate, "Hollywood images of whites—and especially white institutions—have stayed much the same" (ix), pushing images of the superior, brave, fatherly, generous, masculine, and powerful White self as the center of the action, a sort of hero or "messiah figure for people of color" (ix). In modern sports films, the heroes usually save non-Whites from misfortune and mis-education, and teach them life lessons and morals because they are superior men. One would think that these racial motifs would be absent in contemporary American sports films, but it is here that these images thrive. White males are "intellectually superior and meritorious" (ix) as paternal figures who guide unintelligent, lazy, yet flashy individualists, in proper directions. Hollywood has picked up the ball, so to speak, and is scoring points in public perceptions of White dominance in sport. We cannot forget that sport is where constructions and perceptions of masculinity in American culture are largely situated. As Gail Bederman reminds us, for White men, such notions of masculinity have been tarnished since Jack Johnson became heavyweight champion of the world and Jackie Robinson broke the color barrier. Thus, it makes sense that sports films serve as vehicles for image restoration and authentication of notions of racial supremacy. What can we expect from a culture that refused to show the footage of Jack Johnson beating the White champion?

The authors Vera and Gordon interrogate this issue in *Screen*

*Saviors*, explaining: "Hollywood movies are one of the main instruments for establishing the apartheid mind-set that leads people of all colors to automatically consider white to be superior. Hollywood spreads the fiction of whiteness around the world" (1). Sports films are key instruments authenticating the racial contract mentality that leads people to accept White as superior without question, despite the majority of non-White sports heroes in American culture. Meanwhile, it is rare that sports films explore the degrading effects of racism on both White and Black men. Rarely does a non-White achieve a superior position without the assistance, guidance, or counsel of some White figure. Often contemporary American sports films reprise the historic stereotypes such as coons (lazy, harmless, unreliable, crazy, subhuman creatures), Uncle Toms (content slave who obeys his master), and bucks (villainous, hate-filled, violent) (Bogle 7–8), or equally negative one-dimensional depictions of Black men as villains, dumb jocks who are rude, or content with the system and their place within it. These depictions are usually coupled with smart, parental White males, teaching non-Whites how to adhere to "proper" codes of sport ethics and social conduct for success. And because sports play a leading role in situating American masculine identity, these film constructions of Whiteness, which are rarely studied, resituate a flagging masculine identity that has been dethroned by the predominance of non-Whites as sports heroes and dominant males in American culture.

In the imagined world of film, White as superior, physical, and masculine is revived. White males reign. Since the turn of the twentieth century—especially the mid-twentieth century—White males have increasingly assumed lesser roles in high-profile American sports (football, baseball, boxing, and basketball). The response has been a propaganda machine working full throttle to conjure television and film images to sustain the myth of White masculine and cultural supremacy. The predominance of non-Whites depicted as poor, lazy, uneducated, less intelligent, subordinate, unethical, violent bad men, and in need of a

White savior have become common ingredients for a recipe to preserve White male heroism in sport. In fact, in the fictional space of film, White males emerge as the best athletes, leaders, or *real* men.

White heroes reemerge and dominate the fictional world of film. In this world these men occupy space as Horatio Algiers, or cinematic gods, although athletes of color dominate contemporary high-profile sports. Through film America creates White sports heroes, new "White Hopes" who win and resituate the masculinity vanquished in reality. Sports films fill this void, functioning to promotes moral great White coaches (*Glory Road, Hoosiers, Any Given Sunday*, and so on) or all-knowing White male authority figures or leaders and talented/smart White athletes.

Inscribed in sports films are physical low blows aimed at non-Whites, particularly African American aesthetics, masculinity, intellect, morality, and cultural differences. The goal, according to film critic Aaron Baker, is to "relive the past to avoid the social complexities" of modern society. The depictions and moral indictments of Black cultural heritage reflect the racial state of American culture, and the function of sports film as a propaganda tool for upholding the racial contract.

### Rocky, the Great White Hope

Perhaps it is best to begin with the most famous and perhaps the most shameless sports reconstruction of White masculinity or reassertion of "real men" in a fictional space: Rocky Balboa, of the *Rocky* films. Rocky is the modern installment of the Great White Hope made good since Rocky Marciano retired and left boxing and left White supremacy twisting in the wind. During each sequel Rocky's mythical proportions surpassed even Roy Hobbs of Bernard Malmud's novel *The Natural*. Indeed, Rocky's mythology even rivals Homer's great warriors, Hector and Achilles, for a statue of him stands outside the art museum in Philadelphia. It is an example of a fictional representation occupying a nonfictional space and reality. The irony in this is that Philadelphia is the home of one of the greatest heavyweight champions in real life, Joe Frazier. The problem is there are no statutes honoring this real-life hero.

Sylvester Stallone took the story of Chuck Wepner (with a career record of 31–14–2 and known in boxing circles as the "Bayonne Bleeder")—an up-and-mostly-down heavyweight who lasted for fifteen rounds with Muhammad Ali on 24 March 1975 in Cleveland before being knocked out—and turned it into an industry. As I was viewing a replay of the fight on the ESPN Sports Century channel, I could not contain my laughter that this man, fighting a clearly undertrained Ali, bleeding profusely from gashes around and above both eyes from Ali's jabs, inspired the Rocky legend. Perhaps it was because during the fight Wepner is credited with knocking Ali down during his prime (although black-and-white photos and the replay reveal that Ali actually tripped over Wepner's foot in the ninth round). Perhaps what should not be surprising is that the screenplay *Rocky* won an Oscar in 1976 for best script. Suddenly, after all the years of desperately searching for a successor to Rocky Marciano, Stallone, a struggling actor, found fame by giving America its new Great White Hope—in film! Rocky Balboa emerged on the big screen to reclaim late twentieth-century White masculine ideals and supremacy. BNS could not really harm his legacy because Stallone and Hollywood controlled the outcome.

It also reflects the desperation of reasserting White supremacy. Although Ali delivered a brutal beating to Wepner as in 1975, Stallone successfully recasts the tale of Wepner, a mediocre fighter, losing a close match. Wepner was indeed a mediocre boxer whom Foreman disposed of in three rounds; Sonny Liston knocked him out in ten, and among his other twelve losses was a lackluster defeat at the hands of King Roman in Puerto Rico. Yet Stallone culled portions of real fights—along with the real personalities of Frazier, Liston, Foreman, and Ali—to write the first four installments of the *Rocky* industry.

The Wepner/Rocky marriage reflects the desperate state of White masculinity in sport in the modern world. It reveals a masculinity still reeling from the damage Jack Johnson inflicted on the American White male psyche. Gail Bederman's discussion of masculinity and race in *Masculinity and Civilization* is also helpful for understanding why the film industry and American society were willing to embrace Rocky the Hollywood heavyweight champion. According to Bederman, sport, masculinity, and White supremacy are codependent in American culture. Bederman illustrates this by recounting how Jack Johnson's victory "shredded the ideologies of white male power embedded in 'civilization,'" and notes that "it was imperative that white males assume the power to ensure the continued millennial advancement of white civilization" (42). America had nowhere to turn except into the comforting arms of a fictional White heavyweight champion, the Great White Hope it so desperately needed. Since the late twentieth century could provide none in reality, America turned to Rocky Balboa.

W. E. B. DuBois intimated in his *Black Reconstruction in America* (1935) that poor working-class Whites were able to stomach the economic oppression imposed on them because they could always rely psychologically on the public deference that Blacks were forced to pay them. But in modern America, BNS make it plainly clear that no deference will be paid and that, in fact, Whites owe respect to Blacks if they expect any modicum of respect. This has had a damaging effect on the already-weakened myth of White superiority. Novelist William Faulkner was keenly aware of this conflict, often broaching it in his fiction. Thus, film is the only certain salve for a wounded ideal of White superiority and the *Rocky* films are the perfect cure.

The film critic Donald Bogle sums up the Rocky obsession as a case of the absence of "a first-rate White fighter (that familiar great white hope figure) to defeat a loudmouth braggart and reclaim the throne....The *Rocky* movies may have succeeded as great unconscious national fantasies," whereby a successful White boxer can defeat "an Ali-surrogate" and then gain a buddy or sidekick in the process (272).

Indeed, Apollo Creed is Ali, a BNS who personifies all the stereotypes of the modern athlete. In many ways his behavior enhances the greatness of Rocky—increasing Rocky's heroism and power. Although Apollo is cocky, flashy, and obnoxious, he is extremely skilled and bright, yet not fully honoring the spirit of boxing or American opportunity. Although Ali is revered in modern history, it is well known that much of White America resented Ali for his boldness, realness, intelligence, and for refusing the draft on moral and religious grounds. Further, the *Rocky* films make a comment on masculinity in the modern world. Creed's intelligence is his disadvantage. By becoming articulate, educated, and a thriving businessman, he loses his primitive edge. It is an edge that Rocky possesses, which allows him to defeat Creed. Rocky is a raw, inarticulate, semi-literate, but strong-willed Horatio Alger masculinity. However, what is most ironic about Creed is that he is the one who offers the opportunity of the American dream to a White man. Suddenly all that Griffith had predicted in *The Birth of a Nation* (1915) had come to fruition in America post-Reconstruction—the savages had taken control! Rocky's victory has huge implications for American recovery.

Creed's presence confirms not only this fear, but it also encapsulates a myth of racial progress, along with greater gender, race, and class equalities. However, by acknowledging Creed as unbeatable, as the greatest of all time, legitimizes Rocky's claim to the throne as undisputed champ. The Rocky Balboa character in all the films leads the way toward a White return to prominence because he is hardworking, hard-nosed, scrappy, strong-willed, gritty, dedicated, and wise. Actually, he is White masculinity restored in the fictional space of film because of his belief in giving a total effort, unlike BNS (represented by Creed), who have tarnished this American ideal. Rocky achieves what Tommy Burns and Jim Jeffries could not against Jack Johnson. In his *Contesting Identities*, Aaron Baker notes that *Rocky* also reflects a desire to reaffirm the American dream that every man has an opportunity (suggesting that the White male has been displaced) in American society, and to remind the world who the Alpha male really is (130).

To effectively restore this mythology, Black masculinity is first raised to great heights and then emasculated. In the first film, Creed is presented as the best the world has ever seen, an unbeatable man who combines skill, athleticism, and intelligence to situate modern masculinity against the old-fashioned work ethic of Rocky, who with sheer grit manages to go the distance with him. Creed personifies BNS; he is what has gone wrong in sport and America—with the mouth to match. He is also the modern Black bad man who is subtly lazy and undisciplined. At one point during the first *Rocky* film, Creed's corner tells him to quit "shucking and jiving." In the end, Creed escapes with a decision once he finally gets serious about fighting, like Rocky. The film also critiques what is deemed as typically modern Black athletes: angry, undisciplined, pampered, and unappreciative of the opportunities America has given them. Furthermore, literally draping Creed in the American flag sends mixed messages about democracy and opportunity for Blacks in America, but it also symbolizes racial skepticism because of the style and aesthetics Creed brings with him; Creed is a symbol of where America has gone while its original immigrants are still struggling for the crown.

As Aaron Baker correctly points out, Creed wins a narrow decision because he adopts Rocky's more *American*, stable style, which is that of a slugger, in place of his Black aesthetics of speed, guile, signifying, and play. Rocky prevails because he is the antithesis of BNS like Creed. The racial cultural commentary and morality judgments are unmistakable. At the same time, the film dumps onto BNS the tag of immoral, selfish, self-serving, style-without-substance jocks who lack American ideals.

In *Rocky II*, Balboa fills vapid space for all White masculine redemption against all odds by defeating the Ali-like Creed and the aesthetics he represents. Balboa is what John Fiske, in his *Channels of Discourse*, terms a void "between the privileged and deprived and concentrated power in the white male upper middle classes" (320). By humbling the fictional Ali (Creed), Rocky restores manhood and American ideals to their proper place, showing that BNS are culturally, aesthetically, morally lacking.

*Rocky III* (1982) continues to delve into issues of cultural supremacy and morality in the fictional world where a White heavyweight champ reigns supreme. Only this time Rocky is a wealthy, humble, respectful, charitable, loving husband and doting father, who has become civilized and lost his manly edge. Clubber, his opponent, is the uncivilized man Rocky used to be. Rocky represents the modern White male who has been robbed of physical expressions of masculinity by civilization. Black male emasculation and stereotypes take firmer footing after Clubber defeats Rocky in their first bout. Suddenly Creed, once the epitome of masculinity (smart, skillful, handsome, and athletic) becomes a sort of nursemaid (much like the Black shipmate in the novel *Moby-Dick* was to Ahab) to Rocky in his quest to reclaim the title from the raw, hungry, big, brash young Black buck Clubber Lang. Here Creed devolves from noble opponent to Rocky's willing loyal servant, although it is obvious that Creed is the better conditioned and skilled athlete.

By the third film, Rocky has effectively carved out a fictional space, supplanting Creed from this heroic space and resituating notions of bad Black men. Again I turn to Bogle, who suggests that Clubber is "as repugnant as the pimp in *American Gigolo*," representing "black men as perverted street niggers who must go!" (274–75). Clubber is a BNS, and he scares middle-class America, despite his familiar serious work ethic and focus. The dominant image of Clubber is a coarse and vulgar bad man prone to lustful affronts to White masculinity (he flirts with Rocky's wife). Clubber is far from the acceptable *Negro* that Creed has become.

Not only must Clubber be depicted as an out-of-control bad man who is violent, poor, uneducated, and must go, but Creed must be emasculated, become a Tom or a faithful servant to his master, whom he teaches how to win under the guise of racial harmony. In *Rocky III*, Clubber is also raised to great heights as an unbeatable wrecking machine. Rocky's destruction of him restores and solidifies notions of White masculine supremacy.

Clubber is the new "bad nigger" with the big mouth. He is self-serving, representing all the values of BNS. He makes his own way, trains by himself, and is not committed to the American rhetoric of hope and opportunity. He sees the barriers and emerges an angry, isolated Black male unwilling to sacrifice his style, identity, or integrity in the hopes of America embracing him. He is the antithesis of the American dream. Ironically, this allows Creed to emerge as acceptable, despite his South Central Los Angeles roots. The presence of Clubber detracts attention from Creed's Blackness and his distinctive Black fighting style. He becomes Rocky's buddy who deems Rocky his superior.

What makes *Rocky III* so absurd is the premise that Creed—who can defeat Rocky, is a more skilled fighter, and is in better shape—would need Rocky to fight Clubber for him. Nonetheless, Creed trains Rocky to beat Clubber, teaching him all his tricks of the trade, even gives him his shorts from their first fight for good luck (notably outlined in the American flag). In fact, much of the action during the rematch with Clubber is culled from the "rope a dope" tactic employed by Ali during his magical defeat of George Foreman. To defeat Clubber, Rocky must fight "Black" and live in Watts, earning him everything except the burden of being Black and authenticating his existence as a champion without being Black.

But these are minor compromises, for although Apollo changes Rocky's style, at the end the "old Rock" reemerges, paving the way for maximum usage of the new boxing skills that Apollo has taught him. Again, how style is used situates the cinematic and cultural binary battle between Black and White. In the end Rocky's style is most effective, a symbol of the effectiveness of "traditional" American ideals, and that minor, not complete, change is effective—as Paulie suggested earlier in the film: "He can't fight like no Colored." Indeed, Rocky need not fully adopt Blackness to win but merely select bits and pieces of it on the way to a gritty, hard-nosed, physical, yet intelligent victory. Rocky culls from Black style without marring his identity as the new White champion. All the while these racial conflicts and implications are dangled on the fringes of the film, toyed with, then tossed out of the way so that the Black buddy motif and White supremacy reign supreme.

The only thing Rocky's faithful servant (Creed) asks in return for his help is an opportunity to redeem himself against his reconstructed, resurrected White male superior—alone, out of the glare of the public, in a private gym with just the two of them to witness it. The new Apollo wants to prove himself in private without the risk of embarrassing his master or weakening the racial contract. We never learn the outcome.

* * * *

Years ago the comedian Eddie Murphy in his comedy concert film *Raw* poked fun at how the *Rocky* films affected many White men in our culture. Murphy jokes about how a quite diminutive White male, after seeing *Rocky III*, felt so empowered that he tried to bully Murphy in a theater concession line. To paraphrase Murphy, while waiting in line to place his order before going to see *Rocky III* yet again, the man got so wound up, felt so empowered by Rocky's victory over the seemingly unbeatable Clubber, that when it was time to pay, he told the cashier: "The Nigger behind me will pay for it," pointing to Murphy. Although the skit ends with the diminutive man being punched back into his place, Murphy's narrative reveals how these fictions affect nonfictional space. Furthermore, Murphy's anecdote shows the power of sports images in situating masculinity in American culture.

The embracing of Rocky reflects the utter desperation of the racial contract. The city of Philadelphia ignored its own son and champion Joe Frazier, but raised a statue to the fictional Rocky character. In an October 2001 *GQ* magazine profile, Frazier exclaimed: "That Stallone, what a phony scam booger he is. A scavenger. The slaughterhouse, sparring with the sides of beef. I was the one. I was the one who used to run those steps. He stole that story, my story, and they put up a god-damn statute of him. Jesus!" (221). Indeed, Rocky's character ripped off one of Philly's most famous sons, Smokin' Joe Frazier. Rocky is modeled after Joe, who is a throwback, a marvel, a fighter with an engine heart and work ethic to match, a steel chin and a wicked left hook. With so many Black Joes out there, perhaps the film industry felt the American public could better appreciate his grit if a White ethnic version of him (Rocky) was the hero.

## Smart Guys and Flashy Individualists

Besides the search for a White Hope, other common motifs in American sports films are the dumb, flashy, naturally talented, alternative-style Blacks who co-mingle with intelligent White men who lead. A common theme in many sports films is that of the White males teaching non-Whites how to adhere to "proper" sports codes of ethics as well as social conduct for success and maturity. *White Men Can't Jump* (1994) is one such film that again attacks the efficiency of the Black playing style, while promoting an interracial friendship. This is one of the few films where the major Black character is smarter than his White counterpart. Sidney Deane aids Billy Hoyle in finding himself. Billy owes money to gamblers, consistently makes bad decisions, and is on the run with his girlfriend Gloria. To earn money, he hustles basketball games, playing on the myth that White boys can't play to lull his opponents into losing.

After he successfully hustles Sidney, they join forces to hustle others on the playgrounds of South Central Los Angeles. Together they evoke an American racial and cultural binary. Sidney represents the belligerence and f**k-you attitude of BNS, coupled with improvisation, wit, and spontaneity. He has flair and can effectively respond to any situation on the court. Billy, on the other hand, makes his plays without flair, makes the open jumper or lay-up, never risking flash, his eyes singularly on the prize of scoring and winning with a textbook game.

Aaron Baker has summed up this binary in style as "a metaphor for racial identities, the textbook style suggests a White ideology that accepts the rules of the game, broadly defined." Playing by the book means that "Billy avoids traits that mark the Black style that Sidney employs" (36–37). Billy's initial rejection of the improvisation of Black style as part of his own game has a broader cultural significance by implying a rejection of Black style in general in our culture. However, in fairness, Billy's biggest victory on the court occurs when he adopts Black vernacular trash talking to psyche his opponents during a tournament and to score the winning point by improvising with a dunk. A balance is struck between Billy's style and Sidney's style.

But before this occurs, Billy is clearly the antithesis to BNS. He tells Sidney, "You're just like every other brother I've seen on the playground. You'd rather look good and lose than look bad and win." Aaron Baker suggests that Billy's analysis of Black playing style is a view "commonly expressed in media discourse about the supposed ineffectiveness of black, 'playground' style of basketball" (37). In one classic BNS attitude scene in the film, Sidney signifies about outplaying Jordan one day then eschewing Jordan's suggestion that he consider joining the NBA. Hearing this, Billy asks Sidney why he passed on a chance to join the league. Sidney explains that he feared doing so might "mess up" his game. Sidney's rejection has wider social significance, for Sidney knows that the ethnic culture that drives his style and values conflict with those of the dominant culture. It is a very real barrier that is difficult to hurdle in America. He refuses to play that game, opting instead to play under his own rules on the playground. Indeed, Black style is in conflict with the White style that Billy upholds; they are binaries because the racial contract requires one to be superior and the other inferior. Many sports films engage this issue on some level (*Hoop Dreams, Any Given Sunday, Celtic Pride, Above the Rim*). They often depict non-White style, culture, and values in sports films as inferior, and athletes who represent it as insurgent criminals breaking storied traditions.

Near the end of *White Men Can't Jump*, during a big-money game, Billy's improvisational dunk is a semi-acquiescence to an alternative style. In fact, Billy's dunk is yet another example of how he is willing to rise to the challenge of giving his team victory, while simultaneously elevating White masculinity above all others. It is less a show of appreciation for

Black style, than a means of relinquishing racial stereotypes that ground White masculinity and thereby claiming victory. He proves that White men can indeed dunk and improvise—rule the day in the hood—without abandoning the *superior* textbook style of playing ball. Again, Aaron Baker is on the mark in his critique that "the film conforms to Hollywood's pattern of using black characters to define white masculinity. By setting up … [an easy friendship … it] implies that through respect for and loyalty to an African American, a white character can overcome racism" (38). Indeed, Billy maintains his game, adopting what he wants of Black style to complete his masculine presence in the game.

*  *  *  *

When White guys are not outworking the flashy, talented, underachieving (code for lazy) non-Whites in American sports films, they are busy displaying their intellect or acumen. This is nothing new to American sports culture as stereotypes of "smart" White players and "athletic" Black players abound. Who can forget Jimmy "the Greek" Snyder's comment that Blacks are better athletes to begin with because they are bred that way? Or former Los Angeles Dodgers General Manager Al Campanis's assertion that Blacks lack the necessities to be GMs or field managers. In American film, similar sentiments are conveyed.

The film *Celtic Pride* (1996) represents yet another play on the theme of good, hardworking White guy and bad or annoyingly flashy, selfish bad Black. Cultural resentment of flashy individualist BNS is the focus of this film. Luckily, hardworking, honest Average Joes are there to give proper instruction—even if it means breaking the law to restore these American ideals. In this film the culprit is Lewis Scott who plays for the Utah Jazz (from Salt Lake City, a homogenous White American city). Scott is the best player in the NBA and also the epitome of a BNS: a lazy, self-centered, individualistic, ball hog who relies on skill instead of hard work and a team concept. Scott speaks of himself in the third person, is arrogant, and a show-off. He hawks every product under the sun from hot dogs to sneakers because he lacks a moral center and pure love of sport. Scott, not the corporate culture of sports, is what is wrong with America and sports culture.

To punctuate this point, Lewis Scott is the antithesis of Mike and Jimmy (a gym teacher and plumber whose love for sports borders on insanity) who turn him around. In a drunken stupor, they "harmlessly" kidnap the NBA star to ensure their beloved Celtics will win game seven of the NBA finals. They truly represent what Noam Chomsky calls men made pacifist by the inactivity of viewing sport. Glossed over are crime and the ridiculous life of these men (losers) who play football board games, watch and are knowledgeable about sports as mundane as logrolling. They are seemingly unaware of anything else happening in the world besides sport. At one point, Jimmy and Mike compare the integrity of White logrollers and woodcutters with Lewis, whom they criticize for promoting many products. During this discussion, a commercial of the champion woodcutter appears with him hawking chainsaws. This is glossed over because as a privileged White man he does not need to be ashamed about making money from his sports celebrity. The scrutiny quickly shifts back to Lewis Scott for being on television advertisements so often.

However, despite Mike and Jimmy's *crime* of kidnapping, they are not construed as bad men. Instead, the film continues its light-hearted tone, depicting them as team players, committed fans—the Celtic's sixth man, willing to sacrifice their personal freedoms for a championship. Ironically, the real bad man is Lewis, whose morality does not measure that of passionate fans like Mike, Jimmy, and the city of Boston. Lewis is the stereotypical BNS that fails to work hard or cherish his privileged life as a sports superstar. To win, Lewis must learn from Jimmy and Mike how to be a team player. This is the good that comes from his being held hostage. Lewis escapes, and to keep from going to jail, they must root for him to win. At one point Mike yells at Lewis, whose team is trailing by many points, convincing him to pass the ball. Amazingly, Lewis listens to the voice of reason, selflessness, and morality and passes the ball. In the end Lewis wins because he changes his selfish attitude, altering his style of play completely. And, he has Jimmy and Mike to thank for this.

The film borders on the absurd, reeking with the ideology that perpetuates negative perceptions of BNS. The film is not about Lewis Scott, the subject of Mike and Jimmy's heist, but about frustrated, hardworking White males, passionate about sports, bordering on insanity, in desperate need of an outlet to fulfill notions of masculinity, yet resentful of the heroes that do not reflect them. At different points, the insanity of their situation is downplayed because they are doing it for the Celtics. This absolves their kidnapping of Lewis, making them heroes instead of criminals. The film is a cute punch at obsession with sports and a stiff jab at modern athletes. In fact, Mike and Jimmy are depicted as part of a stew of a sport-obsessed town rather than as failed individuals lacking their own identity. This point is illustrated during Lewis's failed escape. He breaks free, leaves Jimmy's house, and tries to get a cab and the help of a police officer, but both the cabdriver and police officer turn their backs on him because he is the opposition. They simply love their Celtics.

At only one point does the film aim a critical eye at sports fans and the psyche behind their obsession. On the first day Lewis is being held hostage, he reads Mike like a book, explaining his life in one minute by calling him a bitter ex–high school athlete who is mad because he wishes it were him out there playing. It hits Mike deep, but the film brushes past the machinations of a fanatic like Mike. In the end Lewis prevails because he finally listens to his newest fans and dumps his dogged individualism and flash for a more team-oriented philosophy that places a premium on hard work and blue-collar ethics instead of the crass individualism attributed to BNS and Black culture. The Bad Man whose style now resembles Jimmy and Mike's beloved Celtics is a likable character at the conclusion of the film—suggesting that kidnapping BNS and talking some sense into them might be good idea.

* * * *

The film *Jerry McGuire* (1996) starts as an innocent commentary on American sports culture, its heightened importance in our lives, the pressure placed on children to play sports, and how winning at all costs is all that matters. However, the film soon wades into the racial waters of a noble, selfless White male. Jerry McGuire is the sports agent, the behind-the-scenes guy who makes all the deals. Jerry, who works for Sports Management International (SMI), narrates the opening scene, disparaging the state of modern sports because of the corporate controls that distance fans from players, athletes' shoe, clothing, car, or soft drink deals, and the questionable morality of players. He even questions his own morality as an agent. The film is, as its title indicates, about Jerry, a selfless, moral White male who wants to take his life as an agent in a new direction. The film reads much like high-profile sports agent Leigh Steinberg's essay "The Role of a Sports Agent," where he explains the importance of agents. Jerry loses his job because he writes a memo, "The Things We Think and Do Not Say," that stresses: (1) More personal relations; (2) More caring; and (3) Less clients.

This leaves him with fewer clients, actually only one client, Rod Tidwell, a New School Baller, who personifies many of the negative stereotypes about modern Black athletes as selfish and money hungry. The first glimpse of Rod depicts him as brash, loud, unreasonable, and full of himself. Rod tells Jerry he will stay with him granted he can: "Show me the money." As poor Jerry is trying to keep his clients, Rod holds him on the phone chanting ridiculous things like: "I love the black man" or "You're my mother fucker!" and "I love black people!" and Jerry loses his entire client list.

This film is full of the myth of the noble, selfless White male. Again, the good White guy persona is juxtaposed against the rebellious Black bad man, hungry for power and money: the racial binary that is punctuated in sports films. A culture filled with avarice, corporate greed, and sharks in suits uses a Black fall guy to take the greed rap.

The film raises the popular perception that athletes are already overpaid, greedy, and generally undeserving of the money they make, especially non-White players. Rod is the classic stereotype of a BNS who has a bad attitude, is selfish, and bitches in the locker room. At one point when Jerry visits Rod at practice and Rod is standing outside the shower, a sign behind him reads "A Positive Attitude Is Better." In fact, this is the focus of their argument; Jerry wants Rod to "bury the attitude" so that he can negotiate better for him. Rod replies to Jerry, "I am an athlete; I do not entertain." Rod sounds very much like the much-maligned BNS Randy Moss, who once told the media that he plays when he wants to play, or the character Sidney in *White Men Can't Jump* who wants to play by his own rules. BNS struggle to negotiate what Todd Boyd calls fusion of "formal" (White) and "vernacular" (Black) styles. It is difficult to achieve, especially when the racial contract is openly rejected. All of the best, most creative players from Dr. J and Magic Johnson to Oscar Robertson were never embraced as Jordan has been because of Jordan's "ability to maintain a difficult balance of white approval and individual identity" (Baker 43).

The truculent nature of BNS like Bonds, Moss, and Rod, is what American sport culture finds so unacceptable. It is also proof that racial strides are negligible. The film proclaims in no uncertain terms that media, coaches, and fans are all fed up with BNS and their attitude. This is illustrated by Jerry calmly telling Rod, "Help me help you." At the end of the film after Rod has a new sense knocked into him during a Monday Night Football game, he does just that. After he regains consciousness, he realizes how fragile his career is and he entertains the people with some good old-fashioned break-dancing moves in the end zone and cries for his wife and his noble, selfless agent.

Calm is restored. Rod is not totally bad. And in the end, viewers see Jerry as the good White guy who is made even more human, despite his role as a sports colonialist (a scavenger of sorts) making money from the sweat of athletes. Jerry McGuire emerges as Rod's ambassador of what he calls "Quam," getting him the contract he desperately wanted, by convincing him to change his bad attitude.

* * *

Even a safe cartoon film starring *the* apolitical poster boy Jordan is not free from racial messages. At first glance *Space Jam* (1996) appears not to be a candidate for my discussion of the racial contract. However, upon closer examination, it raises several alarming issues regarding Black style and stereotypes. Michael Jordan, the best NBA player, has retired from basketball, trying unsuccessfully to make it as a professional baseball player. Aliens come to earth to enslave the Looney Toons characters and take them to their leader on Moron Mountain to make them entertain him and work in his amusement park forever. The Toons agree to a basketball game against the diminutive aliens to decide whether or not they will go. The aliens then go to NBA games and steal the powers of five of the best, well almost the best, players in the NBA and assume their personas as the "Monstars." The term is as loaded as *The Birth of a Nation* images of Blacks as evil, for these Monstars are the athletic wretched of the earth. As Aaron Baker contends, the identities of most of the players that have been stolen reflect "the working-class cynicism and aggressive physicality of the gangsta identity" (41) that Americans fear most. Indeed, Jordan and the Toons' victory against these "Monstars" positions Jordan, like Rocky, as an American champion whose presence is the necessary binary for carrying out the racial critique and criminalization of BNS (41). Jordan achieves this because he has been de-racialized—he is just Mike. This allows him, like Rocky, to reify traditional American ideals that have been sullied by BNS. Oddly, Mike's colorlessness is upheld as the goal for all athletes—a true sign of progress. Those who are unwilling to "Be Like Mike" fall into the historical Hollywood role of violent profane Monstars of this film. Here, Jordan's neutrality or honorary White status is held up as what all should aspire for.

The biggest problem in the film is the characterization of the modern athletes (BNS) whose powers have been stolen as "Monstars." The name is symbolic, transforming once meek little creatures into BNS who are rude, brutish, vulgar, bad men. They parallel the insurgent Blacks depicted in *The Birth of a Nation*. Because the character depictions are cartoons, it seems harmless, but these Monstars represent BNS, who play dirty, are very physical, and lack true skills beyond athleticism. Using two of the NBA's most notorious bad boys at the time (Barkley and Johnson) confirms the subliminal negative commentary on modern basketball players' style, their intellect, and unwillingness to acquiesce to White culture. The film also suggests that if BNS were without their powers—their God-given gifts of extraordinary athletic ability—they would be unable to compete. They lack the mental acuity for the fundamental skills to fill the void left by the loss of their physical skills. Furthermore, Whiteness is disguised in the form of Toon characters that with the help of Jordan (the acceptable standard in the modern athlete) are able to defeat the Monstars (BNS) using courage, hard work, and acute wit. Everything that the Monstars lack or refuse to work for.

However, to be fair, some of the films outlined above do depart somewhat from the monochromatic masculine depictions and stringent racial myths. For example, Jordan, Sidney, and Rod all work hard, take care of their families, and practice a modicum of deferred gratification. For example, it is Sidney who advises Billy in money and love. Still, the stereotypes and critiques of Blackness are undeniable. Most of the films suggest that the bad attitude of BNS is what is wrong in professional sports.

### The Paternal Good Whites and Dumb Jocks

However, when it comes to smart Black guys who are athletes, the paradigm shifts in a different direction. The embrace of smart athletes changes drastically when their hue is much darker, such is the case in the films *Finding Forrester*, *Any Given Sunday*, and *Glory Road*. While my discussion will not engage the latter film, it is certainly steeped in the same formula and ideology of race and paternalism I discuss in *Finding Forrester* and *Any Given Sunday*. As Howard Winant has pointed out, Whiteness has been placed in peril since the arguments for the biological superiority of Whites have come under serious attack during the post–civil rights era.

In response to this, a program of reinterpreting, rearticulating, and representing race and Whiteness has been in action. According to Hernán Vera and Andrew Gordon, "These rearticulations, paradoxically, can only be achieved by conceding dramatic changes in the image of African Americans and other minorities but still reproducing the old image of the heroic white self"( 187).

Let us begin our interrogation of such images in *Finding Forrester*. This film is a perfect example of paradoxical rearticulations and reproductions of old images, despite alterations in the image of the racial other—Black male. Here, the dumb jock motif battles against notions of intellect and physical skills for a Black male. The protagonist Jamal, a brilliant young student, faces harsh scrutiny because the board of trustee members, teachers, and coaches do not believe that Blacks, especially athletes, are capable of succeeding in Malor Callow academically. In fact, they do not believe Blacks are capable of doing anything except putting a basketball through a hoop. Throughout the film, the racial contract is in play. Every intellectual display from Jamal is either questioned, ignored, or the direct result of the influence of his White father figure—William Forrester.

Although Jamal has been offered a scholarship because of intellect, no one at Malor Callow cares about his intellectual promise; in their eyes he is a prized athlete. This is tragically true of Jamal's English instructor, Mr. Crawford, who is completely consumed with notions of Black inferiority. Crawford refuses to believe Jamal's work is authentic or that he possesses any intellect. So after Jamal writes a very good paper, Crawford decides he will schedule time in his office to watch Jamal write the next essay to prove he has done the work himself.

After Jamal is accused of cheating on an essay submitted to a student-writing contest, the chair of the board of trustees allows him to play in the championship game. During halftime of the game, he pulls Jamal aside to tell him that the school is willing to enroll him in easier classes and that he only needs to worry about winning championships for the school. Jamal realizes that they do not see him at all.

Thus, it is not until William Forrester steps to the podium—neo-slave narrative style—to give a public validating statement on Jamal's behalf that his intellectual agency and his skills as a writer are embraced. Forrester's role is validating liberal White voice to prove that the young Jamal is as articulate and intelligent as his voice and essays suggest. The scenario harkens one back to the slave narrative tradition where a White benefactor is needed to vouch for the literacy of the former slave author in question.

Indeed, the film is similar to the eighteenth- and nineteenth-century slave narratives that require an authenticating White abolitionist voice to confirm that the slave had indeed written the text him- or herself. Forrester is the only voice that Crawford, a racist blinded by his conviction or adherence to the racial contract, will believe—even if it means public embarrassment. Racism completely blinds Crawford from ever accepting that any Black, especially a good athlete from the Bronx, can be "this good" of a writer. It is only when William reads Jamal's wonderful essay before the entire school that he is recognized as a good writer—grudgingly authenticated.

While this film struggles to reverse stereotypes that suggest Blacks, especially athletes, are intellectually inferior, it also reminds us that the challenges facing modern non-Whites in the modern world—albeit cloaked, are real. The struggle continues to be one over visibility and subjectivity in the face of racism. Jamal asserts his subjectivity in the championship game that simulates his life and the decision he must make to demand being viewed as more than a dumb nigger and a jock. His life is in flux like the score in the final minutes of the game. As he stands at the free-throw line at the end of regulation, his own fate and the fate of his team in his hands; the game is his alone to win or lose. He is a superb free-throw shooter (earlier in the film he made fifty straight free throws in practice). At this moment his greatest struggle is how to negotiate his identity as a Black male, an intellectual, and an athlete—a supremely difficult task.

Jamal finds an alternative mode of communication. He speaks through basketball. As he stands at the free-throw line with time expired contemplating all that he has experienced, he must navigate a conundrum: if he makes his shot and wins the game he loses his quest to be recognized for his intellect. Jamal's foul shots are also symbolic because several personal fouls have been committed upon his person, his humanity, throughout the film. Missing the free throws is a subversive act of resistance. After Jamal makes his point on the court, the overpowering presence of the paternal "Good White" (Forrester) hinders his quest at the end when he speaks Jamal's words from the letter he has given him. Although he proclaims to the world that Jamal is a brilliant writer, he also assumes credit for Jamal's development as a writer. Thus, in a minor way, Crawford's assertion that a Black kid, without some assistance, cannot write the way that Jamal does is confirmed. In the end, Forrester is positioned as an inspirational White father figure, or as Jamal tells his older brother, his "teacher."

Although Jamal does aid Forrester's reentry into the world, helping him confront his guilt regarding his brother's death, Forrester ultimately functions as Jamal's literary father figure. The film is definitely an improved representation of the racial other and racial contract. Forrester traces the path Jamal marks during the championship game, and it is Jamal's act on the court, coupled with his essay to Forrester, that sparks Forrester's courage to leave his house on his own for the first time in decades. Yet in the final analysis, Forrester's voice echoes the important life lessons Jamal has etched on the pages that Forrester reads. The racial contract, in the end, will not allow Jamal's voice to be completely heard, although his ideas are conveyed. Despite Jamal's power of amazing literacy, only Forrester's White privilege can make that voice audible. And, at the conclusion of the film Forrester's directives to Jamal are among the last words heard.

*Any Given Sunday*

Perhaps one of the most pivotal sports films that engages paternalism along with negative images of New School Ballers is Oliver Stone's film about professional football, *Any Given Sunday*. Stone gets a lot of stuff correct, but he also perpetuates many stereotypes regarding modern athletes of color. The film laments a passing era when White males who "understood" how to play football and realized its "integrity" dominated the field.

In *Any Given Sunday*, race, power, and playing style issues dominate the story as the star Black quarterback, Willie Beamen, plays the game his way: loose, creative, and as an offensive genius. Willie epitomizes a BNS whose style and manner threaten modern society. He is hip-hop on the playing field—innovative and free-styling, displaying an attitude consumed with calling shots on his own terms. His Blackness, expression, and style of play are deemed a direct affront to Coach D'Amato and to tradition; his presence as quarterback threatens all that is good and correct about football and America. But Willie also conveys, perhaps unintentionally, the worldview of BNS who are disgusted with illusions of access and the reality of subtle and not-so-subtle roadblocks to democracy and equal opportunity.

The symbols of this high moral ground are Cap Rooney, a White quarterback, and Tony D'Amato, the old White coach. Both are at the end of their respective ropes, being run out of the game by outsiders: the new female owner, Christina Pagniacci, and Willie Beamen, the upstart Black quarterback. Willie is, in the words of Cap, "breathing down [his] neck," as he vies to be the new team leader. The stereotypes enter as soon as Willie enters the game. Willie, a typical BNS, was previously on the bench eating popcorn, not paying attention to the game, talking to teammates instead of warming up. Upon entry into the game, Willie—the dumb jock, a typical BNS—is hindered because of his poor work poor ethic that has left him unprepared to play effectively, and thus he needs to have things simplified.

Although he plays admirably, the team still loses because Coach D'Amato, representing a man stuck in the past, calls the same play three straight times, the third time resulting in a fumble that loses the game. Nonetheless, the game announcer blames the miscue on the flashy running back Julian Washington's greed (he is to receive a $1 million bonus once he reaches 1,500 yards rushing).

Tony embodies a sports culture reluctant to embrace BNS on their own terms. In *Any Given Sunday*, Willie represents the New School Baller or subversive bad man in African American folklore. But more literally, Willie reflects a generation that does not fear going against the grain, calling its own shots. Ironically, Willie repeatedly calls his own plays in the huddle because he functions best by doing things his way. And the "shots" Willie calls produce points and victories, pulling the team out of a four-game losing streak.

Despite this success, Coach D'Amato is livid that Willie is acting subversively. At one point Willie responds to Tony's anger by telling him sarcastically, "I'm with ya boss," although he is intent on playing on his own terms. In one sequence, Willie changes the play of one formation while violating all the rules of good quarterbacking, and throws off his back foot for a long touchdown. Willie does things his own way and is successful.

Oddly, in a culture that rewards individual accolades over team success, Willie is chided for any displays of individualism, earning him the stigma "hotshot," an inefficient leader. Cap Rooney warns Willie after a victory: "You go out there by yourself, you are gonna die a lonely death." Cap the White, aging quarterback is the antithesis of Willie's rise to the top to emphasize what the change or new breed really means.

At one point, Willie and Cap do a commercial together, and Cap, the consummate team player, gives Willie the "best" line, which draws a flock of kids to Willie at the end asking for his autograph. Cap looks on sadly, a fallen warrior being pushed aside by the New Jack who cares only for himself in a business and society that does not look out for the little guy nor disperse resources equitably. Aware of this, Cap, the consummate team player, explains his line choice to his wife: "No, giving, team sport, those are the lines." To which his aggressive wife replies: "Meanwhile, honey, you used to do this spot alone." Even as he is being displaced, Cap rises to the higher moral ground. He is depicted as completely selfless even when Tony visits him at his sprawling mansion.

Through Willie, the film indicts the disruptiveness of women and hip-hop-influenced modern athletes. BNS are depicted as too "ballerific," with their b-boy street flair, undisciplined prodigious talent, and cocky attitudes. This critique marginalizes Black players and women, making clear that gender and racial parity or diversity is bad for sports culture. For example, a female owner, Pagniacci is depicted as very uncompassionate, business-first, and cold—unlike the many White male owners. And the aging and injured White quarterback, Cap, who fears being supplanted by Willie, complains constantly to Tony that Willie is unprepared, "not doing his homework," does not "give a gee whiz about anybody," and is concerned only "with making the plays himself." I read this as a belief that women and non-Whites lack the populist work ethic and self-reliant masculinity of White males like Cap and Tony.

In response to these complaints, despite two consecutive Willie-engineered victories, Tony calls an informal one-on-one meeting with Willie to discuss suitable leadership models for the team, which better reflect his own ideology instead of Willie's more hip-hop-influenced innovative approach. Tony intends to rid him of selfishness and rebellion and make him more like Cap. During this meeting, Willie and Tony have an honest dialogue about leadership, race, morality, and the business of sports.

In this exchange, director Oliver Stone situates Tony as the good White savior or father in contrast to the greedy, sexist, materialist, undisciplined Black players. During the conversation, Willie—impatient with Tony's nostalgic, narrow-minded paternalistic perspective—stops playing "yes sir man" with Tony midway through their meeting. He finally reproves him, shattering Tony's static notions. His response challenges Tony to recognize the truth about amateur and professional sport culture in modern America. Disgusted with Tony's blindness, he enlightens him by telling him: "It's about the money. Raking in the TV contracts. Fat-cat boosters and coaches trying to up they salary. And all the time what you looking for? You looking for the next Black stud to take you to the next top-ten bowl game. It's the same way in the pros, except in the pros the field hands get paid." Ironically, Willie need not point this out to Tony, for his home is quite lavish, reflecting his wealth. He knows about the money available and at stake; the game has made him wealthy. But again the suggestion is that he, unlike BNS like Willie, has *earned* it. After Tony dismisses Willie's accusation that he might be racist, Willie relents suggesting to Tony that perhaps the problem is "not racism, [but] its placism, a brother has to know his place." Indeed, even if he refuses to sign, Willie understands the terms of the racial contract he must sign for upward mobility.

Tony wants Willie to exhibit a brand of leadership that he approves of, one where sacrifice, taking the fall, is central to success. Meanwhile Willie, who has been the sacrificial lamb of racism, is intent on playing, and leading his way. He says to Tony, "You want me to sacrifice for the greater glory of Cap Rooney? Well, f**k you, coach! I ain't buyin' your brand!" Willie is convinced that Tony is afraid that he will continue to have success playing on his own terms—disrupting the racial contract. The economics of sports culture, the stage he finds himself in his career, force Willie to, as he says, "play my way, up my dollars so that when ya'll go to trade me, waive me, injured reserve me, or whatever the f**k it is ya'll do, I'll be worth ten times what I was worth before I got here."

However, the words of teammate "Shark" resonate most with Willie. After his meeting with the coach Shark chastises him in the sauna after a terrible game preempted by Willie accusing the entire team of being anything but a team. Shark explains to him the rules of manhood and the reality of race: "You led, nigger, but did anybody follow? Let me tell you something, for every sucker who makes it, for every Jerry Rice or Barry Sanders, there is a hundred niggers you never even heard of. Sure, the game has taught you how to strut, how to talk shit, but what else? When a man looks back on his life, it shouldn't just be the time he spent in pads and cleats, it should be all of it. You gotta learn that, Willie, or if you don't, you ain't a man, you just another punk."

Manhood is also a dominant theme of the film, which is why Willie's nomenclature has such symbolic significance. The name (Willie Beamen) begs the question of our protagonist: Will he be a man or more literally will the new generation of athletes (two-thirds of which are Black) be men equal to their White predecessors? Of course the marker of the manhood that Shark outlines to Willie is answered in the very next scene, which begins at the estate of Cap Rooney, who is visited by Tony. In this scene, Cap is spending quality time with his family, having a cookout with his wife and children. His manhood transcends football; he is a devoted husband and father, provider, nurturer. Yet Cap's masculinity, even director Oliver Stone seems to admit, is mythical. As Cap explains to his wife that he plans to retire at the conclusion of the season, she slaps him, telling him, "I will not listen to this bullshit from you," and strides out of the room. The affront to Cap's manhood is complete. First it was the BNS Willie, then a woman. He must redeem himself—and Stone makes certain he does.

The issue of leadership and race are most clearly realized in the battle between Cap and Willie for the starting quarterback position. Willie is stronger, faster, more creative on the field than Cap, yet it is consistently insinuated that perhaps Willie is not smart enough to lead the team or too selfish to be an effective leader. Cap's leadership vision and style is the model Willie is told to emulate or risk being benched.

In the end, Stone does make Willie sign a slightly modified version of the racial contract. As the film draws to an end, Willie, who has been in the background, doing things his own way, suddenly is transformed and joins the group, follows the rules, does things Tony's way with the guidance of Cap. In doing so, he miraculously learns from and supports Cap as the starter. During the second half of the final game Cap announces he can play no more, but he spends the second half guiding his noble young mentee in the ways of leadership. Willie finally becomes Tony's quarterback. He is no longer thought to be like a flash-in-the-pan running back or receiver; he is a quarterback, the top spot, the leader and authority on the field. And, once Willie embraces and signs the racial contract, the conflict of leadership and race dissipate.

The entire film attacks modern Black athletes. They are painted as amoral, greedy, selfish, stupid, violent, irrational caricatures of Stone's imagination. This point is magnified during a fund-raiser supporting eradication of drugs, crime, and so on. Ironically, only the Black members of the team are in a bathroom with groupies and drugs. The film seems to scream "look at what these BNS are doing with our women!" It also situates the new breed as lacking the decorum, ethics, and morals of a previous era of *men* like Tony, who pays expensive prostitutes to come to his home and is willing to date them.

The film is a false embrace of mythical American cultural pluralism and cultural identity. Willie represents the obstacle that BNS pose in the lives of White heroes like Tony and Cap. Tony is disconnected from his players and does not accept Willie's identity, as Willie embraces the *rules of the game*. BNS and modern coaches are a divergent lot. Swept under the rug is the extreme wealth, the lavish homes and mansions of the star White player, head coach, and owners. Oddly, the worst person in the film is new owner Christina Pagniacci, the daughter of the deceased former owner who is depicted as a ruthless bitch. But somehow the White male powerbrokers and owners dodge this characterization.

Although near the end the team comes together around Willie, Stone refuses to allow the BNS to bask in the glory of balling and shot calling too long without making clear that Willie owes his new status and success to his mentors. After the playoff victory, Willie tells Tony, "I can't get over it. I learned more from watching Cap in the first half than I have learned in five years."

Tony's resignation as coach of the Sharks and his new position as GM and coach of another team, along with his signing of his reformed BNS (Willie), is far less a concession or breach of the racial contract, but a slight modification. Tony's masculine superiority emerges unblemished, in fact, as coach and GM he calls even more shots than before. Although Tony makes a slight concession to his BNS, it is still from an even higher position of power than he previously possessed. He embraces Willie only because he realizes it is his best chance for success in the new era. In the end the film trumpets the message that leaders are always White and males. And in this film, any leader who fails to fit this description is fraught with moral and intellectual deficiencies. The Willies symbolize contemporary athletes who with their tattoos, cornrows, "attitude," lack of humility, and edgy Black self-expression, need to be men like Cap and Tony.

Although Willie may be the modern corporate reality of sports culture, the film makes certain to remind us that they are also egomaniacs and villains who have marred the hero image of fans' and sportswriters' boyhoods. Director Oliver Stone parodies BNS in the form of a commercial that has Willie rapping and dancing while selling a product— all the while lauding his greatness after only a few victories. This further suggests that BNS lack class, seek instant fame, and, unlike the Cap Rooneys of the world, lack an understanding of the proper codes of sports hero conduct—even more proof that the racial contract is correct.

\* \* \*

In the end, *Any Given Sunday* is little more than an indictment against BNS that maintains the stereotypes of them as less intelligent, selfish, lazy, purely physical, self-absorbed, and greedy. In many ways it reifies notions that they lack the qualities of a previous era of players. All the while, the film resituates the authority of White males like Tony D'Amato, who struggle in the modern world to teach boys like Willie to be men; to adopt his values, or subordinate their own values and ethnics. Oddly, as Aaron Baker remarks, "Beamen has his best game once he subordinates his outward assertion of ego" (144).

This film captures the essence of the conflicts, themes, and commentary on race in society. Actually this narrative of White male protagonists as heroic men who must struggle against non-White men and women to maintain their rightful status is woven through many sports films. The success of the *Rocky* sequels, the depictions of White coaches as powerful, paternalistic, dominant, moral figures pulsing across the movie screen, coupled with the new White athletes who are physical and smart heroes, conflate to preserve the myth of White masculine dominance in sport via film.

The image of non-White figures in modern sports films is not very far removed from the "Negrophobic" dangers outlined in *The Birth of a Nation*. This point is confirmed in *Any Given Sunday*, as BNS threaten chaos on a once proud and orderly American sports culture. Willie parallels the vicious upstart Black Silas Lynch in *The Birth of a Nation*, who, discontented with his lot, starts war and disrupts the idyllic South. The twist in *Any Given Sunday* is that a White woman also threatens the White male superior status. Meanwhile, Black masculinity maintains a hypermasculine façade of being aggressive, immoral, unruly, and intellectually inferior. Such images in sports films are integral to perpetuating both the racial contract and perceptions of a superior White masculine identity.

# CHAPTER EIGHT

## AVERAGE JOES, COMPLACENCY, POLITICS, AND SPORTS

> *Sports keeps people from worrying about things that matter to their lives that they might have some idea of doing something about. Sports is a major factor in controlling people.*
>
> —Noam Chomsky

Once while giving a lecture on racism in sports and American culture, I was asked why there is so much emphasis placed on sports in our culture. It was the type of question I usually pose to my students during the first week of a class then return to at the end of the semester. It was a question that perplexed ancient Rome. It was precisely the type of question I had hoped my lecture would produce. In a society that prides itself on being filled with intelligent people, the American sports fetish or preoccupation seems in direct conflict with the superior culture signals projected worldwide. One obvious answer is that sport allows an escape from it all—one can let go and root for the home team. Sports also proclaim America as so stable and wealthy that its citizenry can organize and preoccupy themselves with games.

Another answer might be that sports remind us of all of the games we played as kids: kick ball, dodgeball, wall ball, and so on. Sports are youthful, and we take great pleasure in watching talented young men and women at play. Thus, despite the hue or social background of the professional players, we all connect because games allow us to recall a different time in our life—a period when our life went at an easier pace, was less structured and more impromptu. Sports remind us of our childhoods, when we were free and time was actually timeless. Sports are the linchpins to our youth and, sadly, signifiers that we have grown up. Sports remind us to have hope.

Of course, the best answer to why we like sports is a combination of all the above. However, I contend that sports also prove the following: (1) equity and opportunity are never far away, but money, race, and class divisions are real deterrents; (2) sports also divert us from conversations of political, economic, or social criticisms and analysis, while subtly cultivating jingoists; and (3) along with this diversion, sports shape how Average Joes (hereafter "Josina" is inclusive, for I use this term without limiting gender, race, or class) discern these very issues via the heroics of gladiators' exploits on and off fields of competition. The heroes that are conjured or "branded"—compliments of the marketing genius of sports apparel companies like Adidas, Nike, and sports leagues—have more credibility on social issues than a credentialed politician or cultural critic! However, the answer I like best is Noam Chomsky's contention that sport is an important tool for governance because "if you can personalize events of the world . . . you've succeeded in directing people away from what really matters and is important."[1]

In addition to its power to atomize, making obedient nonparticipants, sport is also a unique tool for controlling society. Although fans are nonparticipants, they personalize the events that take place on the playing field, hence sports direct people away from what really matters and is important. Fans empathize with, even feel connected to, Michael Jordan's comeback or to the Chicago Cub's tireless quest for a championship, instead of who has friends on boards of companies that receive multibillion-dollar government military contracts, or no-bid contracts to manage disaster relief, and the lack of sufficient government response to Hurricane Katrina in New Orleans. Indeed, sports pose a dangerous dulling threat, the perfect diversion from matters of importance in the world.

But the question of why sport is so important made me ponder the power of sport in our world. If used correctly it has the potential to provide a platform for resolving the nation's internal and external differences, and can be an effective tool for making a positive impact on the lives of others. As John R. Gerdy alludes in his important study *Sports: The All-American Addiction* (2002), sports can also stifle and reinforce these conflicts.[2] Sports represent public culture, or the enactment of rituals, symbols, and expressions that define social relations and shape public life. The obsession and investment in organized sport encourages and promotes intellectually passive fans, running counter to a culture of intellectualism necessary in the new millennium. The truth is that passiveness in sports encourages passiveness in social life and in politics. Furthermore, the subtle messages it sends can negatively impact the development of a progressive and equitable society.

When the average Joe is sitting on a couch on Sunday watching NFL games, rooting for a team with buddies, downing a few brews, chances are the only thing that crosses his mind are the scores that flash across the bottom of the screen. Of course, he might also be wondering when the pizza guy will arrive with the order he placed twenty-five minutes ago. Perhaps he is considering validity of the myopic views of figures like Mitch Albom and Mike Lupica. But chances are he is distracted from thinking about the North American Free Trade Agreement's impact on developing countries. He might have been pondering if there really were "weapons of mass destruction." But since it is Sunday and nearly noon, all Joe wants is to relax, enjoy the game, a few brews, and block out the distractions and realities of the world. He busies himself with thoughts of his fantasy league team players' stats, schedules, weather conditions, fan noise, time on the clock, and the score of games.

The Average Joe that I envision is a caricature of a dedicated sports fan unable or unwilling to invoke a sophisticated political, social, and intellectual perception of the world equal to that invoked regarding sports topics. Unfortunately, the primary focus of far too many Americans is who won the game last night or how *their* team will fare next season. The discussions are endless, the passion for sports undeniable. It is not uncommon at social gatherings to find sports talk dominating conversations. In fact, it is not uncommon for a heated discussion to erupt over player trades, how much athletes should be paid, or the merits of firing one coach or hiring another one. Average Joe is diverted from pressing issues by sports even when those issues are sports related!

Unfortunately, there is much recent proof of passivity and anti-intellectualism in these United States: (1) the lack of response to diminished Fourth Amendment rights via crime bills in the 1990s; (2) the absent outrage that the vice president was affiliated with a company that was awarded a multibillion-dollar contract for the Iraq War (number two) without bidding; (3) the dissipation of social programs, while military defense spending nears record highs; (4) the shameful display of democracy that resulted in a Bush victory in the 2000 presidential election; (5) little unified public outrage that there were never any weapons of mass destruction in Iraq; (6) scant concern that the behavior of the United States in the Israel-Palestinian conflict has been improper; and (7) little notice or concern that in college sports African American athletes dominate the top revenue-producing sports (football and basketball), while there are few coaches or administrators of color, and that less of these athletes graduate. Instead, even the many intelligent American Joes are immersed in who will win the Final Four, the NBA Finals, the Super Bowl, and the World Series, or celebrating breaking the curse of the Bambino.

Alas, in contemporary society, competitive team games play a significant role in the life of the nation and in the moods of the populace. Unfortunately, too many Average Joes would rather spend weekends, evenings after work, or leisure time escaping into the fantasy world of sports instead of worrying about the complex and contradictory millennial of regressive racial and social politics.

To complicate matters further, we live in a world where for twenty-four hours each day twenty-first-century Joes are bombarded from every angle with sports to escape the doldrums of their "civilized" law-abiding lives. Sports talk is everywhere; sports reporting is always available instantly via Internet sites, blogs, talk radio, fantasy leagues, video games, and of course ESPN, the most profitable programming on television. Furthermore, sports function to instill and reify beliefs, values, and principles of hierarchy while molding jingoists. These jingoists are less prone to question or protest. They are so accustomed to sitting in front of a television eating and watching instead of participating, that it impacts other avenues of their lives. The passive consumption of sport has hindered community action or interest in poverty, education, arts, or discrimination. As Gerdy explains in *Sports*, we are paying a price "for our shift from active participation to passive consumption of sport." For example, there was no outrage that former President George W. Bush made several key Supreme Court appointments that will erode many of the gains of the civil rights movement. Also, the University of Michigan admission policy was a key marker of what the conservative right has been doing for at least twenty-five years to turn back the clock of progress.

No, Joe is too distracted contemplating the playoff status of the home team to worry that affirmative action via the University of Michigan's admissions policy was merely the beginning of civil rights reversals that await the United States in the future. But with less than four seconds remaining on the clock and Joe's team poised to sink the game-winning shot, he is unable to worry that the gains from the landmark 1954 *Brown v. Board of Education* are quickly disappearing. There are no replays on *Sports Center* to inform Joe that only thirty percent of schools are integrated in the twenty-first century—and those numbers are declining! People more often than not want to forget important social or political moments in history, but love to watch the ESPN Classic channel, which replays the most thrilling sporting events in history.

Indeed sport is everywhere, the obsession with sports distract Americans into becoming more concerned with issues such as who will win a championship, athletes' salaries, or whether LeBron James should have gone to college for a few years before turning professional. There was far greater interest in Kobe Bryant's and other non-White athletes' morality in the media than in pressing social and political news. (People are more apt to ask you what you thought about "the game last night" than about war casualties or the war.)

But it is not all Joe's fault. Who can think straight when television networks and sports organizations have designed and packaged sports programs that lure him to watch games and sports news around the clock? Every year ESPN finds new sports programs to whet the insatiable appetite of its sports-hungry American audience. Furthermore, because Joes (of all races and genders) see legions of Black talk-show hosts, rich entertainers, and rich Latino and Black athletes running touchdowns, hitting home runs, and dunking basketballs, they are convinced that racial problems are a thing of America's past. So Joe returns to sports viewing comfortable that equality and social parity have been achieved. Meanwhile, his office or union membership is far from integrated. The games have him trapped on his couch; he can barely find time to get up and *act* or think clearly. The problems of the world seem less important than winning a title or reversing the curse for the Cubs.

## Sport in the Life of Joe

In *The Meaning of Sports*, Michael Mandelbaum contends that sports drama mounts over time. He explains that "in organized sports the tension carries beyond each individual game and tends to increase over time. Each game is part of a designated sequence—a season—the goal of which is to produce a champion. In this way baseball, football, and basketball [and hockey too] resemble the oldest of literary forms, the epic" (5). Sports present weekly, even daily challenges that must be met and defeated as one moves toward the clear goal of gaining a championship. It appeals to what Mandelbaum calls "human affairs of coherence." Just as every literary epic has a hero, sports are no different. In the modern world, the men of action—Ernest Hemmingway-like, standing on the edge of the ultimate; virile men of vigorous outdoor activity, working their masculine "mojo"—have been supplanted. The maleness of the past has lost its way since the twentieth century. The rise of middle-class, "less rugged" occupations and increasing interest in "feminine" occupations—along with deconstruction of White male notions of strength and social authority in modern sports conflate to trouble, racial dominance and plague Joes in the twenty-first century. Although not adequately engaged here, homophobia further complicates the confusion regarding how manhood can and should be understood.

Sport media avoid issues of race, homophobia, and misogyny which is ironic because much of the racial and gender tension in our society is bred in sports culture. What makes this more complicated and frustrating for most American males is that society has shifted from labor-intensive industries to a computer and desk economy of minimal physical exertion. There are fewer physical outlets for measuring masculinity for the Average Joe.[3] Therefore he places the heavy burden of "role model" on the shoulders of his sports heroes. The problem is that in the modern world, White male athletes once personified this manhood (in high-profile sports) but have been supplanted by many non-Whites. Joe is torn. He wants to emulate his hero, but the media message and the hue of modern heroes tells him otherwise.

To make matters worse, Average Joe is trapped in an endless parade of sports programs, slowly dying a premature death without a tangible social structure to define his masculinity. For Joe, a typical Saturday in September morphs into a full day of watching college football and a Major League Baseball game—between running minimal necessary errands during halftimes and the fifth inning, unless, of course, the games are close. Certainly not all Joes are couch potatoes. Some believe in social activity, so they attend college football games instead of watching passively on television. These Joes get an early start by tailgating outside the stadiums early in the morning until game time. Some actually go into the stadium, but others watch on portable televisions from the parking lot. If the team is victorious, they wind down with drinking, more eating, and perhaps a postgame celebration at the local pub with more passive viewing of highlights from the games of the day.

Average Joe spends Sunday recuperating from Saturday while watching professional football games, capped by more Major League Baseball. Just as was the case for college football, fans of professional football also engage in the tailgating ritual. Meanwhile, homebound Joes peruse the Sunday paper and sports shows until the NFL games begin in the early afternoon. Joe spends the day surfing between games, eating, and drinking. By evening, instead of spending time reflecting on society, culture, or politics with renewed insights, or even spending time with his family, our Joe remains immersed in the euphoria from his favorite team's victory or the anguish from their defeat. If his team loses, Joe might suffer from depression for an entire week. But the Joes lucky enough to have cable television are able to review *NFL Primetime* on Sunday night to sort out the events of the day—figure out what their team did right or wrong. Invariably there are Joes who missed the games because they had to work, take care of some chores, or spend time with their family. For those Joes, God was gracious enough to invent *Sunday Night Football* and *Monday Night Football*. And on Thanksgiving, Joe is most thankful for Thanksgiving Day football games.

To get through the week during football season, to ease their sports obsession, baseball games fill the void in September and October. There are pennant races to keep tabs on, races that Joe neglected over the weekend while following football. These "important" baseball games and, with a little luck, *Friday Night Lights* get him safely through each week and into the weekend. Sport permeates American culture.

Before autumn lingers into winter, Major League Baseball playoffs culminates with the World Series in October. With the loss of baseball until April, sports fans are pacified with nightly college and professional basketball games to get them through the week and into more sports-filled weekends. And when the college football bonanza peters out soon after New Year's Day, college and professional basketball edge toward center stage on the heels of the NFL Playoffs and Super Bowl. The week or two prior to the Super Bowl, nothing else really matters and not much else is planned, except for key college and professional basketball matchups on the Saturday and Sunday before the game, which serve as appetizers to the Super Bowl feast.

Soon after a Super Bowl champion is crowned, the marketing cry of either Big Monday, Big Wednesday, or Big Tuesday is heard from the college basketball ranks. This occurs until late February, when eternal conference tournaments decide and redeem the fate of teams hoping to make the big NCAA tournament that will decide who will be national champion of college basketball (known as "March Madness" and "The Road to the Final Four"). During the first week of April when the new national champion is crowned, fans, infected with basketball craziness, suddenly turn their full attention to a professional basketball season that is winding down into very competitive playoff runs.

For the next two months, every NBA game is of "utmost" importance, each outcome determining playoff positioning or home court advantage for the playoffs. Finally, in the first week of June—when a team emerges kissing that NBA championship trophy, and the professional basketball season is over, and when hockey's Stanley Cup is held high—Joe's attention shifts back to Major League Baseball, which began April 1 and is now in full swing. There is also some time to follow the Masters and the British Open and Wimbledon for a few days of the summer. But the spring culminates with NBA playoffs and the daily drama surrounding the road to a championship.

Joes previously too preoccupied with NBA and Stanley Cup playoffs use the early summer to reacquaint themselves with batting averages, ERAs (earned run averages), and perhaps even spend a few lazy summer days at the ballpark with their families. For two months fans settle into La-Z-Boy chairs, box seats, and bleachers to focus on "America's pastime." Family time emerges on the way to ballparks, before games, between innings, while yelling at players and umpires, keeping score, fending off catcalls of "Peanuts!" and "Cold beer here!" and during seventh-inning stretches singing: "Take Me Out to the Ball Game."

But by late August, this romance begins to lose some of its luster to make room for the U.S. Open and the ensuing college and professional regular seasons in September, and the whole cycle starts over again. Every two years the Winter or Summer Olympics are an added bonus for Joe, who adds a variety of Olympic sports to his viewing repertoire.

Within the brief context of the year in sports that I have just described, there is little real time for obsessed fans to give serious thought to issues besides how their teams are doing or whom their teams might trade or acquire to increase their chances at winning a championship. Perhaps it is by design. But it is clear that American culture is programmed to fill all of our leisure time with mind-numbing, passive, leisure activities.

In *Secret Lies and Democracy*, Noam Chomsky best explains the phenomenon of sport in our culture. He contends that "spectator sports make people more passive, because you're not doing them—you're watching somebody doing them." This passive behavior "engender[s] jingoist and chauvinist attitudes."[4] The jingoist part was proven to be true post-September 11, 2001, when the World Trade Center in New York City was destroyed and all teams sewed flags on uniforms and used sports platforms to encourage American patriotism.

When this travesty occurred, sporting events took a brief vacation while security was increased at the ballparks. And like the new ruler of Rome in the movie *Gladiator*, President Bush knew he needed the public's focus to return to the games instead of his foils, namely the ensuing declaration of war without proof of "weapons of mass destruction." Within a week of the bombing, the NFL had all teams back on the field. Barry Bonds stepped back into the batter's box to resume his quest to break the home run record set by Mark McGwire (which he did to the tune of 73 home runs) and things continued as usual. Well, almost. Suddenly players were found giving pro-America statements between commercials of games, while displaying U.S. flags on the shoulders of their uniforms (management was responsible for this) and waving flags before and after games (something many took upon themselves). I watched in disappointment as many big-name football and baseball stars were shown waving flags or reciting written statements subtly endorsing war and engendering blind patriotism—jingoism at its best. My disgust arose from the use of sports an allegedly apolitical space as platforms for encouraging jingoism and filibustering for support of war.

It all contradicted the claim that sport is a apolitical. Sport, I was always told, is the single safe haven of conversation. It is the one thing that allows total strangers to break awkward silences in elevators. However, sport is a wonderful conduit for conveying all sorts of messages from politics and patriotism to fighting racism and notions of supremacy and inferiority. Therefore I was not surprised that football or baseball was used in this manner. In fact, football players participate in the one game that most simulates war. After the 9/11 travesty, Mayor Giuliani and President George W. Bush were present at the World Series—they took center stage, using the games as a platform for patriotism. Led by George Bush, an even bigger deal was made of singing the national anthem before every game, and the seventh inning stretch song "Take Me Out To the Ball Game" was replaced with the Star Spangled Banner. The purpose to increase a loyalist/nationalist and flag-waving spirit. Sports, the space that members of the media and fans proclaim is free from politics, became the catalyst for rallying political or nationalist sentiment.

You see, sports are political; it just depends on what the politics are and who has power in sports culture. For example, a different set of rules applied for former Denver Nuggets guard Mahmoud Abdul-Rauf (Chris Jackson), who was crudely and systematically banished from the NBA during the prime of his career for refusing to stand during the playing of the national anthem because he felt the flag and the song were symbols of American tyranny and oppression. What happened to American democracy and freedom of speech? The justification for the systematic "white-balling" of Abdul-Rauf was that no NBA team or fan wants to deal with politics while attending a sporting event. Meanwhile, many post-9/11 American sports have emphasized the politics of American patriotism. American flags have been sewn onto many uniforms.

If Abdul-Rauf were still in the NBA, how would fans (Joes) have tolerated his decision not to stand? I ask this because at the time of his refusal, fans all over America booed Abdul-Rauf every time he touched the ball—even his own fans. And despite being the best player on the Denver Nuggets team, he was traded because of his idealogical difference of opinion. His punishment spoke to a racist, even jingoist reality filled with contradictions regarding democracy and freedom of speech.

The Abdul-Rauf situation reflects two ugly truths about American sports: (1) political consciousness will not be tolerated from modern athletes; and (2) issues of racism and politics permeate its lifeblood. Sports never have nor perhaps ever will be void of such issues. On the contrary, because sport permeates the facade of the achievement of the American dream, we skim over the harsh truths. Abdul-Rauf's public critique of American freedom, tyranny, and democracy cost him his career—despite being a star on his team. Scant attention is paid to how sports are the most volatile aspect of our society, they gauge how far we have or have not progressed in the way of race, equality, and open-mindedness.

However, this is not to say that sports are an evil entity. Sports are attractive because they reveal hope, courage, human accomplishment, will, and drama—of which organized sports have plenty. Therefore it is not uncommon for sports to provoke conversations between total strangers, easing awkward situations by merging divergent individuals on a common ground. However, its other uses are unmistakably as a tool of propaganda or as a socializing mechanism. For example, the early twentieth-century European immigrants were Americanized via the achievements of their children in sports. It allowed those without a command of English to participate in the celebration of the organized games that their children participated in, especially football and baseball. Lou Gehrig comes to mind as one famous example of the role of sports in helping immigrants melt into American culture—many like Gehrig became heroes.

However, it is disappointing that America's embrace of its more native of sons (Black Americans) has been less than welcoming. Indeed, despite the success and icon status of Michael Jordan, Tiger Woods, or Earvin "Magic" Johnson, non-Whites have endured far more hostility and resistance than "mainstream" embrace. The response to nonconformist contemporary athletes (Ballers of the New School) threatening cultural codes in American sports has been hostile. Since the late 1970s, a significant incorporation of African American presence and culture has made an impact on the framework of mass consumer and sports culture in America—but it has not been without resistance or retooling for "mainstream" embrace. While there are signs non-Whites and women are making progress in American culture via sports, the cost is often high.

Noam Chomsky explains that sports are "designed to organize a community to be hysterically committed to their gladiators."[5] Fans sometimes become cultivated loyalists to their teams and their cities, gauging personal hope and success with every loss or victory. All told, the important political losses and victories occurring in the world are overshadowed by major sporting events and ESPN's twenty-four-hour replays of daily games. Sports function as a distraction from the daily political realities, all the while filled with subtle political, social, moral, racial, and economic time bombs. In the same way that sports and games have enormous power to capture our imaginations, they can also stupefy, even immobilize the populace.

Whether one is politically or socially sophisticated, most will agree that sports are seductive because what athletes create can be quite beautiful to watch. It gives viewers hope that the underdog has a chance to win. However, the danger of sports is varied: (1) sports encourages a racial contract; (2) sports helps cultivate a culture of passive, somewhat obedient, socially and politically nonparticipant Joes who can be manipulated; and (3) while inspiring hope and courage, sport places all of us in danger of being an Average Joe.

One part of me—the Joe, is at times consumed by the playing of games, viewing their outcomes without political, social, or cultural consciousness. But the other half of me—the writer, intellectual, and social critic—pauses to see sport for the problematic, far from apolitical, and dangerous entity that it can be and often is. This part of me is compelled to critically examine a culture where games take place year-round and *SportsCenter* is on all year, twenty-four hours each day. It is this half of me that recognizes how sports can divert us from real news like Darfur's social injustices, that people of color comprise over 60 percent of U.S. prison populations, and that although Whites comprise the majority of U.S. drug users more persons of color go to jail for drug-related crimes. It is the part of me that questions how many White fans are comfortable cheering for Black athletes, yet allow themselves to fear Black men they pass on the streets, and raise little protest when sports media consistently target Black male athletes as criminals.

However, the one thing I cannot deny is that sport's draw is magnetic, bordering on obsessive. It does not discriminate whom it affects because each contest promises an original outcome and hope. No matter who is playing or how unbalanced the matchup, the fans and players believe on that afternoon or evening that "they" can win. This is similar to the American appeal toward meritocracy and democracy, the dream of success and rewards via hard work.

This is the reason sports are so popular. They spin organic narratives supporting notions of the American dream and meritocracy. The underdog can win; the little guy always has a chance. We all want to believe this. That is why in football the Baltimore Ravens, the Pittsburgh Steelers, and the St. Louis Rams can go from terrible one year to Super Bowl champions the very next! It is where the Anaheim Angels, the Chicago White Sox, and the Florida Marlins, perennial doormats, can somehow get it all going and win the World Series; and the Boston Red Sox can "reverse the curse" of Babe Ruth (which they did in 2004). Sports are appealing because there is always a chance the underdog could win. Even failure is rewarded with the optimism that there is always next season. This is why we need and like sports.

However, the sports bombardment is unyielding; there are no holidays or sick days off from sports campaigns. I consider myself as a mixture of sports critic, activist, and sports enthusiast—a self-declared "sportivist" committed to joyful consumption while also raising the issue of race, gender and equality, which is routinely swept under the rug or frequently ignored. Everyone has some "Average Joe" in them, and because sports so permeate our culture, it is easy to understand how nearly everyone is vulnerable on some level.

My aim here has been to disturb the neat, harmless, apolitical corner we paint sport into when it is also a platform upon which White supremacy, racial tensions, sexism, and masculinity stands. While sports are exciting and stimulating, they also place us in danger of passivity, believing stereotypes that gender or racial problems are a thing of a different era. Such thinking is flawed and dangerous. But there is also a chance that sports examined critically will reveal to Average Joe the tremendous odds people of color in the twenty-first century struggle against—even those who achieve "success." If Joes are open-minded enough, they may discover that athletes' struggles might be a metaphor for their personal struggles, while enlightening them to the inequalities of our society.

POST GAME

# CHAPTER NINE

## CHALLENGING ALL BALLERS

> *Questions of color and race have been at the center of some of the most important events in American experience, and Americans continue to live with their ugly and explosive consequences.*
>
> —Barbara J. Fields

In many ways, this book took its original shape during my first visit to the Negro Leagues Baseball Museum in Kansas City, Missouri. While somewhat unorthodox it is necessary that I end by discussing the book's origins. Interested in the emergence and history of this segregated baseball league, I jumped in my car early one Saturday morning and left St. Louis for a day trip to Kansas City. As I neared the area where the museum was located, I slowed down to read the addresses but kept skipping past where the Negro Leagues Baseball Museum was supposed to be! I repeated this three times before I reluctantly got out of the car to walk the street for a better view of the address. What I discovered was that the storefront building with the construction paper forming a man holding a bat was not an abandoned building but the museum! (It has since been replaced by a swank new building)

My struggle to locate the Negro Leagues Baseball Museum symbolizes the notion of race being an invisible relic of the past—its history difficult to locate. The Negro Leagues are a reminder that race is a construct. Just as the museum was difficult to locate, the form that race takes in the modern world can be difficult to articulate, especially in sport. But the museum's existence is evidence against denials of racism in America. It is also evidence that independent institutions and sports can be used to change America's racial problems. The Negro Leagues Baseball Museum is also a reminder that we, like Negro Leagues founder Andrew Rube Foster (a true Baller of the new school), possess the vision, tenacity, and courage to erect institutions to counter the racial contract that threatens to cripple us all. If Foster could, amid great odds, organize a league for Black players who were restricted from playing with Whites, we can do anything.

Visiting the Negro Leagues Baseball Museum was a bittersweet experience because while it revealed the tenacity of the owners and players, it also reminded me of America's harsh racial history as well as the one-sidedness of America's integration. For me, it confirmed the need to write about the perpetuation and validation of racism in sports. Rube Foster, the man who conceived of and successfully ran the Negro Leagues until his health failed him, represents the challenge that this final essay broaches. Foster and the Negro Leagues represent what it means to respond to the racial contract.

Foster and his group, formed a league that reshaped baseball to fit the personality of players and the tastes of fans at the time. They evolved the strategies of baseball, introducing an ingenious, aggressive play (bunting, hit and run, stealing home plate) that was later brought to the White Major Leagues with Robinson, Mays, and others. Like hip-hop's aesthetic that has mutated and affected the world, the Negro Leagues' creativity and its aesthetics altered the way baseball was played in America. Some Black intellectuals seem to disregard the Negro Leagues as a real success story. In *Basketball Jones: America Above the Rim*, scholar Gerald Early has argued that the Negro Leagues were ill conceived and loosely organized, not the romantic picture of progress painted by many contemporary Black nationalists. Although there is some truth to that, it is indisputable that there were several very good teams, owners, and general managers that prospered. Communities and businesses gained financially from these teams as well. If given the opportunity, many of these teams would have competed very well in the White Major Leagues—but this never happened. And Foster's organization and vision were much greater, more significant than Early gives him credit for. Early fails to realize the admirable "Baller" ethos ensconced within the league's struggle and its determination to exist despite racism, discrimination, the Depression, and the eventual raiding by White baseball post–Jackie Robinson.

While meandering through the museum, which is organized in chronological order, it became clear that Foster's failed health led to the failures of the National Negro Leagues. In fact, 1955 was the last season of "quality" Negro Leagues baseball, which officially folded in 1960. But what saddened me more was recalling how historically the rules have applied unequally to reserve spaces for Whites in professional sport. The museum reminded me that White supremacy has and still does reign over the racialized playing fields and rules. But as Davarian Baldwin asserts: "black athletes mastered the 'standard' and improvised based on a given situation by finding tactical loopholes, moving in the gaps, speeding up the tempo, and making new rules within announced rules that didn't consistently apply to them" (230). The existence of the Negro Leagues epitomized the notion of improvisation and mastery of the "standard."

As I finished the tour and neared the lockers marking the Negro Leagues greats who had garnered recognition and acceptance into the Major League Hall of Fame, a tour guide, turned to a small group he was leading, boasted that the lockers represented only a few of the great players who made the Hall of Fame, and the empty lockers were symbolic of those who were yet to be recognized. Hearing this, tears began to form in my eyes; how painful it was to hear that the tour guide felt it necessary to have the White Major Leagues validate the greatness of Negro Leagues Hall of Fame players. "Oh my Lord," I murmured to my self with disgust,

"Rube Foster must be turning over in his grave." It hurt me to hear the racial contract signed, allowing validation of great Negro Leagues players to come through White Major League Baseball. I do not think the great pioneer Andrew Rube Foster, an original Baller of the New School, would approve. Certainly his impetus was to make a league greater than the White league that refused the services of Black players. It is this spirit of self-sufficiency and pioneering attitude—"Baller Mentality" no matter the obstacles—that is a focus of this book.

Indeed, the Negro Leagues Baseball Museum does not need the Baseball Hall of Fame to authenticate the great Black American players of this era. All the gifted players like Robinson, Aaron, Mays, and Campanella who would go on to the Majors and dominate were proof of the greatness of the Negro Leagues talent. The only thing Robinson's crossing over into the White Major leagues accomplished was a swift and effective demise of the Negro Leagues, which was exciting and innovative (lots of base stealing, bunting, and night games). The Negro Leagues was also a place where Black Ballers and outlaws could prosper. For example, numbers hustler Gus Greenlee bought the Pittsburgh Crawfords in the 1930s. The team did well competitively and financially for a while, gaining quite a reputation.

The rise, struggle, and demise of the Negro Leagues due to integration speak volumes of America, its national pastime, and its intense racist culture. The Negro Leagues and the museum that keeps it in our memory confirms sociologist Barbara J. Fields assertion in her essay "Ideology and Race in American History" that:

> The notion of race has played a role in the way Americans think about their history. Race continues to tempt many people into the mistaken belief that American experience constitutes the great exception in world history, the great deviation from patterns that seem to hold for everybody else. Elsewhere, classes may have struggled over power and privilege, over oppression

and exploitation, over competing senses of justice and rights but in the United States these were secondary to the great, overarching theme of race. The determination to keep the United States a white man's country has been the central theme of American, not just Southern, history. Racism has been America's tragic flaw.

Like it or not, the Black athlete—from Jack Johnson to Mahmoud Abdul-Rauf—has historically been connected to the representation of his/her race. And the Negro Leagues Baseball Museum is an important monument—proof that this flaw even extended to sport. It is still difficult to get Americans to have an open and honest discussion about the continued effects of race. The Negro Leagues Baseball Museum never lets us forget that sport has been a significant platform for furthering racism, increasing opportunity, and making America acknowledge triumph over injustices.

As the memorabilia and documents in the Negro Leagues Baseball Museum confirm, race is central to shaping America's history. While progress is indeed undeniable, this book, like the museum, is a reminder that it is a grave error to believe that society has at least transcended race in sports culture. Change cannot ensue unless honest conversations like this text take place.

Any race theory worth its value must historicize the story of American racial history, emphasizing both its progresses and failures. What we cannot allow to elude us is neoconservative falsehoods that absorb racial complexity and contradictions into a narrative of uncomplicated linear progress. To really move forward, we all have to acknowledge the truth regarding neo- and past conservative opposition to racial progress that was achieved under very, very difficult circumstances. Sport is the perfect way to historicize the development and genealogy of American race relations. Here I have attempted to examine a sport past and present to honestly explore the specific conditions under which minorities have been oppressed. I have linked this to an analysis of those conditions via sports culture to enable forms of social theory that can address structural root causes that reproduce oppression over space and time.

Racism as expressed in sports culture is a testament of what has happened and is happening. Sport is a true marker of social conditions; it plays a huge role in cultivating images in American culture, untrue, good, and bad. When we view modern sports, we think that cheering for a team of primarily non-Whites means that White Americans are now eager to make connections or contact with the "Other." bell hooks reminds us in *Yearning* that liberal Whites mistakenly believe that "their desire for contact [is] proof that they [have] transcended racism" (54). The truth is that the desire for this contact dissipates when the clock ticks to zero and the game is over, or if the person sitting next to them is not a famous athlete. While sport may claim credit for progress, it also must bear the blame for perpetuating many of the negative images of Blacks as physical yet anti-intellectual that proliferate the global media at a time when non-Whites remain politically and economically marginalized despite the legal milestones of the civil rights movement.

*The Changing Tide of Progress*
Perhaps it is undeniable that Jackie Robinson reflected some progress, but not as much as O.J. Simpson, the first true Black American sports hero. O.J. constructed the first successful neutral persona for a Black man in America. He was, during the late 1960s and 1970s the most successful color-blind pioneer. He was just "the Juice," a nice guy who could sell Ford cars and Hertz rental cars to White America, as well as to Blacks. O.J. was accepted, embraced by White America. He crossed over as no Black man before him had done, making it in Hollywood, selling numerous products, and carrying the 1984 Olympic torch through Los Angeles. He was a symbol of race in America; he embodied the American

dream, his rising celebrity coexisting with the changing racial relations in America. In doing so, he effectively detached himself from the Black community and literally from being Black. He divorced his first wife of over a decade and found himself the epitome of White beauty in the nineteen-year-old blonde Nicole Brown, whom he married soon after divorcing his first wife.

O.J. was not Black, and he was, as we say, "big pimping." As far as O.J. and America were concerned, O.J. was effectively race-neutral. O.J. was marketable primarily because he was not seen as Black—that is, until 1994 and 1995, when he was charged with the murder of his wife, Nicole Simpson, and her friend Ronald Goldman. Suddenly, O.J. the nice guy, everybody's friend who was colorless, appeared on the cover of *Newsweek* and *Time* magazine literally a shade Blacker than he was in his worst nightmare—and far Blacker than we could ever recall him actually being both mentally and physically. American media wanted to send the message to the American public that had once embraced him that his honorary White card was being revoked and from this day forward he would be perceived for what he has always been—a Black man, violent, a nigger.

O.J. Simpson became the modern thermostat gauging the temperature of race in America. Unlike Jack Johnson, O.J. was once beloved. America held him in a tight embrace because of his racial neutrality. But O.J. violated the rules of acceptance, and since that fateful day in October 1995, when he was found not guilty of the murder of Nicole Simpson and Ron Goldman, the tide changed for him as well as the facade of racial progress. I like to call it "Post-O.J."

The response to the O.J. outcome by Blacks and Whites revealed the depth of America's racial tensions. Othello had betrayed them. O.J. got away with "tupping" then killing the "White Ewe," but unlike Othello, who killed Desdemona and then himself, O.J. did not kill himself; instead, he walked to freedom. (In December 2008 O.J. was convicted of attempted robbery in a Las Vegas hotel room and received nine to twenty years in prison.)

*New School Athletes*

The contemporary sports narrative lulls society into believing that enormous changes have occurred, that prejudiced views are dead, that social and economic inequities are nonexistent. And BNS contribute to perpetuating this myth and the current racial contract. A new sort of abolitionism is necessary that seeks a historical reinterpretation that aims to see race—and more properly, the gestation and evolution of White supremacy—at the center of U.S. politics and culture (especially sport culture). The world must acknowledge that sport culture is infested with racism. Given these realities, I am making a plea for BNS (whose values are steeped in hip-hop's aesthetics) to use their influence to alter the racial contract; to reshape perceptions and worldviews; to defeat xenophobia. BNS must maximize their mass visibility and status as entertainers to become messengers spreading far more than the whims of the marketplace.

These BNS—children of a historical spirit of civil rights generation rebellion and hip-hop's endless innovation—can make a difference. Athletes must envision themselves as influential products whose visibility and influence in the global marketplace can alter consumers' behavior and social attitudes. BNS need to cull the abrasive edginess of hip-hop, its connection to African American and Latino working and underclass, and use that energy to reshape the vision of modern sport culture. While hip-hop has not successfully shaped a contemporary political movement in traditional ways, its spirit of creativity, innovation, and making one's own way is an important current through which to channel ideas of change.

Although BNS embrace some ideology and aesthetics of hip-hop, they, like many hip-hop performers, lack the political convictions necessary to make a change beyond individual goals. Since sport is definitely a socializing mechanism, the visibility of non-Whites in high-profile sports gives Americans a false sense of familiarity with the racial other, which results in a false sense of real progress. BNS in athletics can have a huge impact on youth. In many ways BNS set trends and reach a vast international audience. BNS have a mainstream presence that should be used to alter the parameters of national discussions regarding racial stereotypes, and social, political, and economic inequities.

My hope is that sport culture and BNS can do more to function as tools for dismantling the racial contract and forge real social change. BNS possess the resources to be true agents of change that offer a clearer more focused public voice to youth, who are marginalized and oppressed because of America's racial contract. They can also use their status to help counter images of Black men as criminals or minstrel-esque lovable cartoon characters, and maybe clear the lane for Ballers to enter the administrative levels too.

*Solutions*

While I outlined specific solutions in chapters 4 and 5, I also think athletes have to incorporate Black intellectuals and even activists into their community service efforts to make more meaningful and powerful contributions. They pragmatically address the key issues that impact the youth in these communities. New basketballs and pool tables at boys or girls club are nice, but hardly the most effective resource. I grew up closely affiliated in St. Louis with the Mathews-Dickey Boys Club. It was a safe haven, a great place to develop skills and foster relationships around wonderful people that helped to shape me as a person. The men who started the club, Mr. Mathews and Mr. Dickey (now deceased), are true heroes in the St. Louis community. Although I did not become a professional athlete, the role their organization played in my overall development and life remains significant. Like Mathews-Dickey, which has expanded its outreach beyond sport (they now offer tutoring programs, computer literacy programs and more), BNS must do the same.

I raise this issue because NFL receiver Santana Moss was on the sports show *NFL Access* explaining how happy he was to be hosting a celebrity basketball game because it gave him joy to be able to give back to the community. He explained how as a kid he lamented that he never saw heroes, and how he was happy to help the youth in his hometown, Miami, by organizing such an event. No offense, but come on, man, you can do better than this! Such limited notions of giving something back to poor communities void of educational and economic resources are a testament of the pervasive lack of vision I see in too many contemporary athletes. Although sports helped keep me off the streets as a youth, what every poor youth needs are opportunities to develop professionally, intellectually, and financially.

There is no panacea, but those with privilege, financial resources, and leverage should use this more effectively. The "give back" crap they spin for media and other PR opportunities, pisses me off because many modern athletes know that too many kids lack only access, financial resources, opportunity, and support.

If BNS really want to "give back to the community," why not play a leading role in encouraging internships for non-White youth in different areas of sports businesses, from marketing and team management to equipment management and public relations? Through their charitable foundations, BNS can pay half or all of the wages for two- to eight-week summer programs for youth to work in some area of the sports industry. Since they have affiliations with sports teams and other aspects of the industry, they can use these contacts to orchestrate internships. There are many people like me who are happy to help facilitate these connections. This type of incentive will convince kids to stay in school and study hard. They will see the importance of the skills being taught in school. Most poor kids are very pragmatic people—they have to be. It certainly will take the kids further in life than new basketballs and pool tables. This is strategic community assistance.

I know firsthand that this works. I received an editing job at a publishing company because my college had an internship program whereby they would work with companies to match half the wages. All I had to do was secure the internship. The Press got inexpensive labor, and

I got valuable work experience in the publishing industry at a decent wage. My challenge to BNS who want to give back in ways that really attack and respond to the social ills in poor communities is to help create these types of opportunities. They know that most of their peers from their hoods want to work but need opportunities.

If this is not something that sparks the interest of BNS, then they can help intellectuals and activists address rising incarceration and high school dropout rates. (Forty-nine percent of the nation's prison population are Black and have less than a high school diploma.) Of course, if more BNS followed in the footsteps of Jim Brown, Alan Paige, Kevin Johnson (now Mayor of Sacramento, CA), or Atlanta Falcon running back Warrick Dunn, the world would be a better place for everyone. Dunn, who lost his mom early in life and was a major provider for his siblings, has dedicated himself since the beginning of his career in 1997 to his "Homes for the Holidays" program. This program assists single mothers to become first-time homeowners by providing the down payments and enlisting sponsors to furnish the homes. He has, as of 2005, assisted over fifty mothers in this process.

Dunn is an athlete who understands that "giving back" requires something pragmatic like a place to live comfortably and grow as a person. What he is doing is more life altering than an autograph or charity game to raise money for new pool tables or uniforms at a community center. When I was eleven, a friend of my mom's gave us a zero-interest loan to purchase a three-story house. Prior to that, we were living in a two-bedroom apartment surrounded by crazed violent people. Having our own space, each child with his/her own bedroom, and a backyard changed my life. I had personal space to think, reflect, and grow. It was the sort of pragmatic assistance that Dunn's foundation offers.

Another truth that must be more effectively broached is that sport does not have to be an apolitical space, nor do the successful careers of a handful of athletes make up for the racial bias that contributes to inadequate education, criminality, police brutality, and the terrible economy in the communities where many high-profile athletes hail from. A new narrative must be written that informs kids that sport is not a completely safe zone from the problems of the world. While sport has and can lead the way in ushering real change in society, it will continue to fall short if we are dishonest about the true state of racial and social progress. Hopefully in the future more BNS are willing to communicate "realness" without fearing the loss of multimillion-dollar contracts or endorsement deals. The true test of how far America has evolved is the ease in which BNS display social consciousness and responsibility without being lynched in the media or on Madison Avenue. I mention this to remind BNS that visibility in American sports culture is not progress if they are prisoners of corporate sponsors.

I am of the opinion that the best role models in athletics the last twenty years have been female. They stay out of trouble, complete college at a higher ratio than male athletes in high-profile sports then go on to have professional careers that shatter negative images of intellect, beauty, and gender. Take, for example, Candice Parker, the former University of Tennessee star who was a great student, finished her undergraduate degree early, was the top female player in basketball, and led her team to successive national championships in college basketball her final two years, then went on to win WNBA rookie of the year and MVP in 2008! Then, of course, there is Lisa Leslie of the Los Angeles Sparks whose modeling career is proof that women can be outstanding, competitive athletes and the personification of female beauty simultaneously. Also the Williams sisters, especially Serena, have redefined aesthetics of beauty, creativity and style in the lily-white world of tennis. And, WNBA star Cheryl Swoopes demonstrates that motherhood, beauty, alternative sexual orientation, and athleticism can coexist. Finally, the great Billie Jean King. What has she not done for women in athletics? These are the kinds of role models young fans should look up to.

*A Game Plan*

What I am most concerned about is hard racially tinted facts of American life. For example, more than 50 percent of African American males between the ages of sixteen and twenty-two are out of work and not in school. Those in school because of their athletic ability have roughly a 30 percent chance of graduating in six years. But it gets even better, according to a study by Becky Pruitt of the University of Washington and Bruce Western of Princeton University: at least 60 percent of African American dropouts born between 1965 and 1969 (the hip-hop generation that was supposed to benefit from post–civil rights laws and other advantages) had been incarcerated by the time they reached their thirties. In Chicago, roughly 40 percent of Black males have graduated from high school since 1995. These are just a few examples of the very real problems facing urban America. How many coaches care about this? I want to reverse these trends.

The racial contract is responsible for these grossly imbalanced statistics, especially since Whites comprise over 70 percent of the U.S. population. There is a crisis, and the racial contract has set the social, legal, and economic parameters that have led to this crisis. Change is necessary and possible, but it is something that must be desired.

Change begins with diversity. True diversity on any level involves at least: (1) climate and intergroup relations; (2) access and success; and (3) institutional vitality. Although diversity encompasses more than merely race, gender, and sexual orientation, but also personality and work style, social economic factors, religion, education, and other factors, for consistency with the racial contract, I will limit my focus to race and gender. Clearly on the college level, presidents and athletic directors do not feel comfortable or trusting of non-White head coaching candidates, which would explain why there are so few when non-Whites (particularly Blacks) comprise over half the players.

Again, one thing that prospective college freshman players can do is to query and request that the White coaches heavily recruiting them hire more non-White coaches as offensive and defensive coordinators if they want them to sign. These players wield enormous power, and coaches will do anything to get them to sign letters of intent in football and basketball. Even better, more of the blue-chip players should opt for historically Black colleges that hire Black coaches and athletic administrators. Steve McNair attended a historically Black college, and because his play was so great, his team made it to national television often. Once these colleges begin to sign high-profile high school stars and start defeating the "known" programs, things will change and the media attention will come. One must always remind youth that two of the greatest football players of all time, Walter Payton and Jerry Rice, attended historically Black colleges. If part of the spirit of hip-hop is about taking nothing and making it into something, then Black college athletics present a creative challenge.

*   *   *

For BNS, "giving back" must begin to mean finding innovative and pragmatic ways to circulate money back into the communities from whence they came that will produce real long-term change. The argument that there are not skilled lawyers, agents, accountants, real estate agents, and mortgage brokers of color in these areas will not fly in the twenty-first century. BNS must more avidly explore all options and use their resources to circulate wealth in their communities.

The young Whites who are open-minded, embrace BNS, and who are the movers and shakers within sectors of the sports industry must be challenged to use their power, knowledge, and influence to narrow the racial divide in critical arenas such as coaching, journalism, management, and other areas within the industry. How you "gonna" love Randy Moss, LeBron James, and Kobe Bryant, but refuse to give a contract to a non-White contractor or encourage diversified staffing all around the industry?

Again, I am challenging BNS to provide concrete opportunities for youth, using their influence and leverage with their employers and leagues to provide youth with sport industry internship opportunities. This will have a more lasting impact than a visit to a community center or an autograph. High school and primary school youth are going to make the real changes, but they need assistance in making this happen. Hopefully, the *real* Ballers will do their part. They might consider re-examining ideas like the Negro Industrial and Economic Union.

These types of pragmatic and innovative approaches are the best way to encourage youth to study and see school as a viable option. And they can be run through After School Programs and boys and girls clubs. What kid would not study hard, learn to read and write well, and make certain to study hard in math and science, knowing that to do so can lead to an opportunity to work in sports marketing, management, as a trainer, a journalist, working in a league office, or some other aspect of the sports business? I would have taken such a job over my jobs making pizzas, delivering papers, and flipping burgers for minimum wages.

For many poor youth, the biggest crime they have committed is that they come from rough environments devoid of ample economic growth and opportunities. What can we offer for the young kids who do not have superior athletic abilities to save them from wretched living conditions? Such youth are not criminal or anti-education, but they merely lack concrete resources to make a real difference in their own lives.

BNS can "bling bling" and count their cash all they want, but they have to put up or shut up talking about "giving back" to the community. And for those who do give back, keep this in mind: Racism is real, and it will take creativity to effectively defeat it. Resources must be creatively pooled (economics, contacts, and influence) to create any real economic revitalization or to rebuild in poor communities. I am willing to forge a coalition with athletes, employing the solutions outlined here, to make a difference. How many are game? Whether they want to accept it or not, BNS are an enormous vehicle through which significant changes can be voiced to a national audience—all eyes are on them.

As Bakari Kitwana points out in *The Hip Hop Generation*, contributions from hip-hop-generation entertainers and athletes to larger causes remain few and far between. This has got to change. If the hip-hop culture is about making something from nothing, then this group has to take a greater, more deliberate approach to affecting change. More political consciousness and activism are necessary. Although there are athletes who have founded social programs and foundations that assist the communities that produced them, far more, with the focus outlined above, are necessary. Athletes have to use their influence to help close the racial divide in the sports industry beyond the playing fields. The NBA is making some strides and the NFL is moving slowly, while MLB remains a distant third; but none of what has occurred is sufficient.

At the same time, the question for BNS and communities of color is how to participate in and support a multibillion-dollar industry without ignoring the critical problems facing our generation? No real Baller fears repercussions for using their visibility to make the world better. Real Ballers embody ethics of creativity, rebelliousness, and control public space to truly make a difference with their high-profile public personas. Calling all Ballers, are you out there?

I am not asking BNS to stand on an Olympic podium with a black-gloved fist raised (I am not against this either), but I am asking them not to ignore daily atrocities taking place in communities of color in America. I am asking them to use sport as an instrument to help correct our society. It is not too much to expect them to use their celebrity or "role model" status to fight the racial contract of White privilege and non-White subservience to it. What good are BNS if the only things they stand for are themselves and the products they endorse?

Here is the essence of the challenge: BNS have to strive harder to set the tone for Black and White youth; they have to symbolize the hip-hop mantra of making something of nothing and moving people from semiconscious to conscious. BNS (athletes and young professionals) have to find creative ways to use their resources and visibility to make change for this generation. The challenge for BNS is to decide whether the tone they set will be vapid, self-centered, and weak, or buffed with substance that can make a real (since so many of our generation are into to "keeping it real") difference in the world.

The rapper KRS ONE explains in "The Fundamentals of Hip-Hop" that: "hip-hop is the transformation of subjects and objects in an attempt to describe your consciousness." More BNS must bring this attitude to the playing fields to transform themselves from objects (neutral and criminal) in the American psyche into spokespersons against poverty, limited opportunities for youth of color, mis-education, and disproportionate incarceration rates for people of color.

The majority of Americans would agree that sports have the propensity to help people of different racial and ethnic groups interact. I am among those that believe sport, used strategically, can shift cultural/social attitudes. Just as sports like baseball played an active role in assimilating immigrants and socializing youth into adults, it can reform the racial tensions that still plague America. But, we must be unafraid of tackling tensions head on. For Black Americans, sport has historically been a site to display defiance against White supremacy, from Jack Johnson and Jackie Robinson to Jesse Owens, Mahmoud Abdul-Rauf (Chris Jackson), Tommy Smith and John Carlos. I am challenging all Ballers to continue this legacy in a sophisticated manner that matches modern times and speaks to non-Whites and Whites alike.

This book was written because I love America and I love sports; for this reason I insist on the right to criticize both perpetually. The issues and solutions addressed here are merely a start. I do not expect a consensus. But if we honestly address how the racial contract is upheld in sports, then work to proactively make change, the narrative of sports and racial progress will be more than mythic. Only then can sport help to truly establish a new racial tone in American culture.

# NOTES

## Introduction: Race and Sport in America

1. John Hoberman, author of the controversial Darwin's Athlete, argues that "the black male intelligentsia is generally unprepared to think critically about the role of sports in black life" (xv).

2. See Cornell West's *Race Matters*, where he explains the term "race-transcending prophets" as individuals with courage and political acumen (66-67).

3. The first chapter of Charles Mills's *The Racial Contract* outlines the power parameters of the this contract. Mills provides an analysis of the social contract and historical perspectives of philosophers who have laid the ground work for the privilege that drives the world regarding race relations.

4. I refer here to the fight that took place at the end of a game between the Detroit Pistons and the Indiana Pacers after a fan threw a cup of water on Pacers forward Ron Artest as he lay prone on a scorer's table in the waning seconds of the game. The fan (who happened to be White) threw a cup that hit Artest and he immediately leap into the stands to attack the perpetrator(s). Some of his teammates followed him and some fans ran onto the court as a wild melee ensued that was described in racialized language.

5. One of the most important narratives inscribed in the racial contract is similar to the colonial relationship between Caliban and Prospero in Shakespeare's *The Tempest*. It reflects the relationship

between BNS and media because the text situates the colonial mind-set, which is prevalent in the American media, who adhere to a racial contract. Like Prospero the largely White media deems Caliban (modern athletes) inferior, uncultured, and ungrateful for all that he, Prospero, has taught him, particularly language. In American sports, the feeling is similar in that the media convey the attitude that they have allowed and tolerated integration in professional sports, and athletes of color (primarily Black ones) are not appreciative enough of the opportunities they have received from White America, which has graciously accepted them.

## Chapter One: A Letter to My Cousin

1. Douglass discusses how he learned the importance of literacy in chapter 6 of his narrative.

2. In the film *Finding Forrester*, Jamal hides his writing and reading ability from his friends and the school refuses to acknowledge his intelligence.

3. Gail Bederman reminds us in her *Manliness and Civilization* that, "Late Victorian culture had identified the powerful, large, male body of the heavyweight prizefighter.as the epitome of manhood," (8).

4. Harrison and Valdez reveal in their essay "The Uneven View of African American Ballers" that African American male student-athletes internalize negative stereotypes and low expectations because of a "campus culture that often isolates, exploits and objectifies" them.

5. See Gail Bederman's discussion of historical contradictions of manhood through sports culture.

6. See Toni Morrison's discussion of race in her collection of essays *Playing in the Dark*.

## Chapter Two: Ballers in Contemporary America

1. The term refers to the perception of prestige limited to these

three identities. Or one can also add the label of "scholar-baller" to the list. For more on this see "The Uneven View of African American Ballers," by Keith Harrison and Alicia Valdez.

2. For more on Black style see Davarian Baldwin's discussion of 1930s sporting life and Black style in Chicago's New Negroes(227-28).

3. Robin Kelley discusses this point in greater detail in Yo' Mama's Disfunktional!

## Chapter 3: Original Ballers and New School Ballers

1. Brown, H. Rap. *Die, Nigger Die.* pp. xxxiv-xxxv.

## Chapter 4: Where the Brothers and Sisters At?

1. Charles Mills lays out his premise of the racial contract theory and how it impacts Whites and non-Whites in society and all its polities in his book *The Racial Contract* (p.11).

2. See Richard Lapchick 2007 and 2009 Racial and Gender Report Card for details regarding collegiate and professional sports hiring record.

3. See Lapchick's 2008 Race and Gender Report Card for details about the race implications of these statistics, especially regarding football and basketball.

4. Marcus Allen broaches the reality of racism in NFL in his autobiography, Marcus. He fearlessly broaches issues of race in the world of professional football (206).

5. Allen is critical of modern athletes for remaining silent on the subject of race and discrimination. Feels that they should be more vocal in contemporary America.

6. For more on this see King and Springwood in *Beyond the Cheers.*

7. Thabiti Lewis interview 3 August 2004 with Floyd Keats who points out why basketball has been more progressive but that even sport

culture continues to privilege Whiteness.

8. Thabiti Lewis interview with Keats 3 August 2004.

9. It is important to note that as of 2008, nearly a decade later, the numbers have not improved very much at all. What they show is that progress is minimal, and always slow. Also, Lapchick's study from 1999 is very similar to the numbers for 2007. There has been very little improvement in hiring African American and Latinos in key positions of leadership has manifested at the 119 institutions in Division I-A collegiate sports. Lapchick found that 95 percent of the presidents, 93 percent of the athletics directors, and 91 percent of the faculty athletics representatives at those institutions are White, including the 11 conference commissioners in Division I-A.

10. Carla Williams in her essay "Naked, Neutered, or Noble: The Black Female Body in America and the Problem of Photographic History" reminds us that: "Given the legacy of images created of Black women, it is an especially complex task for contemporary Black women to define their own image, one that necessarily incorporates and subverts the stereotypes, myths, facts, and fantasies that have preceded them" (in *Skin Deep, Spirit Strong* 196).

11. The visibility of non-White athletes and entertainers on television make us think that equality has been achieved. But the National Hockey League (NHL) has perhaps the fewest Black players of any of the major sports leagues. As of 2009 less than twenty Black players could boast playing in the NHL. Astonishingly five of them played for the Edmonton Oilers! The challenges of improving the NHL's racial image are obvious, judging from Marty McSorley's attack on Donald Brashear (Vancouver), hitting him in the head with a stick in 2000. People like Willie O'Ree, the NHL's first Black player and director of youth development for the NHL/USA Hockey Diversity Task Force, agrees that racial tensions exist in the league, as well as a lack of opportunity for playing a sport that requires expensive equipment and access to ice. The game is simply not affordable in poor communities. While progress is occurring, it is slow to take shape; hopefully Canadian hockey fans will

care more about who can score and defend than with skin color.

## Chapter 5: Big Pimpin' in Amateur Sport

1. Peter Keating's essay in ESPN: The Magazine (4/28/03) critiques the NCCA, it s profits, and it status as a non-profit entity.

2. William Rhoden gives a great history of how southern schools became integrated in *Forty Million Dollar Slaves.*

3. Chris Isidore details the revenue and profit of major conference basketball schools that played in the 2006-07 NCAA tournament in his CNNMoney.com column of 4 April 2008.

4. These statistics relate to 2001 salaries and benefits that the NCAA reported; they represent a good estimate of what the NCAA executives officials are paid. As of 2008, all officers' salaries are at least ten percent higher than that reported in 2001.

5. For more on college coaches' salaries, see Mike Fish's article "Sign of the Times," 12/23/03, on SI.com

6. The Witwatersrand story featuring athletes and soccer teams that represent universities for pay appeared in *The Chronicle of Higher Education*, 12 December 2003, A32-33.

## Chapter 6: All About the Benjamins

1. The 3 December 2003 interview was printed in *The Oregonian* republished by the Associated Press. Wallace, who rarely speaks to the press, granted this rare interview to the Oregonian and they used it to seal his fate in Portland. The media were tired of Wallace snubbing them after games and deciding to sit down under pressure and let it all loose, hoping they would leave him alone.

2. Again Rasheed Wallace interview with *The Oregonian* 3 December 2003.

3. Official Dodgers attendance records are the source of this

information.

4. For a clearer picture of Jackie Robinson's financial impact on Brooklyn Dodgers gate revenues, see Dodgers attendance figures from 1941-1949 (on-line documentation).

5. Peter Keating makes this lucid statement in ESPN: The Magazine article 28 April 2003, p. 60.

6. Wallace in The Oregonian discussing how his only concern is being paid (JCC).

7. Quincy Troupe uses this term to describe Miles Davis in his book *Miles and Me* (U of CA Press, 2000).

8. The Telfair interview was conducted in *The Oregonian*, (7/2/04, C5) (Sadly he had minor gun trouble and did not perform well and was traded to Boston who sent him to Memphis).

## Chapter 8: Average Joes, Complacency, Politics, and Sports

1. See Chomsky's *Secrets, Lies and Democracy* where he talks about how sports direct people away from what really matters (54).

2. John Gerdy's study *Sports: The All-American Addiction* makes a compelling argument that sport culture contributes to passive and apolitical citizens.

3. While this point seems to exclude women, the impetus is to focus for a moment on the majority of sport participants-men. They often thrive on physical displays as signs of manhood. Women are a bit more sophisticated and do not rely on sport in this manner.

4. In *Secret Lies and Democracy*, Chomsky really emphasizes the importance of sport as a tool for creating a passive populace. He tends to see it an important tool for maintaining the form of democracy that exists in the United States. See page 52 where Chomsky goes into detail about jingoist behavior and sports.

5. Also see Chomsky's *Secrets, Lies and Democracy* where he explains the gladiator phenomenon in our society. His theory makes inroads into the anger directed at political activist athletes who use the gladiator

# WORKS CITED

platform for social progress.

Adler, Patricia, & Adler, Peter. *Backboards and Blackboards: College Athletics and role Engulfment.* New York: Columbia University Press, 1990.

Allen, Marcus. *Marcus: The Autobiography of Marcus Allen.* New York: St. Martin's Press. 1997. 206, 210.

Andrews, David. "The fact(s) of Michael Jordan's blackness: Excavating a Floating Racial Signifier." *Sociology of Sport Journal* 13 (2), 1996:125-158.

Andrews, Vernon. "African American Player Codes on Celebrations, Taunting, and sportsmanlike conduct. In G. Sailes (Ed.), *African Americans in Sport.* New Brunswick: Transaction Press, 1998: 145-180.

Anthony Neal, Mark. *New Black Man.* New York and London: Routledge. 2005.

Arnold, Geofry. *The Oregonian,* "Rasheed Wallace Cares, Just Not About Fans' Feelings." 11 December 2003.

Ashe, Arthur R., Jr. *A Hard Road to Glory: A History of the African American Athlete* (3 vols). New York: Warner Books, 1988.21-22,

102.

Associated Press. 3 December 2003 (David Stern's response to Rasheed Wallace).

Baker, Aaron. *Contesting Identities: Sports in American Film.* Urbana: University of Illinois Press, 2003. 14, 38, 41-43, 144.

Baldwin, James. "My Dungeon Shook: Letter to My Nephew on the One Hundreth Anniversary of the Emancipation." In *Vintage Baldwin.* Vintage Books: New York, 2004. 7-9.

Barkley, Charles. *Who's Afraid of a Large Black Man?: Race, Power, Fame, Identity, and Why Everyone Should Read My Book.* Riverhead Freestyle: New York, 2005.

Bederman, Gail. *Manliness and Civilization: A Cultural History of Gender and Race in the United States, 1880-1917.* Chicago: University of Chicago Press, 1995. 1-44, 170-198.

Beecher Stowe, Harriet. *Uncle Tom's Cabin.* New York: Chelsea House Publishers, 1996.

Bell, Jarrett. "Union Says Deeper Audit of Owners Books Needed," *USA Today,* May22, 2008. 2C.

Bloom, Jeremy. *New York Times,* August 2003.

Bogle, Donald. *Toms, Coons, Mulattoes, Mammies, & Bucks: An Interpretive History of Blacks in American Films* New York: Viking Press, 1973, 1989. 7-12, 243-272.

Boyd, Todd. *The New H.N.I.C (Head Niggas in Charge): The Death of Civil Rights and the Reign of Hip Hop.* New York: New York

University Press, 2002.

Boyd, Todd and Shropshire, Kenneth (eds). "Mo' Money Mo' Problems" in *Basketball Jones: America Above the Rim*. New York University Press: NewYork, 2000.

Brooks, Dana, and Althouse, Ronald. (Eds.). *Racism in College Sports: The African American Experience*. Morgantown Va: Fitness Information Technology, 1993.

Brown, H. Rap. *Die Nigger Die!* New York: Dial Press, 1969. xxxviv.

Chideya, Farari. *Don't Believe the Hype: Fighting Cultural Misinformation About African Americans*. New York: Plume, 1995.

Chomsky, Noam. *Secrets, Lies and Democracy.* Tuscon: Odonian Press, 2004.

*Chronicle of Higher Education*, 12 December 2003. A32-33.

Cole, Cheryl, L., & Andrews, David. "Look—It's NBA Show Time!: Visions of Race in the Popular Imaginary. *Cultural Studies: A Research Annual*, 1, 1996: 141-181.

Cyphers, Luke and Palmer, Chris. *ESPN: The Magazine*, 28 April 2003: 57-70.

DeArmond, Mike. "Soaring Salaries a Problem." *Kansas City Star,* 22 May 2001.

Dyson, M. Eric. "Be Like Mike: Michael Jordan and the Pedagogy of Desire. *Cultural Studies*, 7 (1), 1993: 64-72.

DuBois, W.E.B. *Black Reconstruction in America: an Essay Toward a History of the Part Which Black Folk Played in the Attempt to Reconstruct Democracy in America, 1860-1880.*

Fiske, John. "British Cultural Studies and Television" in *Channels of Discourse, Reassembled: Television and Contemporary Criticism.* Chapel Hill: University of North Carolina Press, 1992. 284-326.

Early, Gerald. "Collecting the Artificial Nigger: Race and American Material Culture." In *The Culture of Bruising.* Hopewell, NJ: Ecco Press, 1994.

Edwards, Harry. *The Revolt of the Black Athlete.* New York: Free Press, 1969.

Eitzen, D. Stanley. *Fair and Foul: Beyond the myths and Paradoxes of Sport.* Lanham, MD: Rowman and Littlefield, 1999.

Eitzen, Stanley. "Upward Mobility Through Sport?: The Myths and Realities." In Sport in Contemporary Society, ed. Stanley Eitzen. New York: Worth Publishers. 256-262.

Embry, Wayne. *The Inside Game: Race, Power, and Politics in the NBA.* Akron, Ohio: University of Akron Press, 2004.

Emerson, Ralph Waldo. *Self-Reliance and Other Essays.* New York: Dover Publications, Inc., 1993.

Entine, Jon. Taboo: *Why Black Athletes Dominate Sorts and Why We're Afraid to Talk About it.* New York: Public Affairs, 2000.

Engber, Daniel. "Lack of Diversity Among Division I-A Leaders is Reflected in Football Coaches They Hire, Scholars Says." *The Chronicle of Higher Education*, 18 November 2004.

ESPN.Com News Service. "Limbaugh Resigns from NFL Show." 2 October 2005.

Fields, Barbara, J. "Ideology and Race in American History." in *Region, Race, and Reconstruction*, Eds. Morgan Koussar & James Mcpherson. New York: Oxford U Press, 1982: 143-177.

Fish, Mike. "Sign of the Times." *SI.COM*. 23 December 2003. http://sportsillustrated.cnn.com/.

Fiske, John. "British Cultural Studies and Television" in *Channels of Discourse, Reassembled: Television and Contemporary Criticism*. Chapel Hill: University of North Carolina Press, 1992. 284-326.

Foucault, Michael. *Discipline and Punish: The Birth of the Prison*. Pantheon Books: NY, 1977.

*Gentlemen's Quarterly Magazine*, "Joe Frazier, Still Smokin After All These Years." October 2001.

George, Nelson. *Hip Hop America*. New York: Viking, 1998.

Gerdy, John, R. *Sports: The All-American Addictions*. University of Mississippi Press, 2002.

*Gladiator*. Dir. Ridley Scott. Film. DreamWorks-Universal Pictures, 2000.

Guy-Sheftall, Beverly. "The Body Politic: Black Female Sexuality and the

Nineteenth Century Euro-American Imagination" in *Skin Deep, Spirit Strong: The Black Female Body in American Culture*, ed. Kimberly Gisele Wallace-Sanders. Ann Arbor: University of Michigan Press. 2002. 14-17.

Halberstam, David. *Playing for Keeps: Michael Jordan and the World He Made*. Random House: New York, 1999. 410-15

Harrison, Keith and Valdez, Alicia. "Uneven View of African American Ballers." in Ross, Charles (ed.). *Race and Sport: The Struggle for Equality on and off the Field*. University Press of Mississippi, 2004. pp. 183-221.

Hertz, Noreena. The Silent Takeover: Global Capitalism and the Death of Democracy. New York: The Free Press, 2001.

Hoberman, John. *Darwin's Athletes: How Sport Has Damaged Black America and Preserved the Myth of Race*. Boston: Houghton Mifflin Co., 1997.

hooks, bell. *Yearning*. South End Press: Cambridge, MA, 1990.

Hughes, Langston. "The Negro Artist and the Racial Mountain" in *Within the Circle*. Durham: Duke University Press. 1994. 55-9.

Iwamoto, Derek, "Tupac Shakur: Understanding the Identity Formation of Hyper-Masculinity of a Popular Hip-Hop Artist." *Black Scholar.* Summer 2003, Volume 33, Issue 2. 44-50.

Issacs, Neil D. *The Oregonian*, 6 April 2003. E13

Jackson, Scoop. "Game Point." *Slam Magazine*. September 2004.

Keats, Floyd. Thabiti Lewis Interviewed Floyd Keats of Black Coaches Association, 3 August 2004.

Kelley, Robin D.G. *Race Rebels: Culture, Politics, and the Black Working Class*. New York: The Free Press, 1994.

Kelley, Robin D.G. *Yo' Mama's Disfunktional! Fighting the Culture Wars in Urban America*. Boston: Beacon Press, 1997.

Keyes, Cheryl. *Rap Music and Street Consciousness*. Urbana: University of Illinois Press, 2002. 152-153.

King, Richard and Springwood, Charles. *Beyond the Cheers: Race As Spectacle In College Sport*. SUNY Press: Albany, NY. 2001.

Kitwana, Bakari. *The Hip-Hop Generation: Young Blacks and the Crisis of African American Culture*. New York: Basic Civitas Books, 2002.

Kochman, Thomas. *Black and White Styles in Conflict*. Chicago: University of Chicago Press, 1981.

Lapchick, Richard. "Racial and Gender Report Card." Center for the Study of Sport in Society, 1999.

Lapchick, Richard. *Racial and Gender Report Card for College Sport*. Orlando: University of Central Florida Institute, 2001.

Lewis, Thabiti. "Looking for Jackie and Mike: Race, Sport, and Contemporary American Culture. In *Blacks and Whites Meeting in America: Eighteen Essays on Race*. Terry White, (ed.). Jefferson, NC: McFarland & Company, Inc., 2002: 101-110.

———. "Popularizing 'Bad' Black Men." *Oregon Humanities,*
    Spring/Summer (Pop Culture) 2005: 44-47.

Levitan, Mark. *A Crisis in Black Male Employment: Unemployment and
    Joblessness in New York City 2004.* Community Service Society of
    New York, 2004.

Lipsitz, George. *The Possessive Investment in Whiteness: How White
    People Profit from Identity Politics.* Philadelphia: Temple University
    Press, 1998.

Mandelbaum, Michael. *The Meaning of Sports: Why Americans Watch
    Baseball, Football and Basketball, and What They See When They
    Do.* New York: Public Affairs, 2004.

Mills, Charles. *The Racial Contract.* Ithaca: Cornell University Press, 1997.

Nuruddin, Yusuf. "Intergenerational Culture Wars: Civil Rights vs Hip
    Hop" (interview of Todd Boyd). Socialism and Democracy,
    vol.18, No.2 (July-December 2004):51-69.

NCAA Manual, Section 2.9 (2004)

O'Neal, John. "Motion in the Ocean." Black Theatre Drama Review, vol.
    12, No. 4 (summer 1968).

Pennington, Bill. "A Year of Toil and Sweat, Then They Played the
    Game," *The New York Times.* 3 December 2008, B11-12.

Platt, Larry. New Jack Jocks: Rebels, Race, And the American Athlete.
    Temple University Press: 2002.

Powell, Kevin. "The Hip-Hop Generation." Socialism and Democracy, vol.18, No.2 (July-December 2004): 7.

Quick, Jason. *The Oregonian*. 2 July 2005, C5.

"Remolding the Blazers." *The Oregonian*. 24 June 2004, C1.

Rhoden, William. *Forty Million Dollar Slaves*. Crown Books: New York. 2006.

Roby, Peter. "Take Heart: Bad Blazers Could Be Worse."' *The Oregonian*, 4/6/03. E1, E13.

Rochester Review, Summer 2002: 29-36.

Rummel, Jack. Muhammad Ali: Heavyweight Champion. Philadelphia: Chelsea House Publishers. 2005.

Said, Edward. *Culture and Imperialism*. New York: Vintage Books. 1993.

Said, Edward. *Representations of the Intellectual*. New York: Pantheon Books, 1994.

Sailer, Steve. "The Paul Hornung Broohaha." Steve.Com Exclusive Archives, May 2004.

Sage, George H., "Racial Inequality and Sport." in Sport in *Contemporary Society*, ed. Stanley Eitzen. New York: Worth Publishers. 275-284.

Saraceno, Jon. "King James' a one-man gang," *USA Today*, 2/13/2008: C1-2.

*Shaft* Dir. Gordon Parks. Metro-Goldwyn-Mayer, 1971.

Shakespeare, William. *The Tempest.* London: Methuen, 1954.

Shipler, David K. *A Country of Strangers: Blacks and Whites in America.* New York: Knopf, 1997.

Shropshire, Kenneth L. *In Black and White: Race and Sports in America.* New York: NYU Press, 1996.

Shulman, James and Bowen, William. *The Game of Life: College Sports and Educational Values.* Princeton: Princeton University Press, 2001. 4-6, 12-17, 27, 62-64.

Simonich, Milan. "Young Pros Owe Spencer Haywood Large Vote of Thanks." *Pittsburgh Post-Gazette,* 28 November 2003: 2.

Smith-Rosenburg, Carroll. "Surrogate Americans: Masculinity, Masquerade, and the Formation of a National Identity." *PMLA,* October 2004, vol. 119, no. 5: 1325-1335.

Suggs, Welch. "A Color Line for the Grid iron?" *Chronicle of Higher Education,* 14 May 1999: A59-A60.

Suggs, Welch. "Colleges Criticized for 'Poor' Record of Diversifying Staffs of Athletic Departments." *Chronicle of Higher Education,* 6 August 1999. A54

*Superfly* Dir. Gordon Parks. Warner Brothers, 1972.

*Sweet Sweetback's Baadasssss Song* Dir. Melvin Van Peebles. Yeah

Productions, 1971.

*The Chronicle of Higher Education*. 19 December 2003. A37 (topic, Myles Brand).

The Knight Commission Report 2001.

The National Study on Collegiate Sports Wagering and Associated Health Crisis, May 2004.

*The Oregonian*, 2 July 2004. C5.

*The Oregonian*. 4 November 2004. C5.

Thomas, Ron. *They Cleared the Lane: the NBA's Black Pioneers*. Lincoln: University of Nebraska Press, 2002.

*USA Today*, 2 February 2002.

*USA Today*, 27 October 2004.

*USA Today*, 19 November 2004.

Vera, Hernan and Gordon, Andrew M. *Screen Saviors: Hollywood Fictions of Whiteness*. Lanham: Rowman and Littlefield Publishers, 2003 (Needs page numbers)

Ward, Geoffery, C. *Unforgivable Blackness: The Rise and Fall of Jack Johnson*. New York: Alfred A. Knopf, 2004.

Weisman, Larry. "Rivalry takes on new meaning for QBs." *USA Today*, 10 August 2004. C-10.

West, Cornel. *Race Matters*. Boston: Beacon Press, 1993. 157.

Wilbon, Michael. "Qballers: They're Bringing a Whole New Game to the NFL." *ESPN: The Magazine.* 19 April 1999.

Williams, Carla. "Naked, Neutered, or Noble: The Black Female Body in America and the Problem of Photographic History" in *Skin Deep, Spirit Strong: The Black Female Body in American Culture*, ed. Kimberly Gisele Wallace-Sanders. Ann Arbor: University of Michigan Press. 2002. 196.

Williams, Jayson. *Loose Balls: Easy Money, Hard Fouls, Cheap Laughs and True Love in the NBA*. New York: Broadway Books, 2000.

Wilson, Stephen. "After Four Years, Williams Family Relinquishes Wimbledon Title." Associated Press, 3 July 2004.

Zirin, Dave. *What's My Name, Fool?* Chicago, IL:Haymarket Books, 2005.

# INDEX

# ABOUT THE AUTHOR

Thabiti Lewis teaches English and Black studies at Washington State University Vancouver and lectures widely on topics such as hip-hop and film, black masculinity, and race and sports in America. He has been a columnist and a freelance writer for *The Source*, the *St. Louis American* and *News One* and his work has appeared in book anthologies and publications such as *Mosaic Literary Magazine, Oregon Humanities, Crisis Magazine*, the *St. Louis Post-Dispatch*, and *AmeriQuests*. He currently resides in Portland, Oregon